INSIDE

A Witty, Opinionated and Remarkably Useful Guide to Everybody's Favorite City

By Don W. Martin & Betty Woo Martin

Pine Cone Press ● Columbia, California

Other guides by Don & Betty Martin

THE BEST OF SAN FRANCISCO ● Chronicle Books © 1986, revised 1990
THE BEST OF THE GOLD COUNTRY ● Pine Cone Press © 1987, reprinted 1990, revised 1991
SAN FRANCISCO'S ULTIMATE DINING GUIDE ● Pine Cone Press © 1988
THE BEST OF ARIZONA ● Pine Cone Press © 1990

Library of Congress Catalog-in-Publication Data
Martin, Don, 1934; Martin, Betty, 1941—
    Inside San Francisco
    Includes index
1. San Francisco (Calif.)—Description—Guidebooks
    2. Title: 94'610453—dc20

ISBN 0-942053-08-7
Library of Congress card catalogue number: 90-91776

Book design & production ● Charles L. Beucher, Jr. & Jil Weil
Cartography ● Jil Weil
Photography ● Don W. Martin

THE COVER ● Viewed from Yerba Buena Island, the San Francisco-Oakland Bay Bridge frames the city's busy skyline.

Yesterday and today: *San Francisco's Transamerica Pyramid and the 1906 Sentinel building provide an intriguing architectural overlap.*

CONTENTS

MAPS

SAN FRANCISCO—A CITY
IN YOUR POCKET

Virtually all guidebook authors who tilt over a typewriter or boot up their computer approach the task with a common goal—to produce a workable, readable guide to a particular area.

We have attempted—and immodestly claim to have succeeded—in putting San Francisco in your pocket. From the moment you step from your hotel room, blinking into the sunlight or squinting through a cool cloak of fog, this book seeks to untangle the amazing maze that is San Francisco. Streets that seem on a collision course with one another sort themselves out and lead you to fine restaurants, trendy boutiques, museums and galleries. A city that sits at a 45-degree angle to itself begins to make sense.

With this book you become a part of San Francisco—on the inside looking out, not an outsider puzzling over a map scrawled with a tangle of unfamiliar streets.

San Francisco is a diverse collection of neighborhoods fused together to form a surprisingly compact and complex city. A pocket-sized city, if you will, of little more than 700,000 residents, crowded onto a hilly peninsula 46.6 miles square.

On the pages that follow, we explore this diversity in a manageable manner—examining the city one section at a time. In each area, we introduce you to the attractions, shopping, dining, night life and lodgings.

We offer you everything you ever wanted to know about San Francisco, presented logically and simply. Come join us in discovering everybody's favorite city.
—Don W. Martin

THE WAY THINGS WORK

After an introduction telling you more than you ever wanted to know about the city, we have a little fun by selecting its top ten attractions, restaurants and after-hours haunts. This should be useful for visitors with limited time.

We then take you through the city area by area, suggesting what to see and do, where to have a drink when the sun's over the yard arm and where to dine. Maps help you find your way and pinpoint attractions. At the end of each chapter, alphabetical listings offer details of major tourist lures, select restaurants and lodgings.

We then tidy things up with lists of lodgings by price in Chapter 16, and restaurants by alphabet and type in Chapter 17.

HOW WE RATE

We use a simple system, without asking you to memorize a lot of codes, abbreviations and little squiggly figures. We employ three symbols—to indicate quality, price and availability of non-smoking areas.

Attractions

Δ **A cut above boring** ● Worth a visit if you have plenty of time and it's cheap or free.

ΔΔ **Reasonably interesting** ● Worth going a few blocks out of your way.

ΔΔΔ **Very interesting** ● Make it a point to see it unless you're extremely short on time.

ΔΔΔΔ **Outstanding** ● Don't argue; this belongs on your "must see" list!

☺ ● Indicates an attraction that appeals primarily to pre-teens, so be a good parent and let them drag you through it.

Restaurants

Δ **Adequate** ● A clean place with basic but edible food.

ΔΔ **Good** ● An attractive, well-run cafe with tasty food served in a comfy, pleasant setting.

ΔΔΔ **Very Good** ● Substantially above average; excellent fare, served with a smile in a pleasing environment.

ΔΔΔΔ **Excellent** ● An exceptionally well-run restaurant with a distinctive setting and tasty, perhaps innovative dishes.

△△△△△ **Awesome** ● Gourmet quality by every measure; one of the finest restaurants we've encountered.

We occasionally award an extra △ to rather basic places offering exceptionally good, modestly priced food.

Price ranges are based on the tab for an average dinner, including soup or salad (not including wine or dessert). Obviously, places serving only breakfast and/or lunch are priced accordingly.

$ ● Average dinner for one is $9 or less
$$ ● $10 to $14
$$$ ● $15 to $24
$$$$ ● $25 to $34
$$$$$ ● Did you say you were buying?

A few restaurants have dress codes, and we indicate this. Otherwise, we use these guidelines: **Dressy**—coat and ties for gents, cocktail wear for ladies; **Informal**—sport jacket and slacks; **Casual**—laid back; denims will do but leave the shorts packed; this isn't L.A.

Lodgings

△ **Adequate** ● A clean place that meets minimum standards.

△△ **Good** ● A tidy establishment with most essentials, such as private baths, room phones and color TV.

△△△ **Very Good** ● Well-run place with clean, nicely-furnished rooms; may include a pool, restaurant and other amenities.

△△△△ **Excellent** ● An exceptional property with elegant rooms; most such places will have extensive facilities.

△△△△△ **Awesome** ● Outstanding by every measure; one of the best hotels in the country.

Price codes below are for doubles during the summer tourist season. Within the listing, we also show price ranges for doubles, singles and suites.

$ ● a double for under $50
$$ ● $50 to $74
$$$ ● $75 to $99
$$$$ ● $100 to $149
$$$$$ ● $150 or more

It's wise to made advance reservations, since a big convention can tie up most of the city's hotels. If you don't like the place, you can shop around after the first night and—hopefully—find something more suitable. Without advance reservations, the later you arrive, the more likely you'll be stuck with a higher-priced room, or one hanging over a freeway.

You probably know that most lodging chains have toll-free reservation numbers. If you aren't sure, **dial (800) 555-1212** for toll-free directory assistance.

Bed & breakfast inns

We rate them for ambiance, decor, cleanliness and amenities. Bear in mind that many don't offer room phones, TV, private baths, pools and such.

Clearing the air

Ø **No smoking** ● This symbol indicates that lodgings have non-smoking rooms and restaurants have smoke-free areas that are well isolated. In some cases, the entire dining room is smoke-free. San Francisco municipal code requires that restaurants set aside non-smoking tables, but some places are rather casual about enforcing it.

How we pick them

We do not solicit free meals or lodgings, but rely on our own experiences and other unbiased sources. We aren't swayed by recommendations in other guidebooks or brochures, since they may be paid-for listings. We *do* trust recommendations of the American Automobile Association, and we often list them. After eighteen years with AAA's northern California affiliate, I know its ratings are objective and reliable.

Miscellany

Credit card abbreviations should be obvious: **MC/VISA**—MasterCard and VISA; **AMEX**—American Express; **DIN**—Diner's Club; DISC—Discover Card. "Major credit cards" indicates the ubiquitous MC/VISA plus American Express and one or more of the other travel cards.

Prices listed in this book are subject to change, invariably upward. Many were provided by the establishments, so we can't guarantee them.

Find it fast: We've cleverly bordered this introductory section in black, so you can flip back to it for quick reference.

THANK YOU—

Guidebooks, in a sense, are written by committee. The thousands of facts must come from many sources and they're checked by many more. Among those who have been particularly helpful with this and other area guidebooks are:

Sharon Rooney and **Helen K. Chang** of the San Francisco Convention and Visitors Bureau.

Public Information Officer **Diane Palacio** of the Recreation and Park Department.

Nicolas Finck of the San Francisco Railway Community Affairs Department.

Public Information Officer **Michael Feinstein** and assorted rangers of the Golden Gate National Recreation Area.

A BIT ABOUT THE AUTHORS

This is the fifth guidebook by the husband and wife team of Don and Betty Martin, and their third about San Francisco. Don, who provides most of the adjectives, has been a journalist since he was seventeen. He was a Marine correspondent in the Orient, then a reporter and editor for several West Coast newspapers—mostly in California. For eighteen years, he was associate editor of *Motorland,* the travel magazine of the San Francisco-based California State Automobile Association. He now devotes his time to writing, photography, travel and—for some strange reason—collecting chipmunk and squirrel artifacts.

Betty, who does much of the research, offers the curious credentials of a doctorate in pharmacy and a California real estate broker's license. She also is a food expert who has taken courses in culinary arts, and a freelance writer and photographer whose material has appeared in various newspapers and magazines.

CLOSING INTRODUCTORY
THOUGHTS

Nobody's perfect, but we try. This book contains thousands of facts and a few are probably wrong. If you catch an error, let us know. Also, drop us a note if you discover that a cafe has become a laundromat or the other way around. Further, if you find a tourist lure, hideaway or awesome little cafe that we overlooked, please share it with us.

All who provide useful information will earn a free copy of the revised edition of *Inside San Francisco* or any other publication on our list. (See the back of this book.)

Address your comments to:

Pine Cone Press
P.O. Box 1494 (11362 Yankee Hill Road)
Columbia, CA 95310
(209) 532-2699

Isn't it nice that people who prefer Los Angeles to San Francisco live there?
                                        —Herb Caen*

*to whom this book is dedicated, whether he plugs it in his column or not.

SAN FRANCISCO

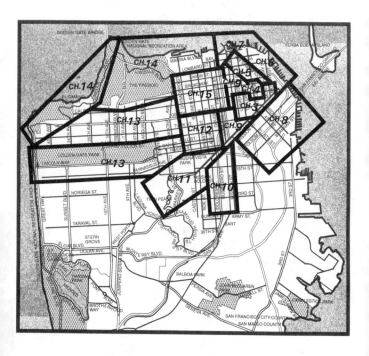

DIRECTORY

One

SAN FRANCISCO

Getting to know you

If you're alive, you can't be bored in San Francisco.
—William Saroyan

IT IS A RARE JEWEL, this San Francisco. Few people disagree with the Convention and Visitors Bureau tag line: "Everybody's favorite city."

It provides everything one would expect in a world-class city: superb restaurants, fine museums, diverse cultural offerings, great drinking establishments, lively night life and luxury hotels. Further, it offers a rich ethnic mix, adding character to its neighborhoods and spicy variety to its restaurants.

All of this bounty has been packaged on a hilly peninsula surrounded by water and tempered by a mild climate. Covering less than 47 square miles, it is second only to New York in population density among American cities. Its Chinatown—the largest outside the Orient—is more thickly populated than Manhattan. It is thus a compact city, and much of it can be explored on foot—which we intend to do in this guide.

Incidentally, despite the city's congestion, San Franciscans are a remarkably polite folk. They line up to board buses and trains. They say "Excuse me" and mean it. They'll pause to give a confused traveler— wrinkled map in hand—directions.

San Francisco challenges Rio de Janeiro as the most beautifully situated city on the planet. Its Golden Gate Bridge is the world's most-photographed manmade object, and the view from the ramparts above the gate is simply awesome.

In a recent travelers' poll, San Francisco was listed as the city they'd most like to visit. Indeed, tourism is the city's leading industry.

This beautiful lady, about whose skirts we've clung for two decades, is not without her blemishes. Parking ranges from difficult to ridiculous. Hotels and better restaurants are probably too pricey. Fisherman's Wharf has succumbed to the carnival gimmickry of wax museums and street hucksters. Like most major American cities, San Francisco suffers the spray can indignity of graffiti artists. The human litter of street people occupies Market Street doorways and the manicured lawns of Golden Gate Park.

We don't claim perfection for the grand lady, as many other tunnel-vision travel guides do. We claim excitement, variety and the pure joy of discovery. And isn't that why people travel?

HISTORY

Pardon the pun, but the city of Saint Francis rarely has been saintly. It began properly enough, as the site for Mission San Francisco de Asis, founded in the auspicious year of 1776. California was part of Spain then, and locals had no interest in all that business back in Lexington and Concord. A few years later, a village called Yerba Buena—the good herb—took root across the peninsula from the mission, near present-day Portsmouth Square. By this time, New Spain had rebelled against its Spanish founders and called itself Mexico.

Then Mexico clashed with the United States and lost. It signed away most of its northern lands—now Texas, Arizona, New Mexico and California—in the Treaty of Guadalupe Hidalgo in 1848. In that same year, itinerant handyman James Marshall accidentally found gold in the American River, about 120 miles east of the city.

An opportunistic Mormon named Sam Brannan bought up every pick, shovel, pie pan and bolt of tent canvas he could find in the city. Then he ran up and down Montgomery Street, waving a vial of nuggets and yelling: "Gold! Gold from the American River!"

Overnight, saintly Yerba Buena became sinful San Francisco, the wildest and wickedest hell-hole in the West. It was a booming metropolis when Los Angelenos were still chasing cows through the sagebrush. In the 1850s and 60s, civilian vigilantes cleaned out the bad guys of the Barbary Coast and things calmed a bit. By the turn of the century, this was a gentler, kinder city. It was a tough city, as well. The 1906 earthquake and fire destroyed 80 percent of its buildings, and it quickly rebuilt.

It has never forgotten its pioneering roots and it remains today on the leading edge of much that is new, daring, creative and often controversial. It's often called "the city that knows how."

San Francisco played host to the creation of the United Nations in 1945 and the influx of flower children in the 1960s. It was here that the Beat Generation was born, that writers Jack Kerouac, William Saroyan and Isadora Duncan were nurtured. Local clubs launched the careers of Phyllis Diller, the Limelighters, Robin Williams, Jefferson Airplane and the Grateful Dead. Dashiell Hammett pursued his imaginary heroes and villains in its shadowy alleys. The city also gave birth to topless dancing and its logical descendant—bottomless.

Here, the gay movement came out of the closet and found acceptance among a tolerant people. And here, the tragedy of AIDS is understood and battled with more vigor than anywhere else on the globe.

San Francisco understands, indulges, forgives, accepts, reaches out, and grins at its sins. It is, as poet George Sterling said in 1921, the "cool, gray city of love."

COMING TO SAN FRANCISCO
Getting Ready

The San Francisco Convention and Visitors Bureau is one of the most active and efficient such agencies in the country. Since tourism is the city's leading industry, the bureau works hard to help visitors prepare for their trip and steer them in proper directions when they arrive.

For an 80-page visitors guide, send a dollar for postage and handling to: **San Francisco Visitors**

Bureau, P.O. Box 6977, San Francisco, CA 94101. For phone information, dial **(415) 391-2000.**

What to pack—Well, a little bit of everything. The city is blessed with a benign climate. It almost never freezes, never snows and temperatures rarely

Variable Today, Probably Followed By Tomorrow

"Night and morning low clouds; otherwise fair. Today's highs from 65 along the coast to the mid-90's inland."

What kind of weather forecast is *that*? It's a San Francisco Bay Area kind, and TV weatherpersons say it with straight faces.

Unlike most of the rest of America's shoreline, northern California's coast is rimmed by hills. In summer, they prevent cool marine air from flowing inland, except through the Golden Gate. It often seeps across the bay, condenses and bathes the city in a chilly fog that dissipates by noon, then returns in the evening.

Inland areas are denied the ocean's cooling effects, so they sizzle with typical summer temperatures. Frequently, the mercury climbs as much as 40 degrees as you travel away from the bay. By September, as inland areas begin to cool, an off-shore flow starts pulling the marine air out to sea.

The result of all this is turned-around seasons. Summer is cooler than fall here; May is cooler than November. September and October are the warmest months of the year.

How does the summer visitor dress for this upside-down climate? Go native and wear knits, light wools and worsteds. Save the shorts for next year's Arizona vacation, or for excursions inland. If you climb to the heights to admire the city's views—to Coit Tower, Twin Peaks or Marin Headlands, for instance—wear a windbreaker to deflect stiff summer breezes.

Best of all, you'll love the fall. Most of the tourists will have packed their goose pimples and returned home. You'll find nobody here but us Bay Area residents, and we promise not to crowd you off the cable cars.

hit 90. Yet, it is a cool, windy city often rinsed by summer fogs. We've seen many an under-dressed, goose-pimpled tourist walking along Market Street on a breezy July morning, wondering what happened to summer.

While it's rather casual, it's not a shorts-and-halter city. You'll feel comfortable in denims and polo shirts, or slacks and sport jackets. You'll feel out of place in Technicolor Hawaiian shirts and cut-offs. The Financial District tends to be dressy, and many better restaurants expect you to show up in tie and cocktail wear. Bring comfy shoes; this is a walking city. And for some of those hills, you may want to consider hiking shoes.

The Bay Area possesses a curious climate (see box below). On any given summer day, it may be 65 degrees in the city and 95 inland. Thus, if you're going to Napa or Sonoma winelands, Sacramento's state capitol, the Gold Country or northern California's many other inland lures, shorts and halter tops *will* be appropriate.

When to come—Anytime, although our favorite season is autumn. The city, often chilly in July and August, basks in a September-to-November Indian summer. The high blue skies enhance those stunning vistas and the tourist crowds have thinned.

Winter and spring are nice, too, if you don't mind occasional rainfall. It comes and goes quickly, with lots of sunny days in between. Annual rainfall is a little over 20 inches; virtually all of that falls between November and May. Surprisingly, this is rated as the fourth sunniest major city in America, after Los Angeles, Denver and Phoenix.

GETTING THERE
By Air

San Francisco International Airport (761-0800) is 16 miles south, in San Mateo County. Virtually every major airline and several minor ones fly there. A cab ride downtown will set you back about $25, or you can catch the **Airporter** bus (495-8404) for $6 one way and $10 round-trip. Coaches leave every 20 minutes (less frequently during off-hours) and drop passengers at downtown hotels.

Super Shuttle (558-8500) is the largest of several van companies providing door-to-door pickup and drop-off. Others include **Good Neighbors** (777-4899); **Lorries,** (334-9000) and **Yellow Airport Shuttle,** (282-7433). They're $9 to $10 each way. The cheapest—but slowest—method is by Sam-Trans (San Mateo County Transit), which charges $1.25 for a pokey bus ride between the airport and Trans-Bay Terminal at First and Mission; call 761-7000.

Oakland International Airport (577-4000) may be a better bet than SFO. It's only slightly farther from the city and it's much less crowded. Air traffic delays, common at SFO, are infrequent here. The "Fly Oakland" reservations number is 444-4444. **Airbart** (832-1464) provides service between Oakland Airport and the Coliseum Bay Area Rapid Transit station every 10 minutes for $1. Hours are 6 a.m. to midnight Monday-Saturday and 9 to midnight Sunday. From there, BART trains running every few minutes will whisk you into the city or elsewhere in the Bay Area.

By Car

Westbound **Interstate 80** crosses the San Francisco-Oakland Bay Bridge and terminates in the city after its long coast-to-coast haul. Off-ramps drop you south of Market in the port and warehousing district; follow signs to the area you want to visit. Fifth Street is the nearest off-ramp to downtown/Union Square; Folsom and Main exits will get you to the Financial District and waterfront.

U.S. 101 cuts a wobbly course through the city, via freeway (the Bayshore) from the south, then along surface streets to the Golden Gate Bridge.

To avoid commuter chaos, don't drive about the city between 7 and 9 a.m. and 4 to 6:30 p.m. And *never* try to enter or leave the city during a rainy commute hour; you will experience the ultimate in gridlock.

Interstate 280 is a better, less crowded and more scenic approach from the south. Like I-80, it has several downtown off-ramps. However, some were closed by the 1989 earthquake and may still be under repair.

The Central Freeway is a spaghetti snarl of the routes mentioned above. It can be useful if you learn its octopus-tangle, but it can be maddening if you tackle it without a map.

Directional signs to Fisherman's Wharf, Chinatown and North Beach have been erected at the base of most Central Freeway off ramps and elsewhere about town. These are particularly useful since the Embarcadero Freeway—the main link to these places—was closed by the 1989 shaker. As we wrote this, officials were still debating whether to repair the ugly thing or tear it down.

By Bus

Greyhound/Trailways (558-6789) launches its cross-country buses from the Trans-Bay Terminal at 425 Mission (at First Street). Those looking for the ratty old Seventh Street Greyhound terminal will find a vacant lot.

By Train

Amtrak service (1-800-USA-RAIL) stops at Oakland's 16th Street Station. From there, buses transport travelers to the Trans-Bay Terminal. Service includes the *Zephyr* from Chicago and the *Coast Starlight*, traveling between San Diego and Seattle.

Once you arrive—by whatever means—start your city exploration at the **San Francisco Visitor Information Center** in Hallidie Plaza near the cable car turntable at Powell and Market. It offers maps, uncounted brochures, videos and helpful advice in English, French, German, Italian, Spanish and Japanese. Hours are weekdays 9 to 5:30, Saturday 9 to 3 and Sunday 9 to 2.

The Redwood Empire Association visitor center (543-8334) at 785 Market Street also offers free literature and information, both on the city and the "Redwood Empire." This includes the counties of Marin, Sonoma, Napa, Lake, Mendocino, Del Norte and Humboldt to the north, plus southern Oregon's Josephine County. Located on the fifteenth floor of the old Humboldt Bank building (next to the new Marriott), it's open weekdays from 9 to 5.

GETTING AROUND
By public transit

San Francisco has the oldest and the most versatile public transit system in America. The **Municipal Railway (Muni)** covers the city with a fleet of 1,000 growling diesel buses, quiet electric coaches, light rail (Muni Metro) and of course, the legendary cable cars. Call 673-MUNI for scheduling information.

Fare is 85 cents per ride and $2 for cable cars. Bus-to-cable car transfer is $1. And yes, the drivers carry no change. The best way to go is to get a Muni Passport ($6 for one day, $10 for three). It provides unlimited rides and transfers throughout the system—including the cable cars. If you plan an extended stay in the city, buy a Muni FastPass for $28; it's good for unlimited rides during a calendar month. That's *calendar* month, so if you buy it on the 15th, you've only got two weeks' worth.

Passports and FastPasses are available at the Muni information booth at City Hall, Polk and McAllister; San Francisco Visitors Information Center in Halladie Plaza; the Cable Car Museum at Washington and Mason and sundry other places. To find out where, call 673-MUNI.

For a Muni street directory by mail, send $2 to: Muni Map, 949 Presidio Ave., San Francisco, CA 94115. While you're about it, ask for the free *Tours of Discovery* and *Muni Passport* brochures. *Tours of Discovery* employs regular bus routes to take you to attractions, intriguing neighborhoods and interesting viewpoints.

Bay Area Rapid Transit (788-BART), heralded as a state-of-the-art transit system when it opened two decades ago, is still one of the globe's fastest and most comfortable people-movers. Over-priced aluminum trains whisk passengers underground, over the surface and on elevated rails at speeds up to 80 miles per hour. Seats are cushioned, floors are carpeted and the 71-foot-long, million-dollar cars have escaped the attacks of graffiti artists, who regularly tattoo the city's buses.

Although BART was designed primarily for commuters, it's a useful visitor tool, as well. Four stations under Market Street can move you quickly between

The city skyline glitters in this nighttime view from Treasure Island.

the waterfront (Embarcadero), Financial District (Montgomery), downtown (Powell) and the City Hall-performing arts center (Civic Center). From there, it swings through the Latin-flavored Mission District and terminates in Daly City, a suburb on the San Francisco-San Mateo County line. Going east, its 71 miles of track dip under San Francisco Bay, then fan out to serve a string of Easy Bay communities and the bedroom towns of the Diablo Valley.

BART's modern ticketing system uses magnetically encoded cards, purchased at vending machines with values up to $20. Entrance and exit gates scan your card and subtract the price of your ride, which varies according to distance.

If you want to explore the system, you can purchase an "excursion ticket," allowing unlimited riding (but no exits) for $3. You can stop and explore stations along the line—some of which are architectural gems—but a trip through the exit gate will nullify your ticket. The most scenic route, incidentally, is through the Diablo Valley on the Concord line.

And if you want to beat the system, simply ride around until you become bored, then exit one station away from where you entered. Your encoded ticket will be debited only for the minimum fare—80 cents at this writing. Once you enter the system, your ticket goes on a time clock and invalidates itself after two and a half hours.

Brochure racks at BART stations offer schedules, tips on riding the system and a touring guide called *Fun Goes Further on BART*.

BART's value as a people-mover was proven after the 1989 "World Series Earthquake" when a chunk of the San Francisco-Oakland Bay Bridge collapsed. Not only did BART survive the shaker unscathed, it kept commuters—and tourists—flowing between the city and the East Bay while the bridge was being repaired. Daily ridership jumped from 218,286 to 253,246 in the days following the quake, and many commuters never went back to their smog-generating cars.

The city's Muni Metro joins BART under Market Street, traveling on stacked tracks between the Embarcadero and Civic Center. It then continues up Market, branching to the south into the Mission District along Church Street and to the west into the Sunset District, terminating at the city's ocean beaches.

Incidentally, Muni's FastPass is good on BART within the city but, for reasons unclear to us, BART tickets aren't accepted on Muni Metro.

By ferry

During the 1930s, the great bridges of San Francisco Bay displaced the romantic old ferryboats. Now the bridges are choked with traffic and sleeker versions of the ferries are back. One system, in fact, is operated by the Golden Gate Bridge District (332-6600). Other passenger ferries are run by Red and White Fleet, which also provides sightseeing excursions (546-BOAT or 800-445-8880). For details on both, see the "Ferry service" listing under "What to see and do" in Chapter 6, and the box on bay cruises in Chapter 7.

By car

Oh, must you? San Francisco has more vehicles per square foot than any other city in the world, and you'd be wise to leave yours home—or in the hotel parking garage. Further, pedestrians are very territorial here, challenging motorists for the right-of-way. Turning across a busy cross-walk can be frustrating. The solution: Don't fight 'em; join 'em. As we've said, this is a compact and walkable city.

If you do choose to drive, bear in mind that South of Market sits at a 45-degree angle to downtown and crossing Market Street is rather complicated. Also, most downtown streets are one-way. Before venturing forth, get a detailed map—with the one-way streets marked.

The **49-mile Scenic Drive** offers a good motoring view of the city and its ramparts to bay and sea, but it can be tricky to follow. A map available from the Convention and Visitors Bureau will help. The route involves scores of turns and takes you through some heavily trafficked areas. Further, a few of the signs may be missing, so keep alert. And don't try it during the rush hour!

Some driving tips:

• Avoid driving into Chinatown on Grant Avenue; it's one of the city's most congested streets. And talk about brazen pedestrians! If you must drive there, use the Stockton Street tunnel from downtown or the Broadway Tunnel from Van Ness Avenue. And good luck finding a parking place once you arrive.

• To move between the Civic Center and waterfront, avoid Market or Mission; take the one-way Howard (inbound) and Folsom (outbound).

• Van Ness Avenue is the city's busiest major street. To miss its congestion, take Franklin (outbound) and Gough (inbound).

Parking is scarce and expensive. Plan on spending up to $20 for all-day parking. Many hotels charge their guests over $20 for their parking garages. (Remember when you could get a room for that?) Cheapest parking is at some of the outdoor lots, although they may fill up with commuters' cars on weekdays.

Some of the less expensive parking garages are **Portsmouth Square**, off Kearny between Washington and Clay (although it's often jammed, and you may have to wait in line to get in), **Union Square Garage**, downtown between Geary, Powell, Sutter and Stockton; **Sutter-Stockton Garage** downtown, next to the Stockton tunnel; **Downtown Cen-**

ter Garage at Mason and O'Farrell; **Fifth and Mission Garage** at 833 Mission, with easy access to the Emporium and San Francisco Centre; **Northpoint Shopping Center Garage** at Bay and Stockton near Fisherman's Wharf and **Pier 39 Garage,** on the Embarcadero opposite Pier 39.

Parking around major tourist lures is difficult, particularly on weekends when thousands of Bay Area residents flock to them. There are ways around this, if act like a native. For instance, if you're going to **Fisherman's Wharf,** try parking along Van Ness Avenue, beyond Ghirardelli Square. For visits to the **Marina Green,** you'll find parking at nearby **Fort Mason Center.** If the **Golden Gate Bridge** viewpoint parking area is full, drive down to **Fort Point** and hike up to the bridge.

GETTING FED

San Francisco is paradise on a plate—the world's dining mecca. It has more restaurants per capita than any other American city—nearly 4,000 at last count. The city's dining tables could accommodate its entire population in less than two sittings! Further, it offers an amazing variety of cafes, from the now ubiquitous California cuisine to Cambodian to classic French.

Bear with us if you find one of our listed restaurants closed. Although we've tried to select durable cafes, nearly a *thousand* open and close each year in the city!

Annually, San Franciscans spend twice as much on restaurant food as New Yorkers, and dine out 65 percent more often than other Americans. Does this mean that nobody here cooks? Not quite. The five million residents from surrounding cities fill a lot of those tables, along with three million annual visitors.

There are historic reasons for this wealth of cafes. Since the days of the Gold Rush, the city has offered a rich ethnic mix, resulting in a cornucopia of cuisine. Chinese and Italians were among the first groups to influence the city's restaurant fare. There are more Chinese restaurants here than any other type, and the city isn't short on pasta palaces, either.

The city also is blessed with a great location. The Pacific Ocean and the rich San Joaquin Valley farm belt offer an unending array of ingredients. Further, it's surrounded by America's finest wine country; interesting wine selections offer more incentive to dine out.

The Bay Area gave birth to a new kind of cuisine a couple of decades ago when Alice Waters of Berkeley's Chez Panisse found innovative ways to combine fresh, local ingredients. She cooked them lightly to retain their original flavors and used curious blends of spices and condiments. This "California Cuisine" has spawned several spin-offs—American regional, American *nouveau* and Southwestern.

Among the better places to sample this new American fare are the original **Chez Panisse** in Berkeley, and **Stars, Square One,** and **Zuni Cafe** in the city.

There is no "restaurant row" in the city; dining places are widely distributed. The thickest concentration is **downtown** and in **Chinatown**. Many fine Asian restaurants are in the **Richmond District**, along Clement Street and Geary Boulevard. For trendy dining, try the places along **Union Street**.

North Beach is a haven for Italian cuisine and you probably know about the **Fisherman's Wharf** chowder houses. However, some of the better seafood places are off the wharf. **Fillmore Street** between Geary and Washington, once a slum, has gentrified itself and offers a good mix of dining spots. Nearby **Japantown** has many Japanese and a few Korean places.

Dining on a budget? Try the hundreds of ethnic Asian restaurants scattered about the city. Vietnamese places are concentrated in the **Tenderloin**, that scruffy triangle between Market, O'Farrell and Larkin. It's best to avoid the inner Tenderloin at night, since it's one of the city's high-crime areas. However, many restaurants occupy the safer fringes. Further, the good efforts of these good people are gradually cleaning up this area.

Some of the city's finest restaurants are in its hotels—both large and small. Most local innkeepers focus on the culinary arts, unlike those in many U.S. cities, who seem to have a coffee shop mentality.

GETTING A NIGHT'S SLEEP

The city is home to nearly 20 world class hotels; expect to pay world class prices. Doubles at top-rated places such as the Westin St. Francis, Four Seasons Clift, Hyatt Regency, Mandarin Oriental, Fairmont, Campton Place and Donatello go for $200 or more.

Obviously, there are less expensive rooms, particularly along the motel rows of Van Ness Avenue and Lombard Street, and in many refurbished older hotels. The city has several bed and breakfast inns offering good value for the dollar; many are in refurbished Victorians.

Lodgings in the city and surrounding communities are detailed in Chapter 16. If you'd like to bed down in a particular area, we provide a quick list at the end of each chapter.

GETTING TICKETED

The city's major ticket agencies for most plays, shows and sporting events are:

BASS, 762-2277 charge-by-phone; (recorded events, 835-3849).

City Box Office in the Sherman Clay building at 141 Kearny (Post), 392-4400.

Downtown Center Box Office in the Downtown Center Garage at Mason and O'Farrell, 775-2021.

STBS, 433-7827; it offers half-price day-of-show tickets from its office on the Stockton Street side of Union Square. It's also a full-service agency selling regular-priced tickets.

Ticketron, 392-SHOW or 243-9001 charge-by-phone.

Tower Records-Video at Columbus Avenue and Bay Street (885-0500), and other Bay Area locations.

GETTING FRISKY?

San Francisco has been a permissive city since the disorderly days of the Barbary Coast. Things have calmed down a bit in recent years, but it's still a good party town. Further, meeting someone of the opposite persuasion is not difficult. It could be risky, however.

Many **massage parlors** in the city tread a fine thread between a proper rubdown and a proposition.

However, our research—in the name of journalism, of course—indicates that most offer little more than a provocative massage at a prohibitive price. Look in the Yellow Pages under "massage." Many offer hotel room service.

Escort services also abound in the city, with subtle names like "Sass with Class" and "Unlimited Fantasy's." Some of the same firms also are listed

---

Some San Francisco Don'ts

● **Don't park on a hill without curbing your wheels.** Your car may decide to leave without you. Further, you could get a ticket. The wheels must touch the curb and the law is enforced on any street with a three percent grade. That's one steep enough for a pencil to roll down, says the city's Traffic Engineering Department.

● **Don't park in a tow-away zone during posted hours.** You'll get hit with a hefty fine and it'll cost up to $100 to bail your car out. Most zones run from 6 a.m. to 9 a.m. and 3 p.m. to 6 p.m. weekdays. If your car shows up missing, call the phone number listed on the tow-away warning sign that you should have obeyed in the first place.

● **Don't park anywhere without checking signs.** Most areas have designated street-cleaning hours, and some have limited parking without a neighborhood decal. You won't get towed, but you will get ticketed.

● **Don't hang around the Tenderloin District at night.** Although Vietnamese and other Southeast Asian immigrants are upgrading the district, it's still a high-crime area and a hang-out for dope dealers and prostitutes.

● **Don't drive into Chinatown on Friday and Saturday nights.** Chinese are drawn here from all over northern California for banquets and family gatherings. The streets are gridlocked and parking is impossible, even in commercial garages.

● **And for hevvin's sake, don't call it 'Frisco!** The city was named for Saint Francis, and it's just poor taste to use that awful slang word. Actually, if you're anywhere within a 300-mile radius, it's quite proper to simply refer to it as "the city."

under massage parlors, so you get the message. And yes, they do take plastic. But don't expect your date to look like the foxy ladies in the ads.

A few **swingers clubs** still function in the Bay Area, and their bawdy newspapers can be found in some news racks, without plain brown wrappers. We aren't recommending this risky way of getting frisky.

Some other adults-only items:

Although topless-bottomless dancing began here, the popularity of going pubic in public is sagging. Most of the surviving clubs are along Broadway and Columbus, near Grant at the edge of Chinatown. They're generally rather scruffy and depressing. The senior citizen of onstage sin—the Condor Club where Carol Doda first dropped her bra in 1964—has closed its doors.

Finocchio's female impersonators have been prancing and dancing about at 506 Broadway (982-9388) for more than half a century. It's harmlessly bawdy and probably would rate a PG as a movie, although the age limit is 21.

The Cake Gallery, with stores at 290 Ninth St. (861-CAKE) and 1045 Polk St. (775-CAKE), will bake you an X-rated pastry for that frisky occasion. For appetizers, serve adult fortune cookies from **Mee Mee** Bakery at 1328 Stockton Street (Broadway), or from **Golden Gate Fortune Cookies** at 56 Ross Alley (off Jackson). Both are in Chinatown.

Want her to slink into something comfortable? Do your shopping at **Midsummer Nights Lingerie** (788-0992) at Pier 39; or **Victoria's Secret,** a classy shop at 395 Sutter Street (397-0521) downtown or 2245 Union Street (921-5444) in the Marina.

If you really want to get steamed up, rent an evening of private and sensual soaking from **Grand Central Sauna & Hot Tub,** (431-1370) or **The Hot Tubs,** 2200 Van Ness Ave. (441-8827).

Single-mindedness

Singles groups continue to be popular and most are legitimate organizations, *not* swingers clubs or fronts for prostitutes.

The best overall source for singles information is **Singles Guide to the San Francisco Bay Area,** by Richard Gosse, published by Marin Publications, 4 Highlands Ave., San Rafael, CA 94901; (415) 459-3817. It's at city bookstores for $9.95, or you can order one directly from the publisher. It offers lists of area singles clubs and bars and even dating etiquette. (How quaint.) The author utters the classic truism about the singles scene: twenty percent of the people get eighty percent of the action.

Although the popularity of singles bars has flagged, some pubs are noted as gathering places for new faces. Here are a few that come to mind.

Balboa Cafe, a relatively quiet conversation bar in the Marina District at 3199 Fillmore St.; 922-4595.

The Chatterbox, a noisy place in the Mission District, with live music on weekends, at 853 Valencia St.; 821-1891.

Chestnut Street Grill, frequented by a flock of faithful followers, many of them single, in the Marina District at 2231 Chestnut St.; 922-5558.

DNA, one of the many South of Market dance clubs, at 375 11th St.; 626-1409.

Hard Rock Cafe, a swinging noise factory at 1699 Van Ness Ave., popular with young singles; 885-1699.

Harry's, a yuppie haven in the gentrified Fillmore District, at 2020 Fillmore; 864-2779.

I-Beam, one of Haight-Ashbury's enduring dance clubs, at 1748 Haight St.; 668-6006.

The Palladium, an after-hours spot at 1031 Kearny St.; 434-1308.

Pat O'Shea's Mad Hatter, the city's best sports bar and a lively singles hangout, in the Richmond District at 3754 Geary Blvd.; 752-3140.

Paradise Lounge, part corner bar and part rock and jazz club, south of Market at 1501 Folsom St.; 861-6906.

Paul's Saloon, a lively country/bluegrass bar just off Lombard Street's motel row at 3251 Scott St.; 922-2456.

Perry's, the ultimate upscale singles bar, in the Marina District at 1944 Union St.; 922-9022.

Pierce Street Annex, perhaps the city's most active singles bar, also in the Marina at 3138 Fillmore St.; 567-1400. "Be cool rules" are printed on a wall.

Rockin' Robbin's, deliberately funky Fifties-Sixties bars popular with young singles. Downtown at 133 Beale St., 543-1961; and in the Haight-Ashbury at 1840 Haight St., 221-1960.

The Saloon, the city's oldest surviving pub and a popular blues place with live music; in North Beach at 1232 Grant Ave.; 989-7666.

GUIDED TOURS

Several firms offer conducted tours around and about the city, the greater Bay Area and the wine country. Here are some examples:

A Day in Nature has half-day outings, including lunch, to Marin Headlands and Muir Woods; **673-0548**.

Betty's Tours runs gaming buses to the casinos of Reno and Lake Tahoe; **495-8430**.

Dolphin Tours has city, Muir Woods and Sausalito tours, some in combination with bay cruises; **441-6810**.

Golden Gate Tours offers city outings that cross the Golden Gate Bridge to Sausalito; **788-5775**.

Gray Line offers its usual assortment of tours within the city and throughout northern California. A double-decker bus ticket office is usually parked at Union Square; **896-1515**.

Great Pacific Tours offers city trips, plus jaunts to Muir Woods, Monterey and the vinelands; **626-4499**.

Napa Valley Wine Train chugs through the vineyards, with stops for tasting and dining; **(800) 522-4142**.

Near Escapes offers a variety of themed tours and activities in the Greater Bay Area, plus self-guiding auto tape tours; **921-1392**.

Pier 39 Cable Car Company runs city tours in motorized cable cars; **39-CABLE**.

WALKING TOURS

Chinatown tours are conducted by the Chinese Culture Center; some include a dim sum lunch; **986-1822**. **Jeanette's Tours** include walks through Chinatown, dim sum lunches and Chinese dinner tours; **982-8839**.

Civic Center, City Hall, Japantown and city tours are conducted free by the Friends of the Library; **558-3981**.

Dashiell Hammett Tours follow the footsteps of the famed writer and his hero Sam Spade; **564-7021**.

Discovery Walks take visitors through Pacific Heights and other Victorian neighborhoods; **673-2894**.

Golden Gate Park strolls are sponsored by Friends of Recreation and Parks, May through October; **221-1311**.

Levi Strauss & Co. tours go through the denimmaker's oldest operating plant, built in 1906; **565-9153**.

Mural tours through the Mission District are conducted by Precita Eyes Mural Center; **285-2287**.

ANNUAL EVENTS

San Franciscans love to party, singly or in organized groups. Here's a list of the city's major yearly events.

January

International Boat Show in Moscone Center, first week of January; **521-2558**.

February

Chinese New Year's Celebration, determined by a complex lunar calendar formula, usually in February (sometimes in early March); **974-6900.**

Great Outdoors Adventure Fair, Concourse Exhibition Center, Eighth and Brannan, late February; **771-1111.**

March

San Francisco International Film Festival at Kabuki 8 Cinemas, Post and Fillmore, early March; **931-3456.**

St. Patrick's Day Parade, downtown, the Sunday before March 17; **467-8218.**

April

Opening Day of the yachting season, first Sunday of Daylight Savings Time; hundreds of sails on the bay; **974-6900.**

Cherry Blossom Festival in Japantown (*Nihonmachi*), middle weekends of April; **922-6776.**

May

Cinco de Mayo, celebrated in the Mission District, closest weekend to May 5; **826-1401.**

Black and White Ball, elegant fund-raiser for the San Francisco Symphony, Civic Center in late May; **431-5400.**

Historic Trolley Festival, May through October; vintage trolleys operate on Muni's Market Street route; **673-MUNI.**

Bay to Breakers race from downtown to Ocean Beach, third Sunday in May; **777-7770.**

San Francisco Music Fair at Showplace Square, 200 Kansas St., dates vary; **864-1500.**

June

Union Street Spring Festival along Union Street, first weekend; **346-4446.**

Haight Street Fair in the Haight-Ashbury, a Saturday in mid-June; **661-8025.**

Stern Grove Midsummer Music Festival in Sigmund Stern Grove, Sundays from mid-June through August; **398-6551.**

Lesbian-Gay Freedom Gay Parade, Market Street to Civic Center, date varies; **864-3733.**

July

Fourth of July Celebration with fireworks off Crissy Field and other events; **556-0560**

San Francisco Marathon through the city's streets, a mid-July Sunday; **681-2322.**

August

Nihonmachi Street Fair in Japantown, weekend in early August; **922-8700.**

San Francisco Hill Stride, scenic walking race over the city's hills, early August; **546-6150.**

September

San Francisco County Fair, at Fort Mason Center and Civic Center, urban version of a county fair (may be in late August); **558-3623.**

San Francisco Blues Festival at Fort Mason's Great Meadow, mid-September; **826-6837.**

KNBR Bridge-to-Bridge Run, eight-mile race in late September; **951-7070.**

Castro Street Fair, in the Castro District in late September; **467-3354.**

Festa Italiana, Italian festival at Fisherman's Wharf and North Beach, late September-early October; **673-3782.**

October
Festival 2000, city-wide ethnic cultural festival, through October; **864-4237.**

Fleet Week, celebration of the U.S. Navy, early October; **765-6056.**

Columbus Day festivities at North Beach and Fisherman's Wharf, nearest weekend to Oct. 12; **434-1492.**

Harvest Festival every weekend from late October to mid-November; **778-6300.**

November
International Auto Show at Moscone Center, late November; **673-2016.**

December
Christmas festivities include poinsettia decorations at **Embarcadero Center** with 17,000 white lights framing the high-rises; window decorations at **Macy's** at Stockton and Geary; large lighted yule trees at **Union Square**, the entrance to **Golden Gate Park** and **Ghirardelli Square**; holiday floral theme at **Conservatory of Flowers; The Nutcracker** performed by the San Francisco Ballet; **Handel's Messiah** by the San Francisco Symphony; and Dickens' **A Christmas Carol** by American Conservatory Theater.

ESSENTIAL PHONE NUMBERS
(All 415 area code)

Emergencies—911

Convention & Visitors Bureau—391-2000/974-6900

Events hotline—English, 391-2001; French, 391-2003; German, 391-2004; Spanish, 391-2122 and Japanese, 391-2101

Redwood Empire Association—543-8334

Muni—673-MUNI
BART—788-BART
Golden Gate Ferry/Golden Gate Transit—332-6600
Red & White Fleet—1-800-445-8880
San Francisco International Airport—761-0800
Oakland International Airport—577-4000
Medical Society referral service—567-6234
Dental Society referral service—421-1435
Senior referral service and information—626-1033
Travelers Aid Society—781-6738
Cityline (free news, weather, stocks, sports and entertainment reports)—512-5000 (sponsored by the San Francisco Chronicle)
Passport information—974-7972
Time of day—POP-CORN or 767-8900
Weather—936-1212

ITEMS FOR YOUR STOREHOUSE OF WORTHLESS INFORMATION

Date of founding—Mission San Francisco de Asis (St. Francis of Assisi) established June 29, 1776; Presidio founded Sept. 17, 1776; city incorporated April 15, 1850.

Motto—*Oro en paz, Fierro en guerra* (Gold in peace, iron in war).

Geology—the city sits on an upthrust of sandstone, shale and volcanic rock.

Government—combined city-county, presided over by a mayor and eleven-member board of supervisors.

City population—727,400 (July 1, 1989); greater Bay Area—5,865,000.

Ethnic make-up—Chinese, 12.9 percent; black, 11.3; English, 10.3; Irish, 8.5; German, 7.5; Italian, 5.7; Filipino, 5.5; Mexican, 4.9; Soviet, 2.8; French, 2.5; Japanese, 2.1; and 26 percent mongrel or smaller ethnic groups.

Total city land area—46.38 square miles.

Total shoreline (bay and ocean front)—8.4 miles.

Size of San Francisco Bay—496 square miles.

Number of foghorns around the bay—26.

Islands within the city limits—11.

Number of hills—43.

Steepest streets—31.5 percent grade: Filbert between Leavenworth and Hyde, and 22nd Street between Church and Vicksburg.

Golden Gate Bridge length—1.7 miles; mid-span is just over a mile.

Actual color of Golden Gate Bridge—International Orange.

Daily vehicle crossings—118,882.

San Francisco-Oakland Bay Bridge length—8.5 miles. (It's actually a suspension bridge, a tunnel and a cantilevered bridge.)

Daily vehicle crossings—220,000.

Number of cable car routes—three: Bay and Taylor, Hyde and Beach and California-Van Ness.

Length of cable car track—8.8 miles, plus 2.2 miles of service and maintenance track.

Number of cable cars—37.

Speed of cable cars—9.5 miles per hour.

Age of cable car system—Began running August 1, 1873; received $60 million overhaul during 1983-84.

Number of cable car riders—12 million annually.

Tallest building—Transamerica Pyramid, 853 feet.

Highest building vista point—Carnelian Room, 52nd floor of Bank of America building, California and Kearny.

Number of hotel/motel rooms—29,000.

Number of Victorian houses—14,000.

Number of colleges and universities—18.

Highest hill—Mount Davidson, 938 feet.

Number of foreign language newspapers—50.

Number of museums—46.

Number of live theaters—60; **nightclubs**—91.

Number of restaurants—nearly 4,000.

Number of bars—2,100.

Number of churches—672; **synagogues**—15.

Tourism

Annual visitors (including convention delegates)—three million.

Median family income of visitor—$54,200 (1989 figure).

Average age of typical visitor—42.

Source of most American visitors—Southern California, followed by Texas, Illinois, Florida and Pennsylvania.

Source of most foreign visitors—Japan, then Germany, United Kingdom, Canada, and Australia.

Two

THE CITY'S TOP TEN
A sampler

IF YOU LIVE IN THE BAY AREA, you can—and probably do—savor the city at your leisure. However, if you're a visitor, your stay may be limited. You'll want to invest your time wisely. So, before we get into our area-by-area explorations, we offer "quick takes"—lists of the best the city has to offer. You'll find more detail in their respective chapters.

The Top Ten San Francisco Experiences

Certainly, you'll want to experience things distinctly San Franciscan. If your stay is brief, forget the zoo (nice, but San Diego's is better) and the wharf (Seattle's is more charming). Here's how we would sample the city if we were on a time budget:

1. Stroll across the Golden Gate Bridge ● There's no better way to witness the grandeur of the city and its setting. If we had only an hour to spend here, we'd grab a cab or drive to the bridge's vista point, and start walking. (See Chapter 14.)

2. Commute on a cable car to Chinatown ● The cable cars *are* San Francisco, and the city's Chinatown is like no other Asian enclave in the world: dynamic, animated, abrim with bright sights and exotic smells. Catch a Bay and Taylor or Hyde and Beach cable car, get off on Nob Hill, then walk down steep California Street to Chinatown. Or take the California line and hop off on Grant or Stockton. (Chapters 3 and 4.)

3. Catch the good ferry to Sausalito ●
Golden Gate ferries sail from a pier near the Ferry Building and offer a city panorama as they cruise across the bay. You'll brush past Alcatraz, parallel the Golden Gate Bridge and skim the shoreline of Marin Headlines before putting into Sausalito, an art colony that resembles a slice of the French Riviera. (Chapters 6 and 7.)

4. Greet the Greenery in Golden Gate Park ● More than a thousand acres of sand dunes have been transformed into one of America's largest, prettiest and most versatile municipal parks. It's a forest in a city, sheltering fine museums, meadows and magnificent gardens. (Chapter 13.)

5. Cruise from the Cliff House to the bridge ● Visit the yapping sea lions of Seal Rocks and the Golden Gate National Recreation Area visitor center near the historic Cliff House. Then drive northeast through Lincoln Park and the Presidio to the Golden Gate. Views of the bridge through wind-sculpted coastal cypress are awesome. (Chapter 14.)

6. Peek at the city from Twin Peaks ● A vista point just below Twin Peaks is popular for city viewing, but it gets crowded during the tourist season. We prefer to climb the peaks themselves; railroad tie steps make the hike easy. From here, your Bay Area view expands to a full 360 degrees. (Chapter 11.)

7. Amble about Alcatraz ● That great grim fortress in the middle of the bay is one of the city's top tourist draws. Once foreboding and unapproachable, the former federal prison is now part of the Golden Gate National Recreation Area. Tour boats transport you there from the waterfront. (Chapter 7.)

8. Visit the Victorians of Alamo Square ● The city is famous for its so-called "Victorians"—narrow homes trimmed with gingerbread gee-gaws and rainbow colors. Natives fondly call them "painted ladies." The best selection is around Alamo Square, a park bordered by Hayes, Scott, Fulton and Steiner streets. It's just up from the Civic Center on Hayes. (Chapter 12.)

9. Meditate in the old mission ● This is where the city's roots were planted—Mission San Francisco de Asis at Dolores and 16th streets. Wander through the hushed chapel and gardens of the 1791 adobe mission, then view the lofty basilica next door, with its Moorish-Corinthian spires. (Chapter 10)

10. Promenade along the bayfront ● An easy three-and-a-half-mile stroll, the Golden Gate Promenade takes you from the historic ships of Hyde Street Pier to Fort Point, in the shadow of the Golden Gate Bridge. Each stride unfurls vistas of ships on the bay and the hilly city skyline. (Chapter 14)

The Top Ten Family Outings

If you brought the tribe along, you'll find that this is a great city for kids. These attractions should keep them occupied. They're listed alphabetically.

1. Academy of Sciences ● *Golden Gate Park; daily from 10 to 5, longer hours in summer; adults $4, less for kids and seniors; 750-7141.* One of America's finest science museums, this extensive complex combines a natural history museum, aquarium, planetarium and *Laserium*. (Chapter 13)

2. Angel Island State Park ● *In San Francisco Bay; sunup to sundown; round-trip fare $7.10, less for kids; 546-2815 for ferry service.* Miles of hiking and biking trails, picnic glens and relics of an old immigration station attract families to this wooded island in San Francisco Bay. The ferryboat ride over is half the fun. (Chapter 14.)

3. The Cliff House, Musee Mechanique and Seal Rocks ● *Great Highway and Point Lobos Avenue; museum open weekdays 11 to 6, weekends 10 to 7; free; 386-1170.* Several lures attract families to this promontory above the Pacific. The Cliff House offers restaurants, curio shops and dramatic ocean views. The mechanical museum features old coin-operated music machines and games of skill. Nearby Seal Rocks earned their name from their barking occupants, usually on hand to entertain visitors. (Chapter 14.)

4. The Exploratorium, ● *Behind the Palace of Fine Arts at Bay and Lyon streets; Thursday-Sunday 10* to 5 and Wednesday from 10 to 9:30; adults $6, seniors $3 and kids 6 to 17, $2 (admissions good for six months); 563-7337. More than 600 science exhibits tempt children and their parents with buttons, levers, keyboards and blinking lights. It's a "how things work" place on the threshold of science. (Chapter 14.)

5. Fisherman's Wharf ● *At the waterfront.* We think once-wonderful Fisherman's Wharf has become schlock city with its wax museums and tacky souvenir shops. But who are we to deny your youngsters admission to the Wax Museum, Haunted Gold Mine, Lazer Maze and Medieval Dungeon? And nearby Pier 39's plastic-horse carousel is fun to ride. (Chapter 7.)

6. Fort Point National Historic Site ● *Beneath the Golden Gate Bridge southern anchorage; daily 10 to 5; free; 556-1693.* Dim corridors and stairways of this ancient brick fort make wonderful hide-and-seek places for youngsters. Park rangers in Civil War-era costume present cannon-loading demonstrations and other Army skills of the day. (Chapter 14.)

7. San Francisco Maritime National Historic Park ● *West of Fisherman's Wharf; daily 10 to 5. Museum free; Hyde Street Pier—adults $3, seniors and kids under 16 free; 556-3002.* Kids who've dreamed of going down to the sea in ships will love this place. The National Maritime Museum at the foot of Polk Street focuses on the history of water transportation with models, artifacts and paintings. Hyde Street Pier exhibits several historic ships, including an 1863 three-masted schooner. (Chapter 7.)

8. San Francisco Zoo ● *Sloat Boulevard at 45th Avenue; daily 10 to 5; adults $6, kids and seniors $3; children's zoo $1; 753-7172.* Youngsters can pet farm animals and admire jungle beasts from a safe distance at the city's zoological gardens. Talk to the animals in Wolf Woods, Gorilla World, Musk Ox Meadows and the excellent Primate Discovery Center. (Chapter 13.)

9. Toy wonderlands ● ***FAO Schwarz Fifth Avenue*** at Stockton and O'Farrell; daily, various hours; 394-8700 and **KinderZimmer**, 556 Sutter Street; Monday-Saturday 10 to 6; 986-0896. FAO

Schwarz offers three floors of youthful delights, with a 24-foot clock tower as a centerpiece. KinderZimmer specializes in classic imported toys, mostly from Europe. (Chapter 3.)

10. U.S.S. Pampanito submarine ● *Pier 45 at the end of Taylor Street; daily 9 to 9 from May to October, shorter hours in the off-season; adults $4, kids and seniors less. 929-0202.* Youngsters can crawl through the echoing steel innards of a battle-scarred submarine and learn of her World War II exploits. (Chapter 7.)

The Top Ten Libation Stations

All right, kids, you've had your fun. Now, plant your little buns in front of the hotel room TV while the folks go out for a nip.

Cocktail hour is a ritual revered by San Franciscans. At the stroke of five, the city's working folk—white collar and blue—adjourn to their favorite pubs to sip something relaxing, slap liars dice on the bar and swap lies with bartenders who know them by name.

We list here our ten choice watering holes and the reasons for their selections:

1. Washington Square Bar and Grill ● *1707 Powell St. (Union), 982-8123.* The "Square" is the quintessential local hangout: a good, noisy bar staffed by friendly barkeeps, and an honest San Francisco-style restaurant with an Italian tilt to the menu.

2. The House of Shields ● *39 New Montgomery St. (Market), 392-7732.* Another local institution, this wood-paneled pub was the city's only surviving stand-up bar until they put stools in a few years ago. It still hasn't lost its earthy, men's club feel, with its high-backed booths, a long main bar and even a mounted trophy or two.

3. The Carnelian Room ● *Atop the Bank of America building, 555 California St. (Montgomery), 433-7500.* From the traditional, we move up—literally—to the city's best sky room bar. (Sorry about that, Top of the Mark). The decor is elegant, the view is stunning and the drinks are only slightly overpriced. (See restaurant listing below.)

4. Spec's 12 Adler Museum Cafe ● *12 Saroyan St. (off Columbus, near Broadway), 421-4112.* We had a choice between Spec's and Vesuvio's, directly across Columbus, for the exemplary North Beach bar. Both are survivors of the Beatnik era, filled with dusty memories and memorabilia. Odd artifacts from around the globe occupy a few small museum cases in Spec's, thus earning the place its curious name.

5. The Penny Farthing Pub ● *679 Sutter St. (Taylor), 771-5155.* The hand-painted wooden sign, brick front, Watney's on tap and bangers 'n' mash mark this as a typical British pub. The place seems to have been moved intact from SOHO to San Francisco.

6. Compass Rose in the Westin St. Francis Hotel ● *Powell at Geary, 774-0167.* In our earlier book, *The Best of San Francisco,* we identified the Compass Rose as the city's most elegant bar. With fluted columns, scalloped drapes and deeply upholstered chairs, it has no peer. Expect the prices to match the decor.

7. The Other Trellis in the Hyatt Regency ● *Five Embarcadero Center (foot of Market Street), 788-1234.* The Hyatt's 17-story atrium—with its *Star Wars* elevator capsules shooting up the walls—is the most impressive hotel lobby in the city. The Other Trellis is a fine place to lounge beneath this lofty canopy of architectural wonder.

8. Pat O'Shea's Mad Hatter ● *3754 Geary Boulevard (Third Avenue), 752-3148.* You'll have to travel far out Geary to experience the city's best and liveliest sports bar. Go on a Sunday during football season and watch the action on a dozen TV sets. Don't worry about the sign outside that says: "We cheat tourists and drunks." Stay sober and tell them you're from Oakland.

9. The Saloon ● *1232 Grant Avenue (Fresno Ally), 989-7666.* The city's oldest bar is an authentic Gold Rush survivor, little changed since it was opened in 1861. Painted ladies no longer steer randy miners up to their tasseled rooms in the adjacent Fresno Hotel, but the place still gets frisky when nightly blues bands begin tuning up.

10. Paul's Saloon ● *3251 Scott St. (Lombard), 922-2456.* Just off Motel Row, Paul's is the town's best country and Western bar. It's not a rhinestone cowboy place, but a San Francisco-style pub where live bands twang out bluegrass and country sounds.

The Top Ten Dining Spots

Talk about being arbitrary! How can one possibly choose the best restaurants among the thousands that the city has to offer?

Obviously, by being arbitrary. What we offer is a balance of interesting places to dine—more of a sampler than a true top ten. Numbering among our selections are establishments which are distinctively San Franciscan.

1. The most elegant restaurant: FLEUR DE LYS ● *777 Sutter Street (Jones), 673-7779. Monday-Saturday 6 to 9:30 p.m. Jacket and tie required; reservations a must. Major credit cards.* A cascading fabric ceiling, lush decor and a contemporary French menu blend beautifully to create a memorable evening out. Indulge yourself and your credit card; this one of the few expensive restaurants that's actually worth the investment. (Chapter 3.)

2. The best hotel restaurant: THE BIG FOUR ● *1075 California St. (in the Huntington Hotel at Taylor); 771-1140. American-continental; dinners $22 to $32; full bar. Daily 7 to 10 a.m., 11:30 to 3 and 5:30 to 10 p.m. Reservations advised. Dressy; jackets for dinner. Major credit cards.* Quietly elegant, decorated with early California memorabilia and offering innovative fare, it's one of the city's finest restaurants. Arrive early and have a pre-dinner drink the stylish 19th century bar, warmed by a cheery fire. (Chapter 3.)

3. The best "new cuisine" restaurant: SQUARE ONE ● *190 Pacific Avenue Mall (Front), 788-1110. Lunch 11:30 to 2:30 weekdays, dinner from 5:30 Monday-Saturday and from 5 Sunday. Informal; reservations essential. MC/VISA, AMEX.* Several restaurants offer varied versions of new American cuisine and we feel that Joyce Goldstein's Square One is the most best. And it's in a nice setting, next to a park near the waterfront. (Chapter 6.)

4. The best seafood restaurant: HAYES STREET GRILL ● *324 Hayes St. (Franklin), 863-5545. Lunch 11:30 to 3 weekdays, dinner Monday-Thursday 5 to 10 and Friday-Saturday 6 to 11. Informal; reservations essential. MC/VISA.* It offers a good selection of perfectly done fish, served with a choice of tasty sauces. And it's not even on the waterfront. To find it, travel to the Civic Center and turn west off Van Ness onto Hayes Street. (Chapter 9.)

5. The best "Joe" style restaurant: LITTLE JOE'S ● *523 Broadway (Columbus and Grant), 433-4343. Monday-Thursday 11 to 10:30, Friday-Saturday 11 to 11 and Sunday 2 to 10. Casual; no reservations. No credit cards.* Distinctly San Franciscan, the "Joe" style restaurant—basic Italian fare with an open kitchen—originated here in the 1930s. Little Joe's is livelier and less formal than its predecessors and it serves some of the best inexpensive pasta in the city. (Chapter 5.)

6. The best sky room restaurant: THE CAR-NELIAN ROOM ● *Atop the Bank of America at 555 California St. (Montgomery), 443-7500. Daily 6 p.m. to 10:30; cocktail lounge opens at 3 weekdays and 4 Saturday; Sunday brunch starts at 10. Jacket and tie required; reservations essential. Major credit cards.* In most sky room restaurants, the prices rise and the food quality sinks as you gain altitude. The Carnelian Room is an exception. While it's not inexpensive, the food is excellent, the service is pleasantly prompt and the wine list is outstanding. (Chapter 3.)

7. The most eye-appealing restaurant: TOMMY TOY'S HAUTE CUISINE CHINOISE ● *655 Montgomery St. (Clay), 397-4888. Lunch 11:30 to 3 weekdays, dinner 6 to 10 Monday-Saturday. Dressy; reservations essential. Major credit cards.* Everything about this place—even the name—is wonderfully pretentious. The restaurant is a vision of Chinese affluence with Asian tapestries, blue porcelains, wood carvings and rare paintings. The food is classic Chinese with strong a French accent. (Chapter 3.)

8. The most lively lunch joint: TOMMY'S JOYNT ● *1101 Geary (Van Ness Avenue), 775-4216. Daily 11 a.m. to 2 a.m. Casual; no reservations. Major credit cards.* Business folk and tourists line up for lunch at this busy, cluttered hofbrau. Order a spicy pastrami sandwich or buffalo stew, find a table and study the faded posters, curios and other doo-dads on the walls and ceilings. (Chapter 9.)

9. The strangest dinner you'll ever enjoy: THE MANSIONS HOTEL RESTAURANT ● *2220 Sacramento St. (Laguna), 929-9444. Dinner shows Monday-Thursday at 6:45 for $35 prix fixe, Friday-Saturday at 6:15 for $40. Dressy; reservations required. Major credit cards.* Irrepressible Bob Pritikin, successful hotelier and musical saw expert, has fashioned two Victorian mansions into an overly-decorated hotel, with a dining room to match. Dinners are preceded by magic shows; on weekends Pritikin entertains with such feats as the "incredible Peking snow duck double transfer" (not a menu item). All this, plus good food. (Chapter 15.)

10. The best Sunday brunch: GARDEN COURT ● *Sheraton Palace Hotel, 639 Market St. (New Montgomery), 392-8600. Brunch from 10:30 to 2 p.m., also regular daily meal service. Dressy; reservations advised. Major credit cards.* Recently renovated, this great open space is a study in Victorian opulence with a lofty glass dome, fluted columns and elaborate chandeliers. It's a wonderful setting for the culinary bounty spread over white-clothed tables every Sunday morning. (Chapter 3.)

The Top Ten Ethnic Restaurants

Perhaps nowhere else in the world can one sample such a variety of exotic foods. The selection includes various European types, Chinese, Japanese, Mexican, Basque, Brazilian, Persian, Nicaraguan, Salvadorean and a wide selection of Thai, Vietnamese and other Southeast Asian places.

Check the Yellow Pages under "Restaurant Guide" for a list of cafes by type. Here are some favorites.

1. The best Arabic restaurant: THE GRAPELEAF ● *4031 Balboa St. (41st Avenue), 668-*

1515. *Wednesday-Saturday 5:30 to 9:30. Casual; reservations accepted. MC/VISA, AMEX.* You'll have to travel far out into the Richmond District (Geary Boulevard, then left onto 41st) to find this intimate Lebanese restaurant. But the spicy fare is worth the trip, and the wriggling belly dancer provides a proper atmosphere. (Chapter 13.)

2. The best Chinese restaurant: BRANDY HO'S ● *217 Columbus Avenue (Pacific), 788-7527; also at 450 Broadway, 362-6268. Daily 11:30 a.m. to 11 p.m. (to midnight Friday and Saturday). Casual; no reservations. MC/VISA.* It's ridiculous to select one Chinese restaurant out of the hundreds in the city. For one thing, there's no such thing as "Chinese" fare; it's either Cantonese, Szechuan, Hunan, Shanghai and who knows what else. Brandy's is the best place to sample this variety; the menu leans toward spicy Hunan, but you can find mild Cantonese dishes as well. (Chapter 4.)

3. The best French restaurant: MASA'S ● *648 Bush St. (Powell), 989-7154. Tuesday-Saturday 6 to 9 p.m. Dressy; reservations essential, well in advance. Major credit cards.* Expect to be separated from $150 and beyond for a full dinner for two; it's the most expensive restaurant in the city. The decor is understated elegance; the service is attentive and not obtrusive. The fare----frankly French----is superb. (Chapter 3.)

4. The best German restaurant: BEETHOVEN ● *1707 Powell Street (Union), 391-4488. Tuesday-Saturday 5:30 to 10:30 p.m. Informal; reservations accepted. MC/VISA.* In this oasis of old Germany, you're lulled by a softly ticking cuckoo clock and the soft strains of a Strauss waltz. The fare is remarkably inexpensive for Beethoven's rather elegant decor. (Chapter 5.)

5. The best Indian restaurant: GAYLORD ● *Ghirardelli Square (900 North Point at Polk), 771-8822; also at One Embarcadero Center, 397-7775. Lunch noon to 2 and dinner 5 to 11 daily. Dressy; reservations essential. Major credit cards.* One of the oldest and still the finest of the city's East India restaurants, Gaylord offers an exquisite setting in which to savor tandoor specialties and spicy curry creations. (Chapter 7.)

6. The best Italian restaurant: BASTA PASTA ● *1268 Grant Avenue (Vallejo), 434-2248. Daily 11:45 a.m. to 2 a.m. Informal to casual; reservations accepted. MC/VISA, AMEX.* A popular late-night spot for locals, Basta Pasta is a lively, attractive cafe serving excellent pasta and other Italian specialties. Try the catch of the day, guaranteed fresh since the management owns part of a fishing boat. (Chapter 5.)

7. The best Japanese restaurant: YOSHIDA-YA ● *2909 Webster St. (Union), 346-3431. Sunday 5 to 10 and Monday-Saturday 5:30 to 11. Informal; reservations accepted. Major credit cards.* You have your choice of floor-seating tatami rooms, American-style tables or a sleek sushi bar at this handsome Marina District establishment. (Chapter 15.)

8. The best Mexican restaurant: CADILLAC BAR AND GRILL ● *One Holland Court (off Howard, between Fourth and Fifth, downtown), 543-8226. Monday-Thursday 11 to 11, Friday 11 to midnight and Saturday 5 to midnight. Casual; no reservations. Major credit cards.* This barn-like place, decorated mostly with noise, may seem an odd choice as the city's best Mexican restaurant. It's better known as a chaotic, Corona-wielding yuppie bar. Yet, lightly done fish, tasty *fajitas*, pork *carnitas* and other savories emerge from its mesquite grill. (Chapter 8.)

9. The best middle European restaurant: VLASTA'S ● *2420 Lombard St. (Scott), 931-7533. Tuesday-Sunday 5:30 to 11. Informal to casual; reservations accepted. MC/VISA, AMEX.* This restaurant on Lombard's motel row features a tasty mix of Czechoslovakian, Hungarian and German fare—ranging from Bohemian duckling to *rouladin*. Prices are surprisingly modest. (Chapter 15.)

10. The best Southeast Asian restaurant: KHAN TOKE THAI HOUSE ● *5937 Geary Blvd. (23rd Avenue), 668-6654. Daily 5 to 11. Informal to casual; reservations accepted. MC/VISA, AMEX.* Scores of Vietnamese, Thai, Indonesian, Malaysian and Cambodian restaurants have opened here recently. Khan Toke Thai is the best of the bunch, with tasty fare served in a handsomely done dining room that's a near-museum of Thailand folk art. (Chapter 13.)

SAN FRANCISCO-STYLE DINING:
Keeping Pace With Yesterday

Well, good grief, who hasn't heard of California cuisine, launched by Alice Waters of Berkeley's Chez Panisse? It has spread to San Francisco, Phoenix, Portland and possibly even Peoria.

However, after years of nibbling feta, polenta, air-dried tomatoes and designer salads without enough greens to keep a rabbit regular, we're returning to an older cuisine. It emerged here more than a century ago, as a shotgun marriage of Gold Rush opulence and frontier deprivation. Gold brought sudden wealth to 1850s San Francisco, but it was still isolated from the rest of the world. Cooks, mostly Italian and Chinese, made do with what they could find— fish from the sea, oysters from the bay, fresh vegetables from hastily-planted gardens and occasional shipments of wine from France.

From this scanty affluence came a special kind of dining. Menus were refined yet unpretentious, often with Italian accents. Restaurants were richly paneled in carved woods. Waiters wore tuxedos; patrons wore pants made of Levi Strauss' tent canvas. The atmosphere was at once formal and casual.

A few such places survive. If you favor fresh fish or chops cooked without odd spices, great wedges of sourdough bread and a glass of respectable wine, served by a waiter who may appear aloof but isn't, patronize one of these places. You'll find common threads of identity. They're generally better for lunch than dinner, they rarely employ waitresses, and they're masculine in decor, yet genteel and somehow not quite chauvinistic.

BARDELLI'S ● *243 O'Farrell (Mason); 982-0243. Lunch weekdays, dinner Monday-Saturday; reservations advised; informal; full bar. Major credit cards.* Established in 1909, this downtown fixture with an Italian tilt specializes in beef and veal dishes.

JACK'S ● *615 Sacramento (Montgomery); 986-9854. Lunch weekdays, dinner nightly; reservations essential;*

The Top Ten Entertainment Spots

Unlike many Western American cities where the downtown area is evacuated after dark, San Francisco is alive with bar-hoppers, party-goers and theater patrons.

---

dressy in evening; full bar. AMEX. With spartan decor, honest steaks and seafood and tuxedoed waiters, Jack's was a Financial District fixture before there was a Financial District. It dates from 1864.

JOHN'S GRILL • *63 Ellis (Powell); 986-0069. Lunch and dinner Monday-Saturday; reservations accepted; informal; full bar. MC/VISA, AMEX.* Dashiell Hammett's Sam Spade put this 1908 restaurant on the map; good chops and seafood have kept it there. Go for the food and the Sam Spade memorabilia.

MAYE'S ITALIAN AND SEAFOOD RESTAURANT • *1233 Polk (Sutter); 474-7674. Lunch and dinner daily, service from 2 p.m. Sundays and holidays; reservations accepted; informal; full bar. MC/VISA, AMEX.* Dating from 1867, this Polk Gulch place serves tasty, affordable fish and pasta. New owners have brightened—yet preserved—its old San Francisco look.

ORIGINAL JOE'S • *144 Taylor (Turk), PRospect 5-4877. Lunch and dinner daily; casual; full bar. MC/VISA.* It's the oldest surviving "Joe" style restaurant, with an open kitchen, black-jacketed waiters and an Italian menu. So, who's Joe? The name came from for Joe Morelio, a nightclub owner who financed the first such place, opened by Frank Venturi in 1937.

SAM'S GRILL AND SEAFOOD RESTAURANT • *374 Bush (Montgomery), 421-0594. Lunch and dinner weekdays; informal; full bar. MC/VISA, DIN.* This slice of yesterday opened its doors in 1867 and hasn't closed them since—except on weekends. With wood paneling, deep booths and fine seafood and chops, it's a local dining landmark.

TADICH GRILL • *240 California (Front), 391-2373. Lunch and dinner weekdays; informal; full bar. No reservations or credit cards.* The California Gold Rush was just getting started when a forerunner of Tadich started serving locally-caught fish and an occasional stray chicken in 1849. Fish is still a specialty.

Our recommended list is eclectic and alphabetical. Theatre is alive and well in San Francisco and having a good time, so we begin there. (See the "Getting Ticketed" section of Chapter 1.)

1. AMERICAN CONSERVATORY THEATRE
● *Geary Theatre, 415 Geary St. (Mason). Call 749-2228 or 749-2200 or write: ACT Subscriptions Office, 450 Geary St., San Francisco, CA 94102.* ACT presents a mix of classic and contemporary plays, usually at the venerable Geary in the downtown Theater Row.

2. ALIVE AND ONSTAGE ● Four other major theaters offer dramas, comedies, musicals, stand-up routines and revues. The **Curran** is just up from the Geary Theatre at 445 Geary St. (Taylor) and the **Marines Memorial Theatre** is at 609 Sutter St. (Mason). The **Golden Gate Theatre** is at #1 Taylor, fronting on Market and the **Orpheum** is at 1192 Market (Hyde and Grove). The number for all four is 474-3800. (See "Getting ticketed" in Chapter 1.)

3. BEACH BLANKET BABYLON ● *Club Fugazi, 678 Green St. (Powell); 421-4222.* The long-running "Beach Blanket Babylon" series is the best of several slapstick song-and-dance comedy shows in the city.

4. COMEDY CLUBS ● The city is noted for stand-up comics, frequently featured on cable TV. Among the more popular clubs are **Cobb's** in the Cannery (2801 Leavenworth at Columbus), 928-4320; **Holy City Zoo,** 408 Clement St. (15th Avenue), 386-4242; **The Other Cafe** at 100 Carl St. (near Cole, in the Haight-Ashbury district), 681-0748; and **The Punch Line,** 444 Battery Street (near Washington, downtown), 397-7573.

5. GREAT AMERICAN MUSIC HALL ● *859 O'Farrell St. (Polk), 885-0750.* A long-popular supper club, it features a variety of live folk groups, light rock, comedy and jazz. Most shows are family-oriented.

6. THE PLUSH ROOM ● *York Hotel at 940 Sutter Street (Hyde), 885-6800.* This handsomely-appointed little cabaret offers lounge acts ranging from comics to small musical revues to rising and fading stars.

7. SAN FRANCISCO BALLET ● *War Memorial Opera House, 401 Van Ness (Grove); 621-3838. Write San Francisco Ballet Company, 455 Franklin St., San Francisco, CA 94102.* One of America's most respected ballet companies, it begins its season with a December presentation of *The Nutcracker,* followed by several major winter-spring productions.

8. SAN FRANCISCO OPERA ● *War Memorial Opera House; 864-3330.* This fine company presents a range of things operatic. Seasons are May to June and September to mid-December; tickets are scarce, so order early.

9. SAN FRANCISCO SYMPHONY ● *Davies Symphony Hall, Van Ness at Grove; 864-6000 (season tickets) and 431-5400 (individual performance tickets). Write: San Francisco Symphony, Davies Symphony Hall, San Francisco, CA 94102.* Before you leave the city, catch a performance in the splendid Louise M. Davies Symphony Hall. Its September-through-June season features 200 programs, ranging from Bach to bop.

10. SLIM'S ● *333 11th St. (Folsom), 621-3330.* This spiffy nightclub-restaurant is co-owned by Boz Skaggs, who occasionally appears on stage as "Presidio Slim." It has a New Orleans look, and features made-in-America jazz, rock and blues. The restaurant serves American *nouveau* and regional cuisine.

DOWNTOWN SAN FRANCISCO

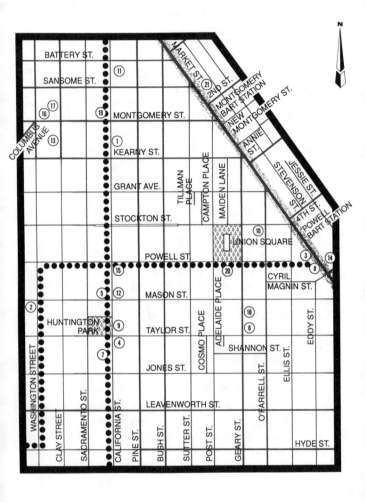

DIRECTORY

1. BANK OF AMERICA (CARNELIAN ROOM)
2. CABLE CAR MUSEUM
3. CABLE CAR TURNTABLE
4. CALIFORNIA MASONIC TEMPLE
5. FAIRMONT HOTEL
6. FOUR SEASON CLIFT HOTEL
7. GRACE CATHEDRAL
8. HALLIDIE PLAZA VISITOR CENTER
9. HUNTINGTON HOTEL
10. MACY'S
11. MANDARIN ORIENTAL
12. MARK HOPKINS
13. PONY EXPRESS PLAQUES
14. SAN FRANCISCO CENTRE
15. STANFORD COURT
16. TRANSAMERICA PYRAMID
17. REDWOOD PARK
18. THEATER ROW: GEARY & CURRAN
19. WELLS FARGO HISTORY MUSEUM
20. WESTIN ST. FRANCIS HOTEL
21. WORLD OF OIL MUSEUM
... CABLE CAR LINES
\\\\ BART

Three
DOWNTOWN/NOB HILL
The city's shopping heart

> **A QUICK LOOK:** Downtown San Francisco is home to several large department stores, upscale shops and luxury hotels, clustered around Union Square. Just to the east is the Financial District, extending toward the waterfront. Above all this is Nob Hill, once home to railroad barons and silver magnates. It's now home to upscale hotels, restaurants and luxury apartments.

LET'S ASSUME you've followed our advice in Chapter 1 and started your visit with a trip to the Visitor Information Center in Hallidie Plaza. It's a large, barn-like structure decorated mostly with information, set in a recessed plaza below the Powell and Market cable car turntable.

Now, map-and-brochure laden, you emerge and stare quizzically at the city swirling busily around you. You're in the heart of town, surrounded by major hotels and most of the city's leading department stores.

Where shall we begin? For that matter, where are we?

Begin by getting your bearings. Take the escalator from the recessed plaza up to the cable car turntable. Powell Street—busy with traffic and cable cars—runs due north from Market, climbing to **Nob Hill**. If you were to continue on Powell, you would brush the edge of **Chinatown** (downhill and off to the right), pass through **North Beach** and eventually hit the waterfront near **Fisherman's Wharf**.

You notice that Market Street runs at a 45-degree angle to Powell and other downtown streets; it travels from the northeast to the southwest. Going down Market, you would shortly arrive at the **Ferry Building,** to the left of the **San Francisco-Oakland Bay Bridge**. Lean into the street—carefully—and you can see the 1896 structure, which appears to block Market to keep it from spilling into the bay.

Heading up Market, you would skim the edge of the **Civic Center** (off to the right) and hit the **Castro District**. There, Market swings westward and climbs rather steeply toward **Twin Peaks**. Near the crest of the city's hilly backbone, Market changes its name to Portola Drive and heads for **San Francisco State University** and **Lake Merced**. The ocean is just beyond.

The city's main residential areas—Richmond and Sunset—lie almost directly west of you, separated by slender Golden Gate Park. If you traveled up Powell a few blocks and hung a left onto Geary Street, you'd cross Van Ness Avenue, pass through **Japantown** and enter the heart of the **Richmond District**. Or if you scooted up Market and did a half-right onto Haight Street, you would go through the **Haight-Ashbury District** of flower child fame and bump into **Golden Gate Park**. To the left of the park, rimmed by Lincoln Way, is the **Sunset District**.

Behind you—assuming you're still standing there, staring curiously up Powell—is the south of Market area, often called **SoMa** or SOMA; take your pick of the spelling. Here, the streets are aligned with Market—either parallel or perpendicular. Also behind you are two of the city's major department stores, **Emporium-Capwell** and **Nordstrom**, which crowns the dramatic new **San Francisco Centre** shopping complex. The "Centre," with its four-story atrium and curved escalators, is certainly worth a browse.

Because SoMa is home to many nightspots, it has been compared with London's SOHO entertainment district. But as you will discover in Chapter 8, there is little similarity. SoMa is primarily an industrial, warehousing and factory outlet shopping area. The nightspots are widely scattered.

DOWNTOWN WALKING TOUR

We've said this is a walking city, so point your Nikes up Powell and start hoofing it. Or queue up for a cable car, after first buying your ticket or transit pass at a vending machine. If the line is discouragingly long, you might do better to walk up Powell a few blocks and try to squeeze aboard at one of the intersection stops.

Immediately to the right of the cable car turntable is formidable old **F.W. Woolworth,** a landmark store in the turn-of-the-century Flood building. It's perhaps the least expensive place in town to buy souvenirs. This all-purpose store also has two budget cafes, check cashing booths, groceries, a deli and general merchandise.

The first three blocks of Powell are lined with a mix of tourist trinket shops, yogurt stands and audio-video stores assaulting your ears with sidewalk speakers. You also brush past street musicians and vendors selling T-shirts, costume jewelry, used license plates and other essentials. This is not one of the city's more tranquil areas.

At the first intersection, walk half a block down Ellis Street to **John's Grill,** a sturdy old chops and seafood place made famous by Dashiell Hammett as Sam Spade's hangout in *The Maltese Falcon.* Stop in for a drink or lunch and inspect the Hammett memorabilia spread over three floors. Most of the stuff is on the third floor, a private dining room that's generally open to browsing.

Continuing up Powell, you'll see **Hotel Villa Florence** and **Kuleto's**—a popular designer restaurant, between O'Farrell and Geary. On your right is the huge **Macy's** department store, sprawling through several buildings.

Above Macy's is **Union Square,** considered the focal point of downtown San Francisco, and the heart of its shopping district. In fact, it ranks fourth in the country in shopping area sales volume.

It's difficult to imagine, but if you traveled back to 1849 during the peak of gold discovery fever, you'd

During Christmas shopping season, holiday streamers glitter from the atrium of the dramatic new San Francisco Centre.

be standing near a good-sized stream, looking at a low, sandy hill where Union Square now sits. Today, it's a landscaped patch of green with a large parking garage beneath. The square earned its name in 1860 when demonstrators gathered to urge Californians to support the Union in the Civil War.

A **Gray Line** ticket office built into a British double-decker bus seems perpetually parked beside Union Square. It can be handy in case you get tired of walking and decide to take a tour.

Opposite the square is the venerable **Westin St.**

Francis Hotel, fronting Powell between Geary and Post streets. Step into the lobby of this bold French Renaissance structure. Admire the great chandeliers, walnut paneling and fluted tapestry that speak silently of the era of grand hotels. An elaborately carved nine-foot walnut clock in the lobby's far right-hand corner is a traditional meeting place. Settle into the lobby bar or the lushly-decorated **Compass Rose,** order a drink and indulge in a bit of people-watching.

From here, stroll up Geary Street, perhaps popping into **Lefty O'Doul's** at 333 Geary to admire a hundred years of sports memorabilia. Founded by the late San Francisco baseball hero, it's a pleasant old hofbrau and saloon. Crossing Mason on Geary, you enter the city's small but active theater district. The venerable stone-front **Geary** and **Curran** theaters are on your left, between Mason and Taylor. This block also might be called Kosher Row. Opposite the show-houses are **Natan's Grill Restaurant** at 450 Geary and **David's Delicatessen Restaurant** at 474. A fixture since 1952, David's is a theater crowd hangout. Natan's is a small Mideastern kosher cafe.

The **Four Seasons Clift** at 495 Geary (Taylor) is one of the city's more refined small hotels with a cozily elegant lobby of floral drapes and carpeting. Its redwood-paneled **Redwood Room** is an upscale bar with an exclusive men's club feel. It's also one of the few pubs in the city with a dress code: jackets please, gentlemen.

At Geary and Taylor, turn right, go up a block and swing left onto Post Street. This is an area of small restaurants and corner grocers—a transition zone between city center businesses and apartments. Mid-block between Taylor and Jones, glance to your right up **Trader Vic Alley** to the near-legendary restaurant of the same name. Victor Bergeron "invented" Polynesian-style restaurants in the 1930s (along with the mai tai). This is the oldest surviving Vic's. With a corrugated roof and plain walls, it looks a bit like an urban shed, but the interior transports you to the tropics. Stop by for a native punch.

Turn uphill again at Post and Jones and walk to Sutter, then loop back toward downtown. This is

The cable car turntable at Powell and Market Streets is a good place to begin a city exploration.

gallery row. Art galleries, antique shops and rare book stores line the street for three blocks. Stop in at any of the galleries for a copy of the **Gallery Guide,** which will direct you to more of them. You'll also pass **Fleur de Lys** (777 Sutter), one of the city's finest restaurants and **Lehr's Greenhouse Restaurant and Florist** (740 Sutter), where you can lunch or sup in a forest of greenery. Also, watch for **Kinder-Zimmer** on the left between Mason and Powell; it's a small wonderland of European toys.

Continue down Sutter, cross the cable car tracks at Powell, then turn right at Stockton and hike down to the **Grand Hyatt** (formerly Hyatt Union Square). Set into its impressive tier of brick steps is the **Ruth Asawa Fountain.** Scores of scampering figures, originally cast in bread dough, offer a whimsical portrayal of life in the city.

From here, drop down to Post and turn left. You're now into serious shopping country. For the next three blocks, as Post slopes gently downhill to Market, you'll encounter **Sak's Fifth Avenue, Burberry's, D. Fine, Alfred Dunhill, Gumps, Gucci, Elizabeth Arden, Eddie Bauer, Brooks Brothers,**

Polo/Ralph Lauren and **Gianinni Versace. Shreve and Company**, an opulent jewelry store at 200 Post (Grant), dates back to 1852; it's been on this site since 1906—one of the few downtown survivors of the earthquake.

More upscale shops line Geary, paralleling Post a block below. You'll find the backside of **Macy's**, plus **I. Magnin** and **Neiman Marcus** with its impressive glass tower and **Rotunda** restaurant. After checking out the Geary shops, return to Post and continue down toward Market. At 50 Post, turn into the impressive glass-domed **Crocker Galleria** with three tiers of shops lining a handsome plaza.

Financial District

Just short of Market, turn left onto Kearny Street and walk beneath the high-rises of the city's **Financial District.** This isn't Manhattan, but some of the skyscrapers top thirty floors. The second highest is the **Bank of America** world headquarters at Kearny and California. The **Carnelian Room** cocktail lounge and restaurant are perched atop this 52-story dark granite monolith. If it's after 3 p.m. on weekdays, 4 on Saturday or 10 a.m. Sunday, catch the high-speed elevator to the top for a drink and a dazzling view.

Continue along Kearny, listening to the slap of cable car cables as you cross California Street, then turn right onto Clay. You're brushing the edge of **Chinatown** here, which we cover in depth in the next chapter.

Mid-block on Clay Street (left side), you'll see several plaques heralding the **Pony Express.** This was the western headquarters of the horseback mail service that scampered between California and Missouri from April 1860 to October 1861. Actually, the San Francisco-Sacramento leg was accomplished by ferryboat. You'll learn that 120 young riders covered more than 650,000 miles with only one interrupted schedule and one lost mail sack. If only the U.S. Postal Service could post such a record!

Incidentally, contrary to what you've seen on film and TV, just one rider died at the hands of Indians.

At Clay and Montgomery, turn and stare at that curious elongated triangle called the **Transamerica**

Pyramid. Considered an architectural outrage by some when it was erected in 1972, it's now regarded—even affectionately—as an integral part of the city's skyline. At 853 feet, it's the tallest building in the city, but the last 212 feet is a windowless spire containing mechanical equipment. The top floor is the 48th, somewhat lower than the neighboring Bank of America. You can catch a view down toward the waterfront from a 27th floor public observation area, open weekdays (except holidays) from 9 to 4.

Redwood Park is a pretty little downtown forest of redwood trees, nestled at the foot of the Pyramid on the Clay Street side. Occasional lunchtime concerts are held here from May through September.

From the Pyramid, walk past huddled banking towers of Montgomery's "Wall Street of the West" toward Market Street. Pause at the **Wells Fargo History Museum** in the bank building at 420 Montgomery (California). It tells the story of the founding of the Wells Fargo Express company during the Gold Rush.

Just beyond, at the corner of California and Montgomery, pass through the impressive lobby of the **Security Pacific Bank** with its rose marble columns and elaborate coffered ceiling. Another imposing old Financial District structure is the **Merchants Exchange Building** at 465 California, half a block down from Montgomery; it shelters First Interstate Bank.

Continue down California to Sansome and turn right for a view of the striking new twin-towered **First Interstate Center**. It's towers are topped by two flagpoles (unkindly called architectural tweezers by some locals); they're linked by a glassed-in pedestrian bridge. At 48 stories, it's the city's third tallest structure. Rooms of the posh **Mandarin Oriental** hotel occupy the top eleven floors. The elegantly simple lobby is off a ground-floor arcade; the hotel's notable **Silks** restaurant is one floor above.

Continue down Montgomery, then cross Market for a peek at the **Sheraton Palace**, an old dowager of a hotel sporting a brand-new face lift. A landmark dating back to 1909, it's noted mostly for its impressive **Garden Court,** with a lofty leaded-glass ceiling.

Across the way, at New Montgomery and Stevenson Alley, is the 1908 **House of Shields,** a typical early San Francisco drinking establishment. Stop in for a libation (or lunch from 11:30 to 3) and admire the rich walnut paneling, turn-of-the-century tulip chandeliers and high-backed booths.

Return to Market and walk just over a block down to **A World of Oil,** a nicely-done museum in the Chevron building at 555 Market (Second Street). A small gallery with changing exhibits is adjacent. As you entered the building, you no doubt noticed the attractive **Chevron floral garden** outside. Now, cross Market and start back uphill, pausing to check out **Lotta's Fountain** on a pedestrian island where Geary and Kearny meet. It was presented to the city in 1875 by celebrated entertainer Lotta Crabtree. Stroll half a block up Kearny, then drop into **Brooks Cameras,** which houses a slightly scruffy but interesting museum of old photographic gear.

Wrap around the corner of Brooks and turn right into **Maiden Lane.** Once a brothel-lined street of sin called St. Mark's Lane, this two-block pedestrian alley offers a nice selection of shops and galleries. It's not quite as pretty as its demure name implies, but plans were afoot at this writing to install bronzed gates at its Kearny and Stockton entrances and spruce up the place a bit. Occasionally, the lane hosts an arts and crafts exhibit and sale.

This shopping alley offers four places of note: the fine **Iron Horse** restaurant and lounge at #19, with its warm woods, plush booths and dim lighting; the **Nosheria,** at 69, which builds enormous pastrami and corned beef sandwiches and other deli fare, then invites you to eat them at outdoor tables; the **Circle Gallery** at 140, the only building in the city designed by Frank Lloyd Wright; and, for yuppie puppies, **Robinson's Pet Shop** at 135, where you can buy Bowser Brittle and Dandy Doggie popcorn.

From the lane, you emerge onto Stockton, staring across at Union Square and the **STBS** discount ticket center (Chapter 1), where you can get day-of-performance ducats at half price. Turn left onto Stockton, walk downhill to Market, take a half-right and you're back at your cable car turntable starting point.

Nob Hill

Unless you *really* like to hike, Nob Hill is best reached by cable car. Take either the Hyde and Beach or Bay and Taylor. Both scramble up steep Powell Street and cross the California cable car line at California. Some of the city's steeper streets fall away from Nob Hill. Taylor is so tilted that its sidewalk is a set of steps.

Why Nob Hill's odd spelling? Because it isn't *Knob* Hill. "Nob" is short for nabob, from the Hindu word "nawab," referring to a person of considerable wealth and power. When the first city-builders came, Nob Hill was a 376-foot scrub-brush promontory. It was pretty much ignored by those teeming about the waterfront below. Later, the era's quick millionaires fancied it as a proper pedestal for their grand abodes.

The "Big Four" of transcontinental railroad fame—Charles Crocker, Leland Stanford, Mark Hopkins and Collis P. Huntington— were among the first to erect mansions here, in the 1870s. Nevada's Comstock Lode silver barons, James Flood and James G. Fair, soon joined them. By the time Robert Louis Stevenson visited the city in 1882, Nob Hill was covered with grandiose symbols of self-indulgence. He called it "the hill of palaces."

Only one of the mansions survives today; many went up in smoke after the 1906 earthquake. The 1886 baronial brownstone of **James Flood** stands at the corner of California and Mason streets. You can admire it only from the sidewalk; it now shelters the exclusive Pacific Union Club.

Although the other palaces are gone, their owners' names live on: Fair's Fairmont Hotel, the Mark Hopkins and Huntington Hotel.

Your cable car has deposited you near the lower entrance to the stately block-long **Fairmont**. Explore its lush, almost overdone lobby, lounges and upholstered hallways. It's a busy study in floriated trim, red velvet settees, plush carpets and impressive marble columns. Does it look familiar? It's the St. Gregory of TV's *Hotel* series.

Opposite the Fairmont at Powell and California is the **Stanford Court**, an upscale mid-sized hotel with large stained glass domes in its carriage way and lobby. The **Mark Hopkins**, at California and Mason, is a bit less imposing than the Fairmont, but it's hardly a Motel 6. The **Top of the Mark** was the first of the city's sky room lounges, a special haunt of World War II GIs. It's still a favorite, open for sipping and viewing daily from 4 p.m. to 1:30 a.m.

Stroll westward past the small, opulent **Huntington Hotel** at California and Taylor. Its posh pillows have been fluffed by Princess Margaret, Alistair Cooke, Pavarotti, Lauren Bacall and other worthies. Its **Big Four Restaurant** offers excellent food and memorabilia of the railroad barons, for whom it was named; plan a dinner or lunch there.

Across the way is **Huntington Park**, a carefully landscaped patch of green where the wealthy still walk their carefully landscaped poodles. Adjacent is **Grace Cathedral,** one of the city's most imposing churches and home to the Episcopal Diocese of California. Its great gothic towers reach heavenward from land donated by the Crocker family. The modern polished granite **California Masonic Memorial Temple** across the way is another impressive Nob Hill edifice. Step inside to view a panoramic glass mural depicting the history of Masons in California.

From here, re-trace your steps to Mason Street and scoot two blocks downhill to the **Cable Car Museum** and carbarn at the corner of Washington Street. Here, you will learn how these fascinating little motorless machines function.

Now you're on the uphill edge of Chinatown, ready to explore our next chapter.

WHAT TO SEE & DO

Cable Car Museum ● △△△△ ☺
1201 Mason St. (Washington); 474-1887. Free; daily 10 to 6. This is a working museum since it's built into a loft of the carbarn, the heart of the cable car system. Here, powerful electric motors turn giant sheaves (pulleys), whose ropes (cables) disappear under the streets to tug the little cars along at 9.5 miles an hour. Photos, models and antique cable cars tell the story of this amazing mode of transit. A museum gift shop sells the usual useless souvenirs, along with useful ones like coffee mugs and T-shirts.

California Masonic Memorial Temple ● △△

1111 California St. (Taylor); 776-4702. Free; open weekdays 9 to 4:30. Two features make this modern marble temple worth a stop. A huge mixed-media mosaic window in the large foyer tells the story of Masonry in California. Also note the exquisitely crafted model of King Solomon's Temple, done on the scale of one-quarter inch to one cubit (20.64 inches).

Dashiell Hammett Tour ● △△

Departs from the public library, Larkin at McAllister, every Saturday from May through August; 939-1214. No reservations; "just show up." Dashiell Hammett aficionado Don Herron guides you along downtown streets and alleys haunted by the famed writer and his legendary detective, Sam Spade. Outings cover four hours and about three miles.

Grace Cathedral ● △△△

1051 Taylor St. (California); 776-6611. Free; doors open 7 a.m. to 6 p.m.; guided tours Sundays at 12:30 and 2, weekdays at 1 and 3 and Saturdays at 11:30 and 1:30. One of the city's grandest churches, it's the largest Gothic structure west of the Mississippi. Note particularly the Doors of Paradise on the Taylor Street side, with ten panels of carved Old Testament scenes. Then step into the main sanctuary and admire its vaulted arch ceiling and brilliant stained glass windows.

Wells Fargo History Museum ● △△△ ☺

420 Montgomery St. (California); 396-2619. Free; open weekdays (except holidays) 9 to 5. The city's best free museum, it tells the story of the Wells Fargo Express Company, the Gold Rush and the development of early California. Displays of gold flakes and nuggets are particularly impressive. The kids can mount the driver's seat of a disassembled Concord stage and snap the ribbons (reins), or climb into the coach and hear a harrowing story of an 1859 crossing to California. Philatelists will like a pull-out exhibit of old letters that traveled by stagecoach.

The World of Oil ● △△

555 Market St. (Second), in the Chevron USA building; 894-5193. Free; open weekdays (except holidays) 9 to 3:30. In this small, neatly arranged museum, you'll learn how the earth is formed, how plate tectonics makes things shake, and how oil is found, pumped out and processed. Exhibits include mean-looking drill bits, models of drilling rigs and a mock-up of an early-day gas station. Test your conservation knowledge at a computerized "Energy Learning Center."

WHERE TO DINE

Bardelli's Restaurant ● △△ $$

243 O'Farrell St. (Powell); 982-0243. Italian-continental; dinners $8.50 to $17; full bar. Weekdays 11:30 to 10, Saturday 5 to 10. Reservations accepted; informal. Major credit cards. Warm woods, stained glass and tuxedo-clad waiters mark this as classic San Francisco. In business since 1909, Bardelli's serves good, honest fare, ranging from fresh fish to Italian veal and pasta.

Bentley's ● △△△ $$$ Ø

185 Sutter St. (Kearny); 989-6895. Seafood; dinners $15 to $25; full bar. Weekdays 11:30 to 10, Saturday 5 to 10. Reservations advised; informal. Major credit cards. A glistening oyster bar is a focal point of this attractive seafood parlor with an impressive etched glass entry. Chef Amey Shaw's seafood, with California and Southwest *nouveau* touches, is excellent. The restaurant is adjacent to the Galleria Park Hotel.

The Big Four ● △△△△△ $$$$ Ø

1075 California St. (in the Huntington Hotel at Taylor); 771-1140. American-continental; dinners $22 to $32; full bar. Daily 7 to 10 a.m., 11:30 to 3 and 5:30 to 10 p.m. Reservations advised. Dressy; jackets required at dinner. Major credit cards. It's one of the city's pre-eminent restaurants, offering attentive service and creative cuisine in an atmosphere of quiet elegance. The stylish decor celebrates the city's glory days, from the Gold Rush to the railroad barons—for whom it is named. The menu is "continental contemporary," and it changes with the seasons. We like to end our meals with dessert and coffee in the oldstyle bar, warmed by a cheery fire and mellowed by a tinkling piano. The dining room, incidentally, is smoke-free.

Carlos Goldstein's ● △△ $$

282 O'Farrell St. (Mason); 397-3356. Sort of Mexican; dinners $5 to $12; full bar service. Daily 11 a.m. to 2 a.m. No reservations; casual. Major credit cards. Take nothing seriously at Carlos Goldstein's—including the food. A Jewish cantina serving kosher burritos? It's a fun place where regulars gather for TV sports events and scrawl their signatures on the walls, between sepia photos of Pancho Villa and his rowdies. Other cafes have copied this light-hearted Latin theme, but this is the original. And those kosher burritos are remarkably tasty.

China Moon Cafe ● △△△ $$$ ∅

639 Post St. (Taylor); 775-4789. California-Chinese; dinners $15 to $25; wine and beer. Lunch Monday-Saturday 11:30 to 2:15, dinner daily 5:30 to 10. Reservations accepted; informal. MC/VISA. Barbara Tropp married Chinese cuisine to California *nouveau* and came up with tasty curiosities such as fried sturgeon topped with roasted bell pepper sauce. It may not sell in Shanghai, but her creations propelled this bright Art Deco (and smoke-free) restaurant into quick popularity.

Ciao ● △△△ $$$

230 Jackson St. (Front); 982-9500. Northern Italian; dinners $12 to $20; full bar service. Monday-Saturday 11 to midnight, Sunday 4 to 10:30. Reservations accepted; informal. Major credit cards. Ciao, Baby; you'll like the upscale Italian look of white tile and brass. The food's also appealing in this popular gathering place. Pastas abound, closely followed by veal dishes and other *entrees Italiano*.

Circolo Restaurant ● △△△ $$ ∅

161 Sutter St. (in Crocker Galleria); 362-0404. Northern Italian; dinners $10 to $18; full bar service. Lunch weekdays 11:30 to 3, dinner Monday-Saturday 5 to 10. Reservations accepted; informal. Major credit cards. Gourmet pizza sounds like a self-canceling phrase, but Circolo's version nearly lives up to its billing. This smartly-decorated restaurant also offers the usual parade of pastas and things grilled Italian style.

Corona Bar & Grill ● △△ $$

88 Cyril Magnin (Ellis); 392-5500. Regional Mexican; dinners $10 to $17.50; full bar service. Daily 11:30 a.m. to 11 p.m. Reservations accepted; informal. Major credit cards. Dressed in requisite salmon and turquoise, Corona features Southwestern fare as well as upscale Mexican. To the uninitiated, Southwestern is California cuisine served with *polenta* and tortillas.

Faz Restaurant & Bar ● △△△ $$

132 Bush St. (Sansome); 362-4484. American; smoked specialties; dinners $10 to $15; full bar service. Lunch Monday-Friday 11:30 to 3, dinner Tuesday-Friday 5 to 9. Reservations suggested; informal. Major credit cards. Faz Poursohi's thing is smoked fish and game, done on the premises. Entrees arrive at your table in neat little fan shapes; most taste as good as they look.

Fleur de Lys ● △△△△△ $$$$ ∅

777 Sutter St. (Taylor); 673-7779. French, with a Mediterranean accent; dinners $8.50 to $35; full bar service. Monday-Thursday 6 to 10, Friday-Saturday 6 to 10:30. Reservations essential. Dressy; jacket required, tie optional. Major credit cards. Gault Millau called this the city's best restaurant; so did a group of chefs we polled in *San Francisco's Ultimate Dining Guide*. Who are we to disagree? Dining under a canopied fabric ceiling, you will experience what chef Hubert Keller describes as "true and simple French cuisine," with lighter sauces and more innovative seasoning than traditional *cuisine de France*. The fare is equal to the legendary Masa's, the setting is more lush and the prices are easier to digest.

Garden Court at the Sheraton Palace ● △△△△ $$$

Two New Montgomery (Market); 392-8600. California nouveau; dinners $18 to $25; full bar service. Daily 7 a.m. to 11 p.m.; Sunday brunch. Reservations accepted; jackets recommended. Major credit cards. A sparkling jewel from yesterday, the Garden Court has re-opened after total renovation. This glass-domed atrium with its marble columns and gilded chandeliers is the most eye-appealing restaurant space in the city. We particularly recommend it for Sunday brunch.

The Iron Horse ● △△△ $$$

19 Maiden Lane (Kearny); 362-8133. Northern Italian; dinners $11 to $21; full bar service. Lunch Monday-Saturday 11:30 to 4, dinner nightly 4 to 10:30. Reservations advised; informal to dressy, jackets optional. Major credit cards. A clubby setting of warm woods, brick and copper provide a pleasant atmosphere for Italian fare that tilts toward *nouveau* cuisine. It's also a popular cocktail hour place with tasty hors d'oeuvres.

Jack's Restaurant ● △△△△ $$$

615 Sacramento St. (Montgomery); 986-9854. Continental-French; dinners $12 to $20; full bar service. Weekdays 11:30 to 9:30, weekends 5 to 9:30 p.m. Reservations essential. Dressy; jackets required for dinner. AMEX only. Nod knowingly to the maitre d' and you'll be spirited into one of the upstairs rooms to lunch with other power brokers. Otherwise, you'll settle for the main dining room with its understated look of old San Francisco. Here, black-jacketed, efficiently taciturn waiters serve excellent, simply cooked fare. A landmark since 1864, Jack Redinger's place is a haven for Financial District brokers and bankers. Please don't dress like you just slid off a hay wagon.

John's Grill ● △△△ $$$

63 Ellis (Powell); 986-0069. American-continental; dinners $16 to $20; full bar. Monday-Saturday 11 to 10. Reservations accepted; informal. MC/VISA, AMEX. Owners of venerable John's Grill probably make a bigger fuss over Dashiell Hammett than the writer ever did about the grill. In his epic, *The Maltese Falcon,* hero Sam Spade dined on lamb chops, sliced tomatoes and a baked potato. The modern version, "Sam Spade's Chops" is rack of lamb plus tomatoes and spuds, for a healthy $21.95. But then, nostalgia has its price. Other fare is less expensive. The place is a virtual museum of Hammett lore, with photos, clippings and other regalia. Most of it is in the Maltese Falcon Room and Hammett's Den, upstairs.

Kuleto's ● △△△ $$$$

221 Powell St. (Geary); 397-7720. Northern Italian with California nouveau accent; dinners $20 to

$40; full bar. Daily 7 a.m. to 11 p.m. *Reservations advised; informal. Major credit cards.* One of the city's trendy power luncheon spots, Kuleto's gets serious about things garnished with air-dried tomatoes and sun-dried cherries. Or is it the other way around? The innovative fare is consistently good, although it comes close to being over-priced. The look is a decorator's dream in upscale Italian deli.

La Quiche ● △△ $$

550 Taylor St. (Post); 441-2711. French; dinners $10 to $15; wine and beer. Monday-Saturday 11:30 to 2:30 and 5:30 to 10. Informal; reservations accepted. Major credit cards. This cute little French cafe, with prim pink tablecloths and linen nappery, offers modestly priced *cuisine de France* and even less expensive crepes. It's handy to the theater district.

Lefty O'Doul's ● △△△ $

333 Geary St. (Powell); 982-8900. Hofbrau; dinners $5 to $10; full bar. Open daily 7 a.m. to 12:45 a.m. Casual, no reservations or credit cards. A century of baseball memorabilia covers the walls of this pub. It was opened by local hero Lefty, who played in the big leagues then later managed the minor league San Francisco Seals before the Giants came to town. It's a folksy downtown hangout, with a hofbrau-deli and oldstyle bar.

Lehr's Greenhouse Restaurant ● △△△ $$$ Ø

740 Sutter (Taylor); 474-6478. American; dinners from $14; full bar. Daily 6:30 a.m. to 10:30 p.m., Sunday brunch 10 to 2. Reservations accepted; informal. Major credit cards. Please don't eat the daisies, but you can dine amidst Boston ferns, palms and hundreds of other plants in this distinctive arboretum cafe. The menu features seafood, light pasta and aged beef.

Masa's ● △△△ $$$$$ Ø

648 Bush St. (Powell); 989-7134. French; prix fixe dinner $68; full bar. Tuesday-Saturday 6 to 9:30. Reservations essential. Dressy; jackets requested, ties optional. Major credit cards. The best French restaurant west of New York, and possibly west of the Seine, Masa's issues impeccably prepared fare in an atmosphere of understated elegance. Service is attentive and never hovering, and the dining room is smoke-free. There is little to dislike here, except possibly the check at the end of the meal. Plan on parting with $150 to $200 per couple for dinner, a proper wine and dessert.

New Joe's ● △△△ $$$

347 Geary St. (Powell); 989-6733. Contemporary Italian; dinners $10 to $19; full bar. Daily 7 a.m. to 11 p.m. Reservations accepted; informal. Major credit cards. It has the look of the "Joe" style restaurants with an open kitchen, mahogany bar and white nappery. The menu, however, is more contemporary—mesquite grilled fish. chicken and chops.

Ristorante Donatello ● △△△△△ $$$$$ Ø

501 Post St. (Donatello Hotel, at Mason); 441-7182. Regional Italian; dinners $35 to $65; full bar service. Daily 7 to 10:30 a.m. and 5:30 to 11 p.m. Reservations essential. Dressy; coat and tie for dinner. Major credit cards. One of the city's premiere restaurants, award-winning Donatello offers intimate dining in small, elegant rooms. We named it as our favorite restaurant in *The Best of San Francisco*. And here's a particular breath of fresh air: smoking is permitted in the bar only.

Rotunda Restaurant ● △△△ $$$

150 Stockton St. (in Neiman-Marcus at Geary); 362-4777. Light continental; lunches from $14 to $20; full bar service. Monday-Saturday 11 a.m. to 5 p.m. AMEX only. The Neiman-Marcus exterior seems patterned after a deck of cheap playing cards, but the rotunda—saved from the building's City of Paris Days—is striking. A comely restaurant has been tucked under the rotunda's stained glass dome, offering a welcome retreat for tired shoppers' feet. It's all a bit pretentious, but the setting and view of Union Square are nice.

Sam's Grill and Seafood Restaurant ● △△△ $$$

374 Bush St. (Montgomery); 421-0594. American; dinners $15 to $20; full bar service. Weekdays 11 to 8:30. Informal; MC/VISA, DIN. Sam's has that almost stark, indefinable ambiance of a classic early San Francisco eatery. Dating from 1868, it's primarily a lunch hangout for Financial District business types; the seafood is excellent.

Sears Fine Food ● △△ $

439 Powell St. (Post); 986-1160. American; breakfast and lunch from $4.25 to $9; no alcohol. Wednesday-Sunday 7 a.m. to 2:30 p.m. No reservations; informal. No credit cards. You haven't done San Francisco until you've done Sears' 18 Swedish pancakes. Not 18 varieties; 18 little pancakes covered with warm maple syrup. This pleasantly funky landmark cafe lures the faithful to hearty fruit-and-pancake breakfasts and old fashioned luncheons of baby beef liver, corned beef hash and Swedish meatballs.

Silks ● △△△△△ $$$$ Ø

222 Sansome St. (California, in the Mandarin Oriental); 986-2020. California-Asian; dinners $25 to $35; full bar service. Breakfast Monday-Saturday 7 to 10:30, Sunday brunch 8 to 2, lunch weekdays 11:30 to 2, dinner nightly 6 to 10. Reservations advised; dressy; coats and ties. Major credit cards. It's difficult to categorize Silks' cuisine, except to say that our meals there have been creatively delicious. Ingredients are perfectly fresh, seasoned with accents of *nouveau* California, Asian—appropriate to the Mandarin Hotel's roots—and hints of French. The menu changes frequently; you may happen across lobster yakitori or grilled ginger chicken with buckwheat noodles. The setting is elegantly subdued: an intimate space in peach, beige and teal, with pastel harbor scenes on silk panels. With service to match the setting, it's one of the city's finest restaurants.

The Thai Stick ● △△ $

698 Post St. (Jones); 928-7730. Thai; dinners $4 to $8; wine and beer. Lunch weekdays 11 to 3, dinner nightly 5 to 10 (until 11 Friday-Saturday). Reservations accepted; casual. Major credit cards. This is one of the tastier of the many Southeast Asian cafes emerging downtown, and it's safely outside the nearby Tenderloin District. Thai cuisine is similar to Chinese, only spicier, with lots of peanut sauces and curries. It comes with unpronounceable names like *nua kra thiam prig Thai*.

Tommy Toy's Haute Cuisine Chinoise ● △△△△ $$$$ ∅

655 Montgomery St. (Washington); 397-4888. Chinese with a French accent; dinners $16 to $45; full bar service. Lunch weekdays 11:30 to 3, dinner nightly 6 to 10. Reservations essential. Dressy; jacket and tie for dinner. Major credit cards. Restaurateur Tommy Toy has created the city's most opulent Chinese dining parlor. This posh place, with a decor reminiscent of Imperial China, features Cino-French curiosities such as pan fried *foie gras* with sliced pear and vanilla prawns with raisins. The effect—visually and culinarily—is pleasantly overwhelming.

Vic's Place ● △△ $

44 Belden (between Pine and Bush); 981-5222. American; lunches $4 to $9; full bar service. Lunch weekdays 10 to 2:30. Reservations accepted; informal. Major credit cards. Vic Parrilla dishes up tasty hamburgers, salads and inexpensive daily specials in this popular warm-wood businessmen's hangout.

Victor's ● △△△△ $$$$ ∅

335 Powell St. (atop Westin St. Francis at Geary); 956-7777. California and contemporary French cuisine; dinners $22 to $30; full bar service. Daily 6 p.m. to 10:30 p.m., Sunday brunch 10 to 2:30. Reservations essential. Dressy; jackets for dinner. Major credit cards. Nestled on the 32nd floor of the Westin St. Francis, Victors is at the same time intimate and grandiose. It's a special occasion restaurant with a constantly-changing menu, lush decor and sweeping city views.

WHAT TO DO AFTER DARK

American Conservatory Theatre ● △△△

Geary Theatre at 415 Geary (Mason); 749-2228. One of the nation's leading repertory groups, ACT presents a season of eight classic and contemporary plays, usually at its Geary playhouse.

Other major legitimate theaters ● △△△

Curran, *445 Geary at Mason, 243-9001;* **Golden Gate**, *#1 Taylor at Market, 474-3800;* **Orpheum**, *1192 Market at Jones;* **Marines Memorial**, *609 Sutter at Mason; phone number for all is 474-3800.* Carole Shorenstein Hays and James M. Nederlander present a year-around series of comedies, dramas, musicals, dance revues and individual performers at these four theaters.

Comedy clubs ● ΔΔ (stand-up comics)

Punch Line, *444 Battery St. (Maritime Plaza), 397-7573; and* **Improv**, *401 Mason (Geary), 441-7787.* Both feature stand-up comics, for a small cover charge and drink minimum.

Greater Tuna ● ΔΔ (comedy show)

Cable Car Theatre, 430 Mason (Geary); 771-6900. Get ready for silly at the city's longest running slapstick show.

The Plush Room ● ΔΔΔ (cabaret)

York Hotel at 940 Sutter St. (Hyde); 885-6800. This attractive room features lounge-type acts and singers on their way up or down.

The Warfield ● ΔΔΔ (nightclub)

982 Market St. (Taylor); 775-7722. Smartly refurbished, this old theater features a variety of entertainers, live music and disco dancing.

WHERE TO SLEEP
(Detailed listings in Chapter 16)

Rooms for $100 or more

Campton Place ● *340 Stockton St. (Post)*
The Donatello ● *501 Post St. (Mason)*
The Fairmont ● *950 Mason St. (California)*
Four Seasons Clift ● *495 Geary St. (Taylor)*
Galleria Park Hotel ● *191 Sutter St. (Montgomery)*
Grand Hyatt ● *345 Stockton St. (Post)*
Handlery Union Square ● *351 Geary St. (Powell)*
Holiday Inn Union Square ● *480 Sutter St. (Powell)*
The Huntington ● *1075 California St. (Taylor)*
Mandarin Oriental ● *222 Sansome St. (California)*
Mark Hopkins ● *One Nob Hill (California-Mason)*
Monticello Inn ● *127 Ellis St. (Powell)*
Pan Pacific Hotel ● *500 Post St. (Mason)*
Parc Fifty Five Hotel ● *55 Cyril Magnin St. (Eddy)*
Park Hyatt ● *333 Battery St. (Clay)*
San Francisco Hilton ● *333 O'Farrell St. (Mason)*
Shannon Court Hotel ● *550 Geary St. (Taylor)*
Sheraton Palace ● *Two Montgomery St. (Market)*

Sir Francis Drake ● *450 Powell St. (Sutter)*
Stanford Court ● *905 California St. (Powell)*
Villa Florence ● *225 Powell St. (O'Farrell)*
Westin St. Francis ● *335 Powell St. (Geary)*

CABLE CARS:
GETTING A GRIP ON HISTORY

"Without cable cars," columnist Herb Caen once wrote, *"San Francisco would be only a lumpy Los Angeles."*

Fortunately, the city will never be without those archaic maroon and golden brown vehicles which—in song, at least—climb halfway to the stars. They were declared a national historic landmark by the Department of Interior in 1964. Further, a 1971 city charter amendment forbids altering or reducing the system without a majority vote of citizens.

That's about as likely as a vote to outlaw San Francisco sourdough bread.

Twelve million people a year crowd onto the rattling little rascals; 60 percent are tourists. If you're here in summer, you'll be alarmed by the long queues at the popular Powell-Market, Hyde-Beach and Bay-Taylor terminals. Here's how to avoid cable car gridlock:

Get an early start ● Cable cars begin running at 6 a.m. If you're willing to do the same, you'll find them virtually tourist-free.

Go to California ● We refer to the California Street line, which isn't as busy as the other two. It runs between Market Street near the Ferry Building and Van Ness Avenue. The least crowded terminal is California at Van Ness.

Go upstream ● If you walk a few blocks from the terminals, you'll find no waiting lines. Stand near a yellow "XX" painted on the street and compete with nimble-footed residents for a spot. On busy days, you'll likely miss the first few over-loaded cars. But you'll catch one more quickly than by standing obediently at the terminal queue.

Many fascinating facts and a few fables are linked to the birth of the cable car. As every guidebook

Rooms for $50 to $99

Amsterdam Hotel • *749 Taylor St. (Sutter)*
Beresford Arms • *701 Post St. (Jones)*
Canterbury Hotel • *740 Sutter St. (Taylor)*
Cartwright • *524 Sutter St. (Powell)*

author knows, the first successful one was developed by Scotsman Andrew Hallidie in 1873.

Historians question a popular legend that Andy was moved to create the cable car after seeing an overloaded horsecar slip backward on a steep grade. More likely, he was moved by the fact that his company made wire rope—or cable—which is the heart of the system. His father invented the stuff in 1835.

He did see a team of horses fall on a steep hill in 1869, but they were pulling a freight wagon, not a streetcar. At the time, Andy was already at work on his system, along with other inventors. He beat them to the market, primarily because his draftsman, William Eppelsheimer, designed a quick-release grip that grabbed onto the underground cable.

The cable car was launched on Clay Street hill at 4 a.m., August 2, 1873. He chose that unearthly hour to avoid embarrassment in case the thing didn't work. It did, and Andy Hallidie became a very rich man.

Soon, seven companies were running their little cars over San Francisco's muddy hills on 103 miles of track. Then the advent of electric street cars and the 1906 earthquake put several firms out of business. Surviving companies operated on 25 miles of track for 40 years, until metal shortages of World War II left the systems in a state of total disrepair.

In 1947, Mayor Roger Lapham announced that cable cars would be replaced by new diesel buses. Feisty socialite Friedel Klussman launched a "Save the Cable Car" campaign that drew national attention. A local ballot initiative to keep the little cars won by a landslide. Other attempts to disband the system have been shouted down with equal vigor.

When the system began to self-destruct again in the early 1980s, $60 million was raised for total renovation. The good people of San Francisco pulled $10 million of that from their own pockets.

Chancellor Hotel ● *433 Powell St. (Post)*
Commodore Hotel ● *825 Sutter St. (Jones)*
King George Hotel ● *334 Mason St. (Geary)*
Pacific Bay Inn ● *520 Jones St. (Geary)*
The Raphael ● *386 Geary St. (Mason)*
Sheehan Hotel ● *620 Sutter St. (Mason)*
York Hotel ● *940 Sutter St. (Leavenworth)*

Rooms under $50
Essex Hotel ● *684 Ellis St. (Larkin)*
Grant Plaza Hotel ● *465 Grant Ave. (Bush)*
Temple Hotel ● *469 Pine St. (Kearny)*

Bed & breakfast inns
Petite Auberge ● *863 Bush St. (Mason)*
White Swan Inn ● *845 Bush St. (Mason)*

Four

CHINATOWN
The Asian Connection

A QUICK LOOK: Chinatown is immediately north of Downtown. Take Stockton Street from Union Square through the Stockton Tunnel, or follow Grant Avenue, paralleling Stockton a block east. These become Chinatown's two main streets. Avoid driving up Grant; it's one of the city's most congested streets and parking is absurd.

IT'S LIKE NO OTHER Chinese community in America—or in the world, for that matter. San Francisco's Chinatown is a crowded, multi-hued Asian feast of restaurants, import stores, herbalists, fortune cookie factories, seafood markets, an occasional sweat shop, dim sum parlors, jewelry stores and tourist junk shops.

Neither high-rise nor spread out, it's a jammed-together collection of three and four-story buildings; some are pagoda-roofed to please the tourists. You won't find this sort of place in China, where most cities are rather drab and low-lying—except for concrete apartment towers. There, pagoda-style roofs are found only on pagodas. Only Hong Kong exceeds the congestion and glitter of San Francisco's Chinatown.

This is the city's most densely populated neighborhood and possibly the most congested urban area in America. Dating back to 1852, it's the country's oldest ethnic enclave. Despite claims of other cities—

CHINATOWN

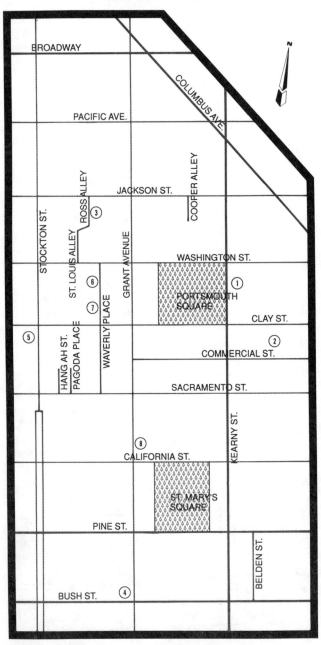

DIRECTORY

1. CHINESE CULTURE CENTER
2. CHINESE HISTORICAL SOCIETY
3. FORTUNE COOKIE FACTORY
4. GATE OF CHINATOWN
5. KONG CHOW BUDDHIST TEMPLE
6. NORRAS BUDDHIST TEMPLE
7. TIN HOU TEMPLE
8. OLD ST. MARY'S

notably Vancouver, B.C.—it's the largest Asian settlement outside the Orient. Population estimates range as high as 100,000 in a 24-block area.

It's a remarkably self-contained community, with its own chamber of commerce, newspapers, banks and political clout. Chinese Americans—inside and outside Chinatown—comprise the city's largest and most affluent ethnic group.

The community's roots go back to the Gold Rush, when immigrants from coastal China came in search of "the Gold Mountain." Some settled around Portsmouth Square, working in shanty hotels as cooks and laundrymen—chores spurned by the macho white miners.

Soon, the ambitious newcomers were operating their own businesses and they began dominating California's early farming and fishing industries. Regarded as an economic threat, they suffered some of the worst discrimination in the country's history. In 1882, Congress passed the Oriental Exclusion Act to prohibit further immigration.

At this point, Chinese men outnumbered women twenty to one. No longer able to import "picture brides" or bring in their families, they turned Chinatown into one of the city's wickedest ghettos. Opium dens and white slavery thrived. Some of the *tongs,* originally benevolent or protective groups, evolved into Mafia-style gangs.

The 1906 earthquake leveled the ramshackle ghetto. As a more stable Chinese community rebuilt, a few timid visitors poked into its narrow alleys and sampled its exotic foods. Accidental tourism had begun. The opportunistic Chinese welcomed these visitors. During the 1950s and 1960s, they dressed up their drab buildings with dragon-entwined columns and turned-up eves. Curio shops and "Chinese-American" restaurants were opened. That incongruity known as San Francisco Chinatown was born.

Virtually all the early immigrants came from a single coastal province—Canton, now called Guangzhou. Thus Chinatown is primarily a Cantonese settlement, presenting a lopsided image of the mother country; China itself is 95 percent Mandarin. Recent arrivals from the Asian melting pots of Hong Kong and Taiwan have tilted the ethnic scales somewhat. Their influence is seen in the proliferation of Szechuan, Hunan and other Mandarin-style restaurants.

Mandarin food is more zesty than the modestly spiced seafood-and-vegetable Cantonese fare. In a town already noted for its many restaurants, Chinatown offers more per square block than any other area. More than a hundred are crowded into a ten-block region.

For a good overview of Chinatown, simply walk up Grant Avenue from Bush to Broadway, then return on paralleling Stockton Street. Then, set yourself free in this Asian colony. Duck into narrow alleys that shelter tucked-away shops, cafes and mystical temples. The map in this chapter will keep you from becoming hopelessly misplaced.

Grant Avenue, incidentally, is the city's oldest street, laid out in 1834 as Calle de la Fundacion (Street of the Founding) when the village was still called Yerba Buena. We'll begin our tour at the "Gate of Chinatown," a green-tiled, dragon-topped portal at Bush and Grant. It was given to the city by the Republic of China (Taiwan) in 1969.

This portal is the only clue that you're entering a Chinese community. The first thing you see is a Mrs. Fields cookie store. A couple of noisy camera-electronic shops and a leather shop are not far away. Zoning indifference and skyrocketing rents that drive out family businesses have permitted this intrusion into one of the city's most historic areas.

Continue your stroll up Grant Avenue and you'll soon surround yourself with the Chinatown we've all come to love: a curious mix of things Chinese and tourist schlock. You can buy fake Samurai swords, back-scratchers, naughty nudie postcards, slinky silk cheongsams, dried black mushrooms and squid, ginseng to ensure extended virility, Alcatraz beach mats and T-shirts.

Check out two rather classy import shops between Bush and Pine. **Tai Nam Yang Furniture Company**, at 438 Grant, offers three floors of beautifully crafted black lacquer and rosewood furniture and huge hand-painted vases. **Dragon House Oriental**

Fine Arts, at 455 Grant, displays exquisite Oriental lacquer-ware, antiques and ivory carvings.

Looking wonderfully out of place is the red brick, Gothic **Old St. Mary's Church** at Grant and California. Chinatown was still huddled around Portsmouth Square a few blocks away when the first stones were laid for this church in 1863. It's still an active parish; try to arrive at 12:30 on a Tuesday to hear noontime concerts in the hushed, balconied sanctuary.

Half a block below the church, on California Street, **St. Mary's Square** is a quiet retreat with a statue of Dr. Sun Yat Sen as its focal point. Unfortunately, the pigeons have shown little respect for this monument to the father of the Republic of China.

McDonald's has invaded Chinatown, squatting guiltily under the second-floor **Cathay House Restaurant** at the corner of Grant and California. Pass on by. The *real* fast foods here are pork buns, mooncakes, rich-tasting glazed pork, almond cookies and honey-sweet Chinese beef jerky. If you're feeling bold, try steamed chicken feet. They look wicked but they taste harmlessly bland. Try not to think about where they've been.

Note the **Bank of America** building at Grant and Sacramento. It's a study in deliberate Chinese architecture, with dragon-entwined columns and 60 dragon medallions across its facade. One of our favorite Chinatown stops is **Eastern Bakery** at Grant and Commercial. It's San Francisco's oldest Chinese-American bakery, dating from 1924. The display cases are abrim with a diet-denting mix of Chinese and American pastries. Try the assorted mooncakes, almond cookies, crispy bow ties and rubbery-yet-tasty almond soybean cakes.

Kee Fung Ng Gallery at 757 Grant Avenue (Clay) exhibits the works of its owner, a Chinese-born artist who creates fetching, almost too cute paintings of Chinese children. Note the beautifully-carved elephant tusks and other ivory work in the window of **Arts of China** at 843 Grant (between Clay and Washington).

Drop half a block down Washington Street to **Portsmouth Square,** the city's first plaza, then follow a pedestrian bridge to the **Chinese Culture Center** in the ugly, spraddle-legged Financial District Holiday Inn. A museum there features changing exhibits of Chinese art, culture and history. Return to Grant and continue northward. At **TenRen's Tea Company,** 949 Grant (Jackson), get a free sip of assorted teas and learn about the questionable curative powers of ginseng.

As you cross Pacific Avenue, Chinatown begins looking less like a tourist gimmick and more like an ethnic neighborhood with grocers, fish markets and herbal shops. The sights and smells will transport you to a busy Hong Kong back street.

Canton Market at Grant and Pacific is a good example of a typical Chinese market. Step inside to view slippery mounds of fish, recently demised and ready for the steamer. Live ones thrive in tanks along one wall. Outside, curious produce such as hairy melons, Chinese long beans and *bock choy* intrude upon the sidewalk. Next door at **On Sang Poultry Company,** glazed ducks hang in the window; they're as tasty as they look.

The topless and bottomless joints of Broadway form a bawdy barrier to Chinatown. So swing left, go up a block, go left again onto Stockton and return to the Orient. Actually, Stockton is more typically Chinese than popular Grant Avenue. There are no curio shops selling back-scratchers here. The street is lined with Asian produce shops, fish and poultry markets, mom and pop cafes, dim sum parlors and jewelry stores.

Jade Galore Jewelry at Stockton and Washington is particularly stylish, with its stainless steel exterior, matched golden lions guarding the entrance and display windows glittering with jade and gold. Continue along Stockton, poking into its array of Asian markets.

Between Clay and Sacramento, pop into the **Kong Chow Buddhist Temple** above the Chinatown Post Office at 855 Stockton (fourth floor via elevator). Next door is the **Chinese Six Companies** building with its multi-colored Oriental facade. The Six Companies are combined business-benevolent societies that once controlled much of Chinatown's economy and looked after the welfare of its residents.

The friendly folk at **Ellison Enterprises herbal shop**, 805 Stockton (Sacramento), will explain the mystical medicinal powers of hundreds of herbs and potions, including—ugh—dried human placenta.

You're now facing the Stockton Tunnel, so turn left and head down Sacramento Street. Pop into **Clarion Music Center** at 816 Sacramento, with several ancient gongs, drums and other Chinese musical devices on display, along with modern instruments. Many local children attend Chinese schools as well as public ones. Note the traditional architecture in the green tile-roofed **Nam Kue School,** set just off the sidewalk at 755 Sacramento, between Grant and Kearny.

Having completed your loop, it's time to begin your random wandering. Discoveries await you in every side street and narrow alley. Here are some suggestions:

Waverly Place runs two blocks from Sacramento to Washington, between Stockton and Grant. It's often called "the street of painted balconies" because of the cheerful red, yellow and green paint jobs on the upper floors. These buildings shelter two incense-laden temples, **Norras Buddhist Association of America Temple** at 109 Waverly and **Tin Hou Temple** at 125. Both are open to the public; they can be reached via narrow stairways.

Ross Alley, running between Jackson and Washington, is a busy retreat of small trading companies, sewing shops and cottage industries. Step into the **Golden Gate Fortune Cookies Company** at 56 Ross and discover how they get those little messages inside. You can buy a big bag of cookies—including some with harmlessly naughty messages—for $4. Nearby, at **Sam Bo Trading Company** (14 Ross), admire the brilliant red and gold temple objects, home altars, tasseled lanterns and stacks of stick incense.

Jackson Street between Grant and Stockton is lined with old country herbal shops, selling curious things such as dried squid, sharks fin, deer's tail extract and assorted varieties of ginseng. Note the interesting banks of little wooden drawers, like library card catalogues, where herbs and spices are kept. Some merchants still use balance scales to weigh your pinch of powdered deer's horn; they tote up your bill on an abacus.

If you're wearing your hiking shoes, climb four steep blocks to **Jackson Market** at Jackson and Jones, and buy a bag of Chinese beef jerky. It's a real San Francisco treat, known only to virtually every Chinatown resident and now, to readers of this guidebook.

WHAT TO SEE & DO

Chinese Culture Center ● △△△

750 Kearny St. (in the Financial District Holiday Inn); 986-1822. Free. Tuesday-Saturday 9 to 5; gallery open 10 to 4. Reached by a pedestrian bridge from Portsmouth Square, the center features changing exhibits relating to Chinese culture and history. Note display cases of ancient puppets in the lobby; Chinese puppetry goes back to the 12th century B.C.

Chinese Heritage Walk & Culinary Walk ● △△△ ☺

Meet at the Chinese Culture Center. Call 986-1822 or write 750 Kearny St., San Francisco, CA 94108. Reservations required for Culinary Walk. Docents take you behind the scenes of Chinatown in two-hour Heritage Walks, starting every Saturday at 2 p.m. The price is $9 for adults and $2 for kids under 18. The Chinatown Culinary Walk focuses on Asian cuisine, with stops at markets, stores and food factories, then ends with a dim sum luncheon. Three-hour tours depart the Chinese Culture Center at 10:30 a.m. Wednesday; $18 for adults and $9 for kids under 12; luncheon included.

Chinese Historical Society Museum ● △△△

650 Commercial St. (Kearny); 391-1188. Free. Wednesday-Sunday noon to 4. Although it's in modest quarters, this small museum offers attractive, uncluttered exhibits. Its primary focus is the early migration of Chinese from Canton to America and the growth and development of Chinatown. Exhibits include

Busy Chinatown, gleaming with nighttime neon, is like no other Asian enclave in the world.

photos of opium dens and early Chinatown and artifacts such as temple altars and ancient lanterns.

Chinese temples ● △△

Kong Chow Buddhist Temple, 855 Stockton St. (above the post office at Sacramento); Norras Buddhist Association of America Temple, 109 Waverly Place; Tin Hou Temple, 125 Waverly Place. Chinese temples don't conduct scheduled services. They're places of sanctuary, where folks send prayers and pretend money to ancestors or simply sit in quiet reflection. Most are open from 9 to 4. **Kong Chow** is the oldest and most attractive of Chinatown's temples—an intriguing study in red, gold and black lacquer carvings. From the balcony, you'll get a nice overview of Chinatown. **Norras** and **Tin Hou** temples in Waverly Place (off Washington between Grant and Stockton) also welcome visitors. Follow signs up narrow stairways, then ring a buzzer for entry.

Temple-keepers will appreciate a dollar or two in the offering box. Or you can by a parcel of stick incense and paper money and communicate with your ancestors.

Fortune cookie factory ● ΔΔ ☺
Golden Gate Fortune Cookies Co., 56 Ross Alley (off Jackson); 781-3956. Daily 9 to 9. We won't tell you how they get those little slips of paper inside fortune cookies, but you can find out by stepping into this cluttered place. The manager will ask you—with nagging persistence—to buy a bag, hot off the griddle. You can choose between "R" and "G" rated messages.

Jeanette's Walking Tours of Chinatown ● ΔΔΔ ☺
Call 982-8839 or write: Jeanette's Walking Tours, 812 Clay St., San Francisco, CA 94108. Tours depart daily. Led by Chinatown native Linda Lee, these tours take you through the area's streets and alleys, with stops at temples, fortune cookie factories, herbal shops and historic sites. The "Heart of Chinatown" tour is $20 (kids 5 to 11, $7). With lunch, it's $30 (kids $10). A nightly dinner tour is $35 (kids $15).

Old St. Mary's ● ΔΔ
Grant Avenue at California Street; 986-4388. Noontime concerts Tuesdays at 12:30. San Francisco's first cathedral, this brick edifice was dedicated on Christmas Day, 1854. It's now an active parish, playing host to tourists and the downtown business community. The Paulist Book and Gift Shop is next door at 614 Grant Avenue.

Portsmouth Square ● ΔΔ
Kearny, Clay and Washington streets. Somewhat scruffy but historically interesting, this was the city's birthplace; the American flag was raised here on July 9, 1846. Back then, Yerba Buena Cove extend to the base of the square as the city's first landing. Today, the square is a favorite haunt of Chinatown's old men, who play mahjong, talk of yesterday and conduct graceful, slow-motion *tai chi* rituals. Pagoda-style structures erected in 1990 give the square a proper Asian look. A parking garage lurks beneath.

St. Mary's Square ● Δ
California and Quincy streets. A statue of Dr. Sun Yat Sen by noted Bay Area sculptor Beniamino Bufano is the centerpiece of this small, tree-shaded plaza

just off Grant Avenue. Another monument honors Chinese-American victims of world wars I and II.

WHERE TO DINE

Advice from my Chinese-American wife and co-author: If you want authentic food, go where the Chinese go. Wander the streets during the lunch or dinner hour, and note which places are most crowed with locals. Don't be put off by the shabby look of some cafes. You may find the best food at the lowest prices there.

We usually avoid large tourist-oriented China-town restaurants in favor of small family-owned places. The food is fine at many of the larger spots, but they're more expensive and their menus are often compromised for honkey tastes. Most smaller places don't take reservations and some don't take credit cards. Just show up with an appetite and a little money. Best time to catch a table is after 8:30 on week nights; most Chinese like to eat earlier.

Brandy Ho's ● ΔΔ $$

217 Columbus Avenue (Pacific); 788-7527; also at 450 Broadway (Kearny); 362-6268. Mandarin (Hunan); dinners $9 to $16; wine and beer (full bar at Broadway restaurant). Daily 11:30 to midnight. No reservations; casual. MC/VISA, AMEX. Decorated with tasseled lanterns and "NO MSG" signs, lively Brandy Ho's is one of Chinatown's spicier cafes. It's a good place to sample Hunan-Szechuan food because the helpful waitstaff will explain the menu—and the kitchen will go easy on the peppers if you ask.

Choi Kee Restaurant ● Δ $

1365 Stockton St. (Vallejo); 788-7071. Cantonese; dinners $5 to $10; wine and beer. Daily 10 to 10. Casual; no reservations or credit cards. For an authentic family-style restaurant, walk a block off China-town's beaten path and dine at this little corner place. The interior is basic Formica, the food is remarkably inexpensive and very good for the price. The odds are you'll be the only round-eye in the place.

Far East Cafe ● ΔΔ $$

631 Grant Ave. (California); 982-3245. Cantonese; dinners $7 to $12; full bar. Weekdays 11:30 to 10, *weekends noon to 10. Informal to casual. Major credit cards.* This large place with dark-wood panels and Asian chandeliers has a been a Chinatown fixture for decades. We like its 1930s look of slightly shabby elegance. The fare is Cantonese and generally excellent.

Grand Palace and Little Palace ● △△ $

950 Grant Ave. (Washington); 982-3705. Cantonese; dinners $5 to $10; full bar in Grand Palace, wine and beer in Little Palace. Daily 9 a.m. to 10 p.m. Casual; MC/VISA, AMEX. The "Palaces" cater to both tourists and locals; the menu is bi-lingual. The glitzy and only slightly shabby Grand Palace serves tasty won ton, Hong Kong style noodles and barbecued meats over rice at quite reasonable prices. Little Palace is a less formal, somewhat noisier basement place.

EAT YOUR LITTLE HEARTS OUT

Any Chinatown travel guide worth its salted egg should discuss **dim sum**. Translated as "little hearts," dim sum is both a kind of food and a style of serving.

In a dim sum restaurant, waiters and waitresses parade past your table with steam carts or platters laden with small dishes of assorted morsels. Select what interests you and sip chrysanthemum or green tea between bites.

You won't recognize some of the items, but what's life without surprises? Selections may include spring rolls, potstickers, deep-fried dumplings filled with all manner of things, fried taro, steamed pork buns and sweet, gelatinous desserts that feel funny going down.

Originated in Canton and made popular in Hong Kong, dim sum is served from morning to mid-afternoon. The earlier you arrive, the better your odds for a table and a good selection. Weekdays are best. Some places are crowded and chaotic; you take a number and wait your turn. Others are quiet and informal; a few are elegant and expensive.

Here are five of our preferred dim sum parlors:

Hang Ah Tea Room ● △△ $ ∅

One Hang Ah St. (off Sacramento); 982-5686. Cantonese, dim sum; dinners $5 to $10; wine and beer. Daily 10 a.m. to 9 p.m., dim sum 10 to 3. Casual; no reservations or credit cards. Dating from the turn of the century, Hang Ah claims to be Chinatown's oldest dim sum parlor (see box). It serves these "little hearts" until 3 p.m., then switches to Cantonese entrees. Lunch patrons can either do dim sum or order from the menu. Other than a small room off to one side, the dining area is smoke free.

Hunan Homes ● △△ $$

622 Jackson (Grant); 982-2844. Mandarin/Cantonese; dinners $9 to $15; wine and beer. Sunday-Thursday 11:30 to 9:30, Friday-Saturday 11:30 to 10. Casual; MC/VISA, AMEX. This attractive, modestly-priced place with mirrored booths offers an eclectic

---

Hang Ah Tea Room ● *One Hang Ah St. (in Chinatown, off Sacramento); 982-5686. Dim sum served daily 10 to 3. Inexpensive; no credit cards.* The helpful waitstaff aids your selections in this small, rather quiet place.

Harbor Village ● *#4 Embarcadero Center (lower Market); 781-8833. Dim sum served weekdays 11 to 2:30, Saturdays 10:30 to 2:30 and Sundays 10 to 2:30; reservations advised. Moderately expensive; MC/VISA, AMEX.* Dim sum for the BMW set? It's innovative, tasty and pricey in this elegant place.

Hong Kong Tea House ● *835 Pacific Ave. (in Chinatown, near Stockton); 391-6365. Dim sum daily 8:30 to 3. Inexpensive; no credit cards.* It's large and chaotic, with good variety. Take a number and wait.

King of China ● *939 Clement St. (in the Richmond District, near 11th Avenue); 668-2618. Dim sum daily 9 to 3. Moderate to inexpensive; MC/VISA.* Ignore the garish Tokyoesque decor and enjoy what may be the tastiest dim sum in town.

Tung Fong ● *808 Pacific Ave. (in Chinatown, near Stockton); 362-7115. Dim sum served from 9 to 3 daily except Wednesday. Inexpensive; no credit cards.* Small and not too noisy, it's a favorite of many Chinatown residents.

Asian menu ranging from spicy Hunan and Mongolian hot plates to subtly flavored Cantonese fish and vegetable dishes.

Hunan Village ● △△△ $$

839 Kearny St. (Jackson); 956-7868. Mandarin (Hunan); dinners $8 to $14; wine and beer. Daily 11 to 9:30. Casual; MC/VISA. A simple, prim little place, Hunan Village is a bit of a sleeper. Although not well-known, its kitchen has won culinary awards for its spicy Hunan fare. Try the hot braised whole fish, General Tsou's chicken or Mongolian lamb, which is rather rare in Chinatown restaurants.

Kum Yuen ● △ $

1247 Stockton St. (Pacific); 434-1128. Cantonese; dinners $4 to $7; no alcohol but it may be brought in. Daily 8 a.m. to 11 p.m. Very casual; no reservations or credit cards. We voted this one of the city's ten best budget restaurants in *The Best of San Francisco*. You can get remarkably tasty and filling dishes for $3 or $4. This is a *very* scruffy place; you'll see only natives here, but they're quite friendly.

Lotus Garden New Vegetarian Restaurant ● △△△ $$

352 Grant Ave. (California); 397-0130. Cantonese; dinners $7 to $10; full bar. Lunch Tuesday-Friday 11:30 to 2:30, dinner Tuesday-Sunday 5 to 9, closed Mondays. Informal to casual. MC/VISA. This attractive upstairs place, highly regarded by area food critics, is Chinatown's best vegetarian restaurant. Try hearty dishes such as mushrooms with Chinese broccoli or straw mushrooms with chili and sesame flavor.

The Pot Sticker ● △△ $$

150 Waverly Place (Washington); 397-9985. Mandarin; dinners $8 to $12; wine and beer. Daily 11:30 to 4 and 4:30 to 9. No reservations; casual. MC/VISA, AMEX. Like Brandy Ho's, this is a good place to venture into spicy Mandarin cuisine, and it serves the best potstickers in town. For the uninitiated, these are meat-filled, spiced dumplings that are steamed, then pan-fried. Pour over a little Hunan hot oil (very little) and enjoy!

Sam Wo ● Δ $

813 Washington St. (Grant); 982-0596. Canton-ese; dinners $5 to $10; no alcohol. Daily 11 a.m. to 3 a.m. Very casual; no reservations or credit cards. Slumming yuppies, starving students and lovers of a rice gruel called *jook* have made this shabby, skinny, three-story place legendary. Much of the legend was the work of the late Edsel Ford Wong, whose rude waiter act was the talk of the town. The food varies, from excellent *jook* and noodle dishes to rather greasy stir-fried veggies. So tramp through the noisy ground-floor kitchen, climb the stairs, find a seat and hope the cook's in a good mood. And remember to order Chinese doughnuts (actually crullers) with your *jook.* They're for dunking.

Yuet Lee ● Δ $$ to $$$

1300 Stockton St. (Broadway); 982-6020. Chinese seafood; dinners $8 to $20; no alcohol but it may be brought in. Daily except Tuesday 11 a.m. to 3 a.m. Casual; no reservations or credit cards. This shabby place is the darling of underground diners, but the food can be erratic. It has served us some of the best—and some of the worst—steamed fish in town. It offers Chinatown's widest selection of seafood and some of the dishes are very pricey. Should you need a bottle of wine, there's a liquor store just around the corner on Stockton. Yuet Lee will provide the glasses—water glasses.

WHERE TO SLEEP
(Detailed listings in Chapter 16)

Rooms over $100
Holiday Inn ● *750 Kearny St. (Washington)*

Rooms for $50 to $99
Royal Pacific Motor Inn ● *661 Broadway (Grant)*

Rooms under $50
Grant Plaza Hotel ● *465 Grant Ave. (Bush)*
Temple Hotel ● *469 Pine St. (Kearny)*

Bed & breakfast inn
Obrero Hotel ● *1208 Stockton St. (Pacific)*

NORTH BEACH

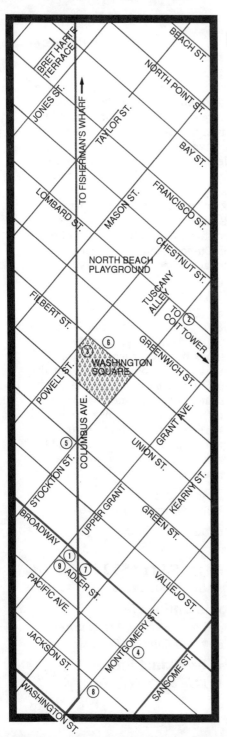

DIRECTORY

1. CITY LIGHTS BOOKSTORE
2. COIT TOWER
3. FIREFIGHTERS' MONUMENT
4. JACKSON SQUARE
   HISTORIC DISTRICT
5. NORTH BEACH MUSEUM
6. SAINTS PETER &
   PAUL CHURCH
7. SPEC'S 12 ADLER
   MUSEUM CAFE
8. TRANSAMERICA PYRAMID
9. VESUVIO'S

Five

NORTH BEACH
Now, that's Italian?

A QUICK LOOK: North Beach is the city's Italian enclave, also called Little Italy, dotted with ethnic cafes and delis. It once sheltered the notorious Barbary Coast red light district and later Beat Generation artists and writers. With Columbus Avenue as its main artery, North Beach lies next to Chinatown which, in fact, is seeping into the neighborhood. Parking is at a premium, so it's best explored on foot.

WHERE'S the beach?

It's moved east. North Beach is a name left over from the 1800s, when Yerba Buena Cove reached inland between Telegraph and Russian hills. As the city grew, this shallow inlet was filled, with rotting ships abandoned during the Gold Rush serving as a foundation. They're still down there.

Along with adjacent Chinatown, North Beach is the city's oldest neighborhood. It was settled by Italians, who returned from the gold fields to go into the fishing and produce business. Later generations opened restaurants and delicatessens, which still predominate.

During the 1950s, North Beach and the steep slopes of Telegraph Hill became refuges for starving artists and free-thinking writers. It gave birth to the Beat Generation of Jack Kerouac and Allen Ginsberg.

Many Chinese are now moving into North Beach, spilling out of overcrowded Chinatown. It would be neat to imagine old Chinese and Italian gentlemen sharing a Washington Square park bench, quietly debating whether China or Italy invented noodles. In reality, the two groups stoically ignore one another.

Despite this Asian invasion, much of the flavor of Italy survives. A walk through North Beach will be rewarded by the good smells of garlic, fresh pasta and cappuccino, visions of spicy sausages dangling from ceilings of cluttered delicatessens and perhaps the sound of an aria from *Le Figaro*.

Or was that a Chinese opera?

North Beach's centerpiece is **Washington Square**, a mis-named grassy piazza that is neither on Washington Street, nor a square. A pigeon-spotted statue of Ben Franklin—not the father of our country—occupies its center. But never mind that. Like Chinatown's Portsmouth Square, it's a refuge for reminiscing old men, giggling children and others seeking solace from the surrounding city. On the northern edge, the elaborate twin spires of **Saints Peter and Paul Church** reach skyward—hopefully toward heaven.

Columbus Avenue is North Beach's main street, running diagonally from the Financial District to Fisherman's Wharf. For the newcomer, its oblique route only aggravates the confusion of the area's congestion.

Begin your North Beach stroll near the **Transamerica Pyramid**, where Columbus, Washington and Montgomery streets merge at the edge of the **Financial District**. Follow Montgomery north a block, into **Jackson Square Historic District.** It's not really a square, but a section containing some of the city's oldest and most handsome brick buildings. Once the heart of the wicked **Barbary Coast,** it's now a gentrified district of upscale furniture, antique and design shops and professional offices. Redevelopment threatened these venerable structures until the city designated Jackson Square as an historic preserve in 1971.

Notice the Transalvania-style brick edifice at 722-28 Montgomery; it houses the offices of flamboyant attorney **Melvin Belli.** Turn right onto Jackson, stroll past an assortment of expensive antique and furniture shops, go left onto Sansome, then left again onto Pacific. You've essentially circled the heart of the square, and you emerge onto Columbus.

Look to your left at the marvelous little copper green **Sentinel Building** at Columbus and Kearny. This flatiron-shaped charmer, built in 1907, shelters movie producer Francis Ford Coppola's Zoetrope Studios. Stop in at the **San Francisco Brewing Company,** a dark-wood pub at 155 Columbus (Pacific). Have a pint of Emperor Norton lager and admire the curious horizontal ceiling fan resembling a paddlewheel.

Continuing onward, you encounter two saloon survivors of the Beatnik era, **Vesuvio** at 255 Columbus and **Spec's 12 Adler Museum Cafe,** across the way at 12 Saroyan Street. Perch on stools once warmed by Jack Kerouac and William Saroyan and study the eclectic scatter that passes for decor in these venerable watering holes.

Next door is another durable landmark, poet Lawrence Ferlinghetti's **City Lights Bookstore** at 261 Columbus. It's perhaps the most literate and certainly the most liberal book shop in America. Chairs invite you to sit and thumb through translated European classics, Kerouac's ramblings and gay and lesbian works.

Just beyond is another expression of local liberalism—Broadway's bawdy shops, birthplace of topless and bottomless dancing. On opening night of the 1964 Republican National Convention, waitress Carol Doda wriggled into a one-piece bathing suit and jiggled onstage at the **Condor Club** at 300 Columbus. Five years later, she went bottomless. A gag historical plaque on an outside wall of the Condor—looking suspiciously authentic—heralds these two debuts.

Carol has since covered her assets and—at last report—was promoting lingerie fashion shows. The Condor has closed its shabby doors, but several other palaces of perversion offer "wall to wall sex" and "continuous erotic love acts."

Hawk-faced hawkers will try to lure you off the street, promising no cover and no minimum as you take a peek at the pink. But unless you're tempted to pay hefty prices for watery drinks and watch a flabby-breasted, bored-looking woman gyrate in a smoke-filled room, you'd best keep moving.

At the former Condor corner, take a half-right onto Grant Avenue as it begins climbing the flanks of Telegraph Hill. This leads to another Beatnik sanctuary known—during my shaggy-hair days—as **Upper Grant.** Little remains from that wonderfully disoriented era when we hung out at the Co-Existence Bagel Shop and the Cellar, reciting or listening to bad poetry. They're gone now, replaced by faceless polyglot: a junk shop, a health food store, Chinese bakeries, laundromats and a video shop. (Who on *earth* watches all those video movies?)

Fortunately, a few fragments of yesterday remain. Check out **The Saloon,** at the corner of Grant and Fresno Alley, the city's oldest pub, dating from 1861. Across the street is **Caffe Trieste** (Vallejo and Grant), a pleasantly shabby coffee house filled with faded photos and memories. **Figoni's** (1351 Grant) is an old fashioned hardware store in delightful disarray. At **Savoy Tivoli,** a coffee house and bar open to the sidewalk (1434 Grant), you can sip espresso and watch Chinese merchants walk by.

Two business up here still offer savory tastes of old Italy: **Panama Canal Ravioli Factory** at 1358 Grant (Green), and **R. Iacopi Delicatessen** at 1462 Grant (Union). If you want to write home on something more original than a "wish you were here" post card, stop in at **Quality Postcards,** 1441 Grant (Union). Its stock of 15,000 cards ranges from California citrus label reproductions to old movie queens.

Return to Columbus and continue your trek through Little Italy. **Molinari Deli** at 373 Columbus (Vallejo) is another tasty clutter of edible things Italian. Across Columbus are the twin Gothic towers of **St. Francis of Assisi,** San Francisco's namesake church, dating from 1860.

Step into **Caffe Roma** at 414 Columbus (Vallejo) and admire the pink cherubs and other heavenly

Coit Tower has been a Telegraph Hill sentinel since 1933; modern condos now cluster at its base.

bodies on walls and ceiling. The iced *caffe latte* served here is quite refreshing. At the juncture of Columbus, Green and Stockton, cross over to the **North Beach Museum** on the mezzanine of Eureka Federal Savings, 1435 Stockton Street. It offers yesterday displays of North Beach and Chinatown.

As you approach **Washington Square,** check out **Mario's Bohemian Cigar Store.** This dusky old hangout isn't a stogey shop, but a landmark bar and bistro serving some of the least expensive cannelloni, frittata and other Italian fare in the neighborhood. Across the way at 1707 Powell is a landmark of a different stripe, **Washington Square Bar and Grill.** It's the city's unofficial press club and penultimate pub.

Beyond Washington Square, Columbus Avenue heads into Fisherman's Wharf, shedding what's left of its Italian identity. Stop and catch your breath at

North Beach Playground, where local boy Joe DiMaggio once played sandlot baseball.

Look eastward and you'll see the fluted column of **Coit Tower** atop Telegraph Hill. This slender cylinder was built with funds left by Lillie Hitchcock Coit, a cigar-smoking eccentric who loved fire engines and the men who ran them. Despite its suggestive fire nozzle shape, it wasn't intended as Lillie's memorial to her beloved heroes. She *did* provide for such a monument—a sculpture on Washington Square, of three firefighters rescuing a lady in distress.

Tighten your shoelaces and begin climbing toward the tower. If you drive, you'll become imprisoned in a logjam of muttering motorists waiting for one of the limited parking spaces up there. As you hike up Lombard, then spiral around Telegraph Hill Boulevard, your effort will be rewarded with nice city views. If you aren't up to the climb, the **39-Coit** bus follows the same route.

Once atop the hill, you'll discover that thick vegetation obscures much of the city view. You'll see more after a $3 elevator ride to the tower's top. There, the city presents itself in slices through narrow arched windows. Back outside, pause to admire the statue of a caped Christopher Columbus, looking as though he'd discovered San Francisco instead of an obscure Caribbean island.

Local columnist Herb Cain likes to call San Francisco "Baghdad by the Bay." He could have said Babylon, for it does have its hanging gardens. They drape dramatically down the northeast slope of Telegraph Hill. You can explore them by taking the precipitous **Greenwich Steps** down from Coit Tower's parking lot. Look for the "Greenwich" sign where idling cars await their turn for a parking place.

It's a stunning stroll, offering swatches of the city framed in flowering plants and trees. Midway down, you'll pass the turreted **Julius Castle,** an upscale restaurant with city views. Jog to your right here, start down a set of concrete steps and you'll shortly emerge onto Sansome Street, opposite the handsome brickwork of **Levi's Plaza.**

This ends our North Beach tour, and we're ready

to steer you along the waterfront. However, if you feel up to the challenge, you can pick up the **Filbert Steps** at Filbert and Sansome, and hike back to Coit Tower.

It's only 494 steps. Meet you at the top.

WHAT TO SEE & DO

Coit Tower ● △△△△ ☺

Atop Telegraph Hill (via Lombard Street); 362-8037. Adults $3, seniors $2, kids (6 to 12) $1. Daily 10 to 4:30. When Lillie Hitchcock Coit bequeathed $125,000 "for the purpose of adding to the beauty of San Francisco," designers came up with this fluted Art Deco column, completed in 1933. Study interesting WPA murals on the inner walls, depicting Californians at work. Then take the clunking old elevator to the top for impressive city views. You can buy souvenirs at a small ground floor shop and feed a machine that smashes a penny into a Coit Tower token.

North Beach Museum ● △△

1435 Stockton St. (Eureka Federal Savings mezzanine, near Green); 391-6210. Free; Monday-Thursday 9 to 4, Friday 9 to 6 and Saturday 9 to 1. Operated as a community service by Eureka Federal, this attractive, well-lighted museum seeks to preserve memories of North Beach and adjacent Chinatown. Exhibits of photos and artifacts are changed twice yearly.

Saints Peter and Paul Church ● △△

666 Filbert St. (on Washington Square); 421-0809. Built in 1924 in a classic European filigree style, this church anchors the northern side of Washington Square. Step inside and study the busy complex of arches and columns and the domed altar with an eerily three-dimensional face of Christ.

Vesuvio ● △△△

255 Columbus Ave. (near Broadway); 362-3370. Free, but be civilized and by a drink, f'Chrissake. Daily 6 a.m. to 2 a.m. This 1948 relic is a valid visitor attraction. Stare quizzically at the works of local artists hanging on the walls, try to commune with the departed vibes of Jack Kerouac and otherwise lose yourself into North Beach's Beatnik era. When you've done that, cross Columbus (carefully) to **Spec's 12**

Adler Museum Cafe for more Sixties immersion. Adults only at both, please.

Washington Square ● △△ ☺
Cradled by Columbus, Filbert, Stockton and Union. Statues of Benjamin Franklin and heroic firemen adorn this large patch of grass. Turn the kids loose with their Frisbees, relax on a bench and admire surrounding North Beach.

WHERE TO DINE

Basta Pasta ● △△△ $$ Ø
1268 Grant Ave. (Vallejo); 434-2248. Italian; dinners $8 to $14; full bar. Daily 11:30 a.m. to 2 a.m. Reservations for six or more; informal. Major credit cards. Sporting a handsome new tiled interior, this long-time North Beach establishment is one of our favorite Italian cafes. Try tasty veal dishes, excellent fresh fish or pizza and calzone done to a proper turn in an imposing wood-burning oven.

Beethoven Restaurant ● △△△ $$
1701 Powell (Union); 391-4488. German; dinners $10.50 to $16; wine and beer. Tuesday-Saturday 5:30 to 10:30. Reservations accepted; informal. MC/VISA, AMEX. What's a fine German restaurant doing in the middle of Little Italy? Very well, *mein herr*. Wainscoting, soft music and a quietly-ticking cuckoo clock put you in a properly pleasant mood for hearty German fare such as *wienerschnitzel* and *rindsrouladen*.

Bix ● △△△ $$$
56 Gold St. (between Stockton and Pacific); 433-6300. American; dinners $12 to $25; full bar. Lunch weekdays from 11:30, dinner Sunday-Thursday 6 to 10 and Friday-Saturday 6 to midnight. Reservations accepted; informal. Major credit cards. Tucked into an alley in Jackson Square, this upscale little supper club captures a bit of old San Francisco ambiance. The menu tilts toward fresh seafood. Live jazz or vocalists are featured nightly.

Caffe Roma ● △△△ $$
414 Columbus Ave. (Vallejo); 391-8584. Italian; dinners $8 to $12; full bar service. Daily 7:30 a.m. to 11 p.m. (to 1 a.m. weekends). Reservations for five or more; casual. MC/VISA. Pastel pink cherubs decorate

the walls and high ceilings of this old bistro. Dining room windows open to the sidewalk on warm days, and you can adjourn to a sunny patio out back. The food's surprisingly tasty for the modest prices.

Caffe Trieste ● ΔΔ $

601 Vallejo (Grant); 392-6739. Coffee house; light meals $5 to $9; wine and beer. Weekdays 7 a.m. to 11:30 p.m. and weekends 7 a.m. to 12:30 a.m. No reservations; casual. No credit cards. Inhale the aroma of fresh coffee and nibble a piroshki, pizza or deli-style salad in this seedy survivor of the Beat Generation.

Calzone's Pizza Cucina ● ΔΔΔ $$

430 Columbus Ave. (Vallejo); 397-3600. Italian, specializing in pizza and calzone; dinners $6 to $14; full bar. Daily 11 a.m. to 1 a.m. Informal, Major credit cards. Calzone vies with Basta Pasta as North Beach's most attractive restaurant, with a distinctive ceramic tile and deli theme. Try the calzone—sort of a pizza that's been folded over and sealed shut.

Des Alpes Basque Restaurant ● Δ $$

732 Broadway (Stockton); 391-4249. French Basque; dinners $11; full bar service. Tuesday-Saturday 5:30 to 10, Sunday 5 to 9:30. Reservations accepted; casual. MC/VISA. One of the city's few surviving Basque restaurants, Des Alpes will fill your tank with nightly *prix fixe* dinners for $11, including soup, salad, appetizer, coffee and ice cream.

Fior d'Italia ● ΔΔ $$

601 Union (Stockton); 986-1886. Northern Italian; dinners $9 to $18; full bar service. Weekdays 11 to 10:30, weekends 5 to 10:30. Reservations accepted; jackets requested; Major credit cards. Like George Burns, Fior d'Italia earns plaudits simply for longevity. The city's senior North Beach restaurant, it's been around since 1886. Caught in a comfortable time warp of black-jacketed waiters and polished woods, its fare is rather ordinary oldstyle Italian.

The Gold Spike ● ΔΔΔ $$

527 Columbus Ave. (Green); 421-4591. Italian; six course dinners $12.95; full bar. Monday-Tuesday-Thursday 5 to 10, Friday-Saturday 5 to 10:30, Sunday 4:30 to 9:45, closed Wednesday. Informal. MC/VISA,

DISC. A wonderful scatter of eclectic clutter adorns the walls of this hangout, which dates back to Prohibition. Tummy-topping six-course dinners include everything from antipasto to dessert. Friday is crab cioppino night; all you can eat for $14.95.

Il Pollaio ● △ $

555 Columbus Ave. (Union); 362-7727. Italian-Argentinian; dinners $4 to $13; wine and beer. Daily except Tuesday 11:30 to 9. Casual. Major credit cards. This tiny Italian *rosticceria* (roasted meats) offers the best meal prices in North Beach. Four dollars gets you half a chicken; add salad or fries and it's still only $5.50.

Julius' Castle ● △△△△ $$$

1541 Montgomery St. (Telegraph Hill); 362-3042. Contemporary European; dinners $17 to $24; full bar service. Nightly from 5 to 10. Reservations advised; dressy; jackets for men. Major credit cards. One of the city's most stylish dining rooms has been inserted into a fanciful 1920s turreted mansion perched on the shoulder of Telegraph Hill. The atmosphere is romantic; the menu is Italian and French; the city views are grand.

La Bodega Restaurant ● △△ $$

1337 Grant Ave. (Vallejo); 433-0439. Spanish; dinners $10 to $15; wine and beer. Wednesday-Sunday 7 to 10 p.m. Reservations accepted for four or more; informal. No credit cards. This cute little place specializes in hearty *paella* and other Spanish-flavored fare. Live guitarists and flamenco dinner shows are held several nights a week.

Little City Antipasti Bar ● △△ $$

673 Union St. (Powell); 434-2900. Italian-Mediterranean-California; dinners $8.75 to $15; full bar service. Daily 11:30 a.m. to midnight. Reservations for six or more; casual. MC/VISA, AMEX. This attractive brick and brass place features international "little plates" running the culinary gamut from baked brie to *baba ghanoush*. Enough appetizers and you've got a meal; wash them down with a little *grappa*.

Little Joe's ● △△ $$

523 Broadway (Columbus); 433-4343. Italian; dinners $8 to $12; wine and beer. Thursday 11 to

11:30, Friday-Saturday 11 to 11, Sunday noon to 10. *Casual; no reservations or credit cards.* Get a glass of wine, then get in line for tasty Italian fare in this bustling bistro. Joe boasts that "rain or shine, there's always a line." For faster service, take a counter stool and watch the chefs at work in the open kitchen.

Mamma Tina ● ∆∆ $$$ Ø

1315 Grant Ave. (Vallejo); 391-4129. Italian; dinners $15 to $20; full bar service. Daily 5:30 to 11. Reservations accepted; informal. MC/VISA, AMEX. A large Italian pottery collection adds color to this cozy place, which specializes in pastas, veals and such. It offers a separate dining room for non-smokers.

Mario's Bohemian Cigar Store ● ∆ $

566 Columbus Ave. (Union); 362-0536. Light Italian; meals $4.75 to $5.50; wine and beer. Sunday 10 to 6, Monday 10 to 11, Tuesday-Saturday 10 to midnight. Casual; no reservation or credit cards. This isn't a cigar store and the last Bohemian was seen hitchhiking toward L.A. with Jack Kerouac in the 1960s. It's mostly a scruffy little pub that qualifies as a restaurant by serving tasty, inexpensive sandwiches on *focaccia.* (That's a type of bread that started out as a pizza, then changed its mind.)

North Beach Restaurant ● ∆∆ $$$

1512 Stockton St. (Columbus); 392-1700. Northern Italian; dinners $20 to $30; full bar service. Daily 11:45 to 11:45. Reservations accepted; casual. Major credit cards. Homemade pastas and veal dishes are this long-time establishment's trademark. The food is consistently good and the decor is pleasantly Italian, although we find it a bit pricey for the neighborhood.

Ristorante Grifone ● ∆∆∆ $$$

1609 Powell St. (Green); 397-8458. Regional Italian; dinners $20 to $30; full bar service. Daily 5 to 11 p.m. Reservations accepted; casual. MC/VISA, AMEX. Grifone exudes old Italian ambiance with mirrored glass and Venetian crystal, although it's only a few years old. The homemade pastas, table side Caesar salads and lightly-sauced veal and fish dishes are quite tasty—if a little on the high side.

San Francisco Brewing Company ● ∆∆ $

155 Columbus Ave. (Pacific); 434-3344. American;

light fare from $5 to $7.25; beer and wine. Weekdays 11:30 to 10 p.m., weekends noon to 10 (bar open until 2 a.m.). No reservations; casual. AMEX only. We stretch credibility by calling this brewpub a restaurant, but we need an excuse to list it. Hearty beers and ales are brewed in a big copper kettle right before patrons' eyes. Pub grub such as fish and chips and assorted sandwiches accompany your pint of Albatross or Emperor Norton lager.

The Shadows ● △△△△ $$$

1349 Montgomery St. (on Telegraph Hill); 982-5536. French-continental; dinners $17 to $24; full bar service. Nightly 5 to 10. Reservations suggested; dressy to informal; jacket optional. Major credit cards. Occupying a century-old house in the steep slope of Telegraph Hill, the Shadows has been refurbished and brightened, offering a *nouveau* menu to compliment its striking city views.

Washington Square Bar and Grill ● △△△△ $$$

1707 Powell St. (Union); 982-8123. American with an Italian accent; dinners $15 to $25; full bar. Lunch Monday-Saturday from 11:30; dinner Sunday 4 to 10, Monday-Thursday 5:30 to 10:30, Friday-Saturday 5:30 to 11:30. Reservations essential; informal. Major credit cards. It's the classic San Francisco restaurant, with honest food served by knowledgeable waiters, a great bar, live music and a good crowd of regulars. All this ambience is squeezed into a high-ceiling Victorian. In this city, the "Square" is very in.

What's Your Beef? ● △ $

759 Columbus Ave. (Greenwich); 989-1852. Hamburgers; dinners $5 to $9; wine and beer. Daily 11 a.m. to 7 p.m. No reservations; casual; no credit cards. San Francisco's only restaurant ending with a question serves thick, juicy burgers and homemade chips. Take them out or eat in a snug dining room.

WHAT TO DO AFTER DARK

Club Fugazi ● △△△ (comedy revue)

678 Green St. (Powell); 421-4222. Steve Silver's zany "Beach Blanket Babylon" slapstick song-and-dance show is in its second giggling generation; shows Wednesday through Saturday.

Finocchio's ● ΔΔ (revue)
506 Broadway (Columbus); 982-9388. Female impersonators have been mincing around this scruffy old theater for more than half a century.

La Bodega Restaurant ● ΔΔ (flamenco)
1337 Grant Ave. (Vallejo); 433-0439. This small cafe features dinner shows with flamenco dancers and Spanish guitarists.

The Saloon ● ΔΔ (blues, rock)
1232 Grant Ave. (Fresno Alley); 989-7666. Local groups perform at this scruffily historic pub most nights of the week.

Washington Square Bar & Grill ● ΔΔ (jazz)
1707 Powell St. (Union); 982-8123. Live jazz and piano music happens nights and Sundays.

WHERE TO SLEEP
(Detailed listings in Chapter 16)

Bed & breakfast inns
Millefiori Inn ● *444 Columbus Ave. (Vallejo)*
Obrero Hotel ● *1208 Stockton St. (Pacific)*
Washington Square Inn ● *1660 Stockton (Filbert)*

WATERFRONT/LOWER MARKET STREET

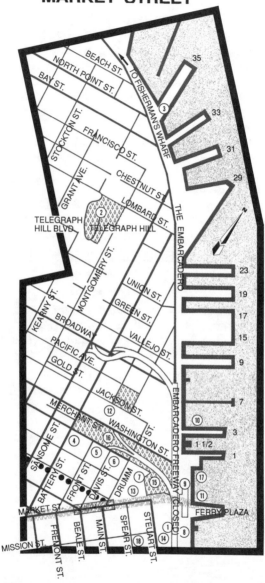

DIRECTORY

1. AUDIFFRED BUILDING
2. COIT TOWER (SEE CHAPTER 5)
3. CRUISE SHIP TERMINAL
4. EMBARCADERO #1
5. EMBARCADERO #2
6. EMBARCADERO #3
7. EMBARCADERO #4
8. EMBARCADERO PROMENADE
9. FERRY BUILDING

10. FERRYBOAT SANTA ROSA
11. GOLDEN GATE FERRY DOCK
12. GOLDEN GATEWAY
13. HYATT REGENCY
14. JEWISH COMMUNITY MUSEUM
15. JUSTIN HERMAN PLAZA
16. MARITIME PLAZA
17. RED & WHITE FERRY DOCK
18. RINCON CENTER
... CABLE CAR LINE
//// BART

Six

THE WATERFRONT
Sunny lunches and sea gulls

A QUICK LOOK: The waterfront area along the foot of Market Street is a mix of old piers, an Orwellian high-rise complex and upscale shopping. The area we cover extends from the Ferry Building north along the shoreline toward Fisherman's Wharf. Its main drag is the Embarcadero, Spanish for "place of embarkation." The earthquake-crippled Embarcadero Freeway straddles it for several blocks before swinging inland.

MUCH OF THE CITY'S WATERFRONT is landfill. Until Andy Hallidie invented the cable car, the muddy slopes were difficult to negotiate, so expansion reached its eager fingers into the bay. Today, of course, those ramparts are the city's choicest home sites.

Often, when a waterfront site is excavated to lay foundations for yet another high-rise, workers will burrow into buried remnants of yesterday. They've found hulls of ships deserted by crews during the Gold Rush, then covered with landfill. You'll see relics from such digs at **Rincon Center,** which we will visit shortly.

San Francisco lost most of its shipping business to the more aggressive Port of Oakland decades ago. Some say the waterfront never recovered from violent strikes led by labor leader Harry Bridges in the 1930s.

Many of the cavernous cargo piers are now empty, reaching into the bay like giant, chubby-fingered gloves. Some piers are used as parking lots; others house professional offices or they host cruise ships instead of cargo-heavy freighters. A few of the old wharves have vanished; rotting pilings—useful now only as sea gull perches—mark their sites.

Our stroll leads along this waterfront-in-transition and inland through the city's most ambitious redevelopment complex.

Begin at the **California Street cable car** terminus, where California, Market and Drumm streets converge. BART's **Embarcadero Station** is adjacent. Cross Market to Spear Street and follow it to **Rincon Center** (Spear and Mission), the city's finest architectural marriage of past and present. Once the Art Deco Rincon Annex post office, it has been fashioned into an atrium shopping center, with office and apartment towers rising behind.

The old post office facade and the lobby with its New Deal **California history murals** by Anton Refregier have been preserved. Display cases exhibit photos and artifacts of early-day San Francisco. After scanning the restored and brightened murals, step into the center's atrium and admire the unusual 80-foot "rain column" cascading from the glass roof to a decorative concrete splash basin. Chairs, tables and assorted snack shops will tempt you to linger.

From the center, walk down Mission Street to the waterfront. The elaborate mansard-roofed French Renaissance **Audiffred Building** at 100 Mission dates from 1889 and once housed the offices of fiery labor leader Harry Bridges. An exhibit in the foyer recalls the history of this area.

At the foot of Mission, cross under the cracked, shored-up **Embarcadero Freeway** to the bayfront. The San Francisco Port Commission, having lost most of its cargo business, now busies itself with waterfront redevelopment. A recent addition is the **Embarcadero Promenade,** a series of concrete risers and walkways along the Embarcadero just south of the Ferry Building. It's a good vantage point for views of the East Bay and the **San Francisco-Oakland Bay**

Bridge, whose great oval piers seem to float on the glistening gray-green water.

Walk along the promenade toward the Ferry Building, swinging bay-ward to explore Ferry Plaza East, a concrete pier built over ventilation ducts of BART's trans-bay tube. Two restaurants, **Sinbad's** and **Gabbiano's** offer bay view dining. Nearby, you can catch **Golden Gate** commuter ferries to Sausalito and Larkspur. A bronze statue of **Mohandas K. Ghandi,** garbed in his sack cloth of suffering, rises from the middle of the plaza. And no, we don't know what he's doing on the San Francisco waterfront.

Hike over to the 1896 **Ferry Building**, survivor of two major earthquakes, with its four-faced clock tower. More than a 100,000 commuters a day once poured through here before the bridges put the ferryboats out of business. During their heyday, fifty ferryboats plied the bay, carrying passengers, vehicles, cargo and freight cars between San Francisco and neighboring cities. Now the bridges are jammed and ferry transit has come full circle. (See "What to See & Do" below.)

The Ferry Building is home to the **World Trade Center** and noteworthy agencies such as the Prune Marketing Commission. Step inside and study the **Pacific Rim picture maps**, charmingly simple murals painted for the 1939 Golden Gate International Exposition.

Then, cross back under the freeway and you'll emerge onto **Justin Herman Plaza,** named for the redevelopment agency boss who spurred waterfront development. It's a busy place for street artists and crafts people, occasional outdoor concerts and perennial skateboarders who seem to have found it unnecessary to work for a living.

Squarish and garish **Vaillancourt Fountain,** apparently assembled from concrete packing crates, occupies one end of the plaza. It's as ugly as the dead freeway behind it, but it's fun to crawl among its innards and tip-toe across square stepping stones of the dirty reflection pool.

Cast your eyes now upon a more attractive vision, the thin high-rises and tiered shopping galleries of

Embarcadero Center. Started in 1968, it's the commercial heart of the Golden Gateway Project, the most ambitious redevelopment effort since post-1906 earthquake reconstruction.

The $645 million project includes five high-rises—four with arcaded shopping malls at their feet, the surrealistic **Hyatt Regency Hotel** with its soaring atrium lobby, the new European-style **Park Hyatt Hotel** and the restored **Federal Reserve Bank** building. It spreads over several waterfront blocks that once sheltered a shabby produce district.

With its landscaped patios, elevated shops, monumental artworks and slender high-rises, Embarcadero Center has the feel of an Orwellian city of the future. Crosswalks link it to both Hyatt Hotels and to the adjacent Golden Gateway residential towers. Except for schooling, you could grow up, find a job, retire and expire here without your feet ever touching the sidewalks below.

Begin your exploration with the Hyatt Regency. Its backside, facing Herman Plaza, is a curious thing resembling a giant typewriter keyboard. However, its seventeen-story atrium lobby is the city's most dramatic inner space. Pause for an afternoon cocktail at **The Other Trellis** and admire the spill-over fountain, hanging gardens on the terraced upper floors and the space capsule elevators scaling the inner walls. This bit of architectural drama was created by new wave architect John Portman.

The Hyatt's **Equinox** is a revolving restaurant bar above it all, but it's rather a disappointment. For some odd reason, Portman enclosed this glass bubble inside bands of concrete, so the view isn't that awesome. The drink prices are, unfortunately.

From the Hyatt, cross over to **Embarcaderos Four, Three, Two** and **One**. They're lined up between Sacramento and Clay streets in that order. More than 140 shops, restaurants and take-outs occupy tiered shopping plazas at the base of each. Handy kiosks have "you are here" maps, lists of merchants and brochures to keep you from going astray in this complex.

If you like *al fresco* dining, you'll want to spend time here, since most restaurants have outdoor seating. A dozen sidewalk cafes and take-outs line the base of Embarc Four, with bolted down tables on adjacent Herman Plaza. Benches and picnic tables are scattered throughout the center.

When your wanderings have carried you to **Embarc One,** you can take a crosswalk to the right—over Clay Street—to **One Maritime Plaza**. The Alcoa Building, looking still unpacked in a curious crosshatch crate, rises from an elevated park. Across the way is **The Punch Line,** a comedy club.

Another crosswalk bridges Washington Street, taking you to the elevated Utopian people capsules of the Golden Gateway. Beyond is the attractive brick condo complex of **Bridgeway Plaza,** across Jackson Street. A gate bars idle strollers, so you must reluctantly drop down to the reality of a Jackson Street sidewalk.

Take Jackson a short block bayward to Drumm, turn left and stroll through a landscaped walkway that emerges onto the Embarcadero near **The Waterfront** restaurant. Adjacent **Pier 7** was opened in late 1990 as a pubic access fishing pier. From here, you can continue along the waterfront to **Fisherman's Wharf** and our next chapter, or go back to the Ferry Building.

If you head the back up the Embarcadero, note the old **Ferryboat Santa Rosa**, permanently berthed at Pier 3. It houses the offices of **Hornblower Dining Yachts** and other firms, and a sign invites strollers. From its roof deck, you'll get a gull's eye view of the bay and the glistening city that rises abruptly from it like a tourist brochure Atlantis.

WHAT TO SEE & DO

Audiffred Building ● △△

100 Embarcadero (Mission). Small history exhibit in foyer open during weekday business hours. This 1886 French Renaissance building was erected by Hippolite d'Audiffred, who began his fortune by peddling charcoal to Chinatown merchants. After the 1906 earthquake, the operator of a downstairs saloon bribed firefighters with whiskey to prevent its destruction for a firebreak. It was from here that Harry Bridges called the 1934 waterfront strike that erupted into bloody violence.

The Ferry Building, survivor of two earthquakes, is one of the city's most enduring—and endearing—landmarks.

Embarcadero Center ● △△△△

Just off the waterfront, between Sacramento, Sansome and Clay streets; 772-0500. Most shops open weekdays 10 a.m. to 6 p.m., 10 to 5 Saturday and noon to 5 Sunday; restaurant hours vary. Validated parking; free parking on weekends. Shops and restaurants line three levels of the four Embarcadero Center complexes. Elevated walkways, basins of flowering plants, artworks, fountains and patios make this the city's most attractive shopping area.

Ferry Building ● △△△ ☺

Foot of Market Street on the Embarcadero; open to the public weekdays 7 a.m. to 6 p.m. It rivals the Golden Gate Bridge as a San Francisco landmark. The 230-foot clock tower was modeled after the campanile of Seville's cathedral. Youngsters will enjoy the oversized wall maps depicting the people, animals and native shelters of the nations of the Pacific Rim.

Ferry Service ● △△ ☺

Golden Gate ferries depart the south side of the Ferry Building; call 332-6600. Red and White ferries leave from a north side dock; dial 546-BOAT locally or (800) 445-8880 elsewhere in California. The ferries are intended to haul commuters, but they make great excursion boats as well. Particularly appealing are the Golden Gate run to Sausalito, the Red and White ferry trip to Tiburon and Red and White's long haul across the bay and up Carquinez Strait to Vallejo. Red and White initiated runs to Oakland and Alameda after the 1989 earthquake. It may or may not be in service by the time you read this. (See box in Chapter 7.)

Ferryboat Santa Rosa ● △△

Pier 3 at the Embarcadero. Monday-Saturday 9:30 to 4; free. Although it houses private offices, this restored ferryboat invites visitors. Built in 1927, it ran between the Ferry Building and Oakland until 1939, then it sailed Puget Sound for Washington State Ferries. The 251-foot double-ended ferry could carry 1,200 passengers and 65 vehicles.

Hyatt Regency Hotel lobby ● △△△ ☺

Five Embarcadero Center (California at Drumm); 788-1234. The Hyatt's atrium soars dramatically skyward and a gigantic lacy steel ball hangs over a reflection fountain. Don't just stand around and gawk like a tourist. This stunning space is best enjoyed from a table at **The Other Trellis** lobby bar. Or ride a *Star Trek* people capsule up to the **Equinox**.

Jewish Community Museum ● △△

121 Steuart St. (Mission); 543-8880. Adults $3, seniors $1. Tuesday-Friday and Sunday 10 to 4. Changing exhibits in this small, modern museum focus on past and present Jewish life. A gift counter sells Judaic books and crafts.

Rincon Center ● △△△

Mission Street between Spear and Steuart. Daily 7 a.m. to 11 p.m. The old Rincon Annex post office, a national architectural landmark, is the handsome frontpiece of this new shopping-business-residential center. Twenty-nine California history murals line the historic lobby and museum cases contain artifacts found in local excavations. New murals depicting contemporary city life rim the walls of an adjacent atrium lobby.

WHERE TO DINE

Harrington's Bar & Grill ● △△ $$

245 Front St. (opposite Embarcadero Center); 392-7595. American; dinners $7 to $12; full bar. Monday-Thursday 11:30 a.m. to 9 p.m., Friday 11:30 to 10:30, Saturday 11:30 to 4. No reservations; informal; no credit cards. The food in this honest old Irish pub is hearty and the drinks are as stiff as a lonely sailor's document. Hamburgers, corned beef, fresh seafood and liars' dice lure white collars, blue collars and an occasional tourist.

Harbor Village ● △△△△ $$$ Ø

Four Embarcadero Center (Drumm and Clay); 781-8833. Chinese; dinners from $16; full bar service. Lunch weekdays 11 to 2:30, weekends 10 to 2:30, dinner daily 5:30 to 9:30. Reservations accepted; dressy for dinner. Major credit cards. This handsome Asian restaurant is both resplendent and understated, with touches of rosewood, teak and crystal in small, canopied dining areas. Many tables offer bay views and the food is upscale Hong Kong, consistently well-prepared.

The Holding Company ● △△△ $$

Two Embarcadero Center (Front and Clay); 986-0797. American; dinners $7 to $15; full bar. Daily 11 a.m. to midnight. Reservations accepted; informal. Major credit cards. This is primarily a well-dressed bar that serves excellent hamburgers and other American fare. We like the wood and brass ambiance and the sunny outdoor dining; it' a favored lunch spot.

Hornblower Dining Cruises ● △△△ $$$$

Pier 33, off the Embarcadero; 394-8900. Continental; prix fixe dinners $50 ($65 on weekends), including *bay cruise and band for dinner-dancing; lunch cruises $25; full bar service. Dinner voyages depart 7:30 daily, lunch cruises at noon Fridays only. Reservations essential; dressy to informal. MC/VISA, AMEX.* Hornblower's dining yachts are nicely done in turn-of-the-century brass and glass, with stylish table service. Dinners are ample, sometimes uneven but generally tasty. The splendid setting may be tarnished by yappie (not yuppie) tour bus groups, and the dance band can get loud. But the views are marvelous, especially the city lights at night—and you can escape the noise by going out on deck. The itinerary varies, depending on the captain's whims. The ship may skim the Marin coastline, ply Raccoon Straits near Angel Island or cruise up the Oakland-Alameda estuary.

Schroeder's Restaurant ● △△△ $$

240 Front St. (California); 421-4778. Bavarian; dinners $8.75 to $15.50; full bar. Monday-Friday 11 a.m. to 9 p.m., Saturday 5 to 9. Reservations accepted; informal. Major credit cards. Schroeder's is an authentic antique dating from 1893, trimmed in Old World murals and beer steins; the food is predictably hearty. Start with German-style potato salad, then loosen your belt.

Square One ● △△△△ $$$$

190 Pacific Avenue Mall (Front Street); 788-1110. International; dinners $28 to $40; full bar. Lunch weekdays 11:30 to 2:30, dinner Monday-Thursday 5:30 to 10, Friday-Saturday 5:30 to 10:30, Sunday 5 to 9:30. Reservations essential; informal. MC/VISA, AMEX. An early graduate of Alice Waters' school of new California cuisine, Joyce Goldstein creates innovative fare with a Mediterranean accent. It's served in a handsome space of light woods, brick, glass and autumn colors, off Walton Park.

Tadich Grill ● △△ $$$

240 California St. (Front); 391-2373. American, mostly seafood; dinners $14 to $20; full bar. Weekdays 11 a.m. to 9 p.m., Saturday 11:30 to 9. No reservations; informal. MC/VISA. Despite its revered status as the city's oldest restaurant, Tadich isn't one of our favorites. It's too crowded and noisy and we're unnerved by people milling around like nervous collies, waiting for a seat. Why the crowds? The seafood is unfailingly fresh and properly cooked. Tadich traces its roots—in a roundabout manner—to 1849 when a Yugoslavian immigrant opened the New World Coffee Stand in a tent. Somehow, according to the fine print on the menu, that ties to a place opened by another Yugoslav, John Tadich, in 1887.

Umberto Ristorante ● △△△ $$$
141 Steuart St. (Mission); 543-8021. Italian; dinners $10 to $19; full bar. Lunch weekdays 11:30 to 2, dinner Monday-Saturday 5:30 to 11. Reservations accepted; informal. Major credit cards. Seafoods, pastas and veal dishes are served in a handsome brick setting that passes for a Financial District Mediterranean villa.

The Waterfront ● △△△△ $$$
Pier 7 (foot of Broadway); 391-2696. Seafood; dinners $20 to $25; full bar. Monday-Saturday 11:30 to 10:30, Sunday 10 to 10:30. Reservations advised; informal. Major credit cards. The city's classiest looking seafood restaurant, the Waterfront offers terraced bay views and fresh, properly cooked fish. Trimmed with brass and glass, it's a favored spot for business entertainment.

WHAT TO DO AFTER DARK
Pier 23 Cafe ● △△ (jazz, dixieland)
Embarcadero at Pier 23; 362-5125. Local groups perform Tuesday through Saturday afternoons.

The Punch Line ● △△ (stand-up comedy)
444 Battery St. (Maritime Plaza); 397-7573. Local and out-of-town comics do stand-up routines Tuesday through Sunday.

WHERE TO SLEEP
(Detailed listing in Chapter 16)

Rooms for $100 and up
Hyatt Regency ● *Five Embarcadero Center (Market)*
(Also see Fisherman's Wharf)

Seven

FISHERMAN'S WHARF
Must there be clowns?

A QUICK LOOK: For tourist purposes, Fisherman's Wharf begins at the Pier 39 shopping complex and continues west along the waterfront to Aquatic Park and Ghirardelli Square. Its lures extend three blocks inland along Jefferson, Beach and North Point streets to include the Cannery and Cost Plus. To reach the wharf, take either a Hyde and Beach or Bay and Taylor cable car from downtown, or travel north and west along the Embarcadero.

PICTURE, IF YOU CAN, early-morning mist shrouding the masts of fishing boats, like a surreal forest; Sicilian fishermen in their slickers and thick stocking caps, fussing with nets, sipping strong black coffee; their women clattering about kitchens of small bayside cafes.

Smell the salty bouquet of fresh-caught fish, the spicy tang of cioppino.

This was the Fisherman's Wharf of yesterday. In the years following the Gold Rush, Chinese set sail from here in high-prowed junks, seeking bay shrimp. They were nudged aside by Genoese with their triangular-rigged *feluccas,* then Sicilians and southern Italians. First called Meigg's Wharf, Fisherman's Wharf became an extension of North Beach, with Italian-run fish canneries and restaurants. Eventually, a boat basin was built in Jefferson Street Lagoon

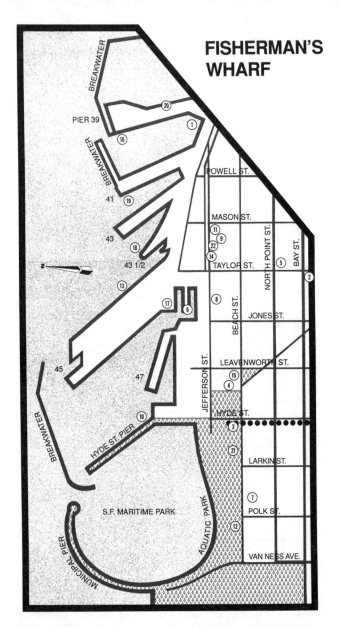

FISHERMAN'S WHARF

BREAKWATER

PIER 39

BREAKWATER

41

43

43 1/2

BREAKWATER

MUNICIPAL PIER

45

47

HYDE ST. PIER

S.F. MARITIME PARK

AQUATIC PARK

POWELL ST.

MASON ST.

TAYLOR ST.

BEACH ST.

JONES ST.

LEAVENWORTH ST.

JEFFERSON ST.

HYDE ST.

LARKIN ST.

POLK ST.

VAN NESS AVE.

NORTH POINT ST.

BAY ST.

DIRECTORY

1. BLUE & GOLD FLEET
2. CABLE CAR TERMINAL (BAY & TAYLOR)
3. CABLE CAR TERMINAL (HYDE & BEACH)
4. THE CANNERY
5. COST PLUS
6. FISHING FLEET
7. GHIRARDELLI SQUARE
8. GUINNESS MUSEUM OF WORLD RECORDS
9. HAUNTED GOLD MINE
10. HYDE STREET PIER HISTORIC SHIPS
11. MEDIEVAL DUNGEON

12. NATIONAL MARITIME MUSEUM
13. PAMPANITO SUBMARINE
14. RIPLEY'S BELIEVE IT OR NOT MUSEUM
15. SAN FRANCISCO INTERNATIONAL
    TOY MUSEUM
16. SEA LION HERD
17. SEAMEN'S MEMORIAL CHAPEL
18. RED & WHITE FLEET
19. ALCATRAZ FERRY
20. SAN FRANCISCO EXPERIENCE
21. VICTORIAN PARK
22. WAX MUSEUM AT FISHERMAN'S WHARF
... CABLE CAR LINE

for the fishing fleet and a beach and pier at Aquatic Park for residents and visitors.

By the 1950s, the wharf had become one of the city's most appealing areas—a John Steinbeck scene of weathered packing sheds, chowder houses and brightly-painted fishing boats.

Today's Fisherman's Wharf is a pathetic parody of itself. It's a gaudy potpourri of wax museums, novelty rides, fake cable cars, rickshaws, sidewalk T-shirt vendors and souvenir shops. Hawkers try to peddle tours on fake cable cars or lure visitors into their so-called attractions. It has all the charm and character of a cheap carnival midway.

It's also the most popular visitor lure in San Francisco, so who are we to be so imperious?

It does offer several legitimate attractions, mixed in with the glitz and gimmickry. Boats still bob in their slips at Jefferson Street lagoon—although many of them are party boats. Glittering catches of fish are still hauled into processing plants of Pier 45, and steaming crab pots permeate the salty air with their special aromas. The wharf also offers the city's largest selection of seafood restaurants.

The **National Maritime Museum** provides a wonderful cargo of nautical lore, and the yesterday ships of **Hyde Street Pier** are fun to explore. Visitors can test their resistance to claustrophobia as they crawl through the cramped metallic innards of the *U.S.S. Pampanito*, a battle-scarred World War II submarine.

The wharf is the launching point for an assortment of bay cruises by the **Red and White Fleet,** berthed at piers 41 and 43 1/2 and Pier 39's **Blue and Gold Fleet**. (See box for details.)

Alcatraz, that grim-looking rock fortress in the middle of the bay, is served by Red and White from Pier 41. Once a notorious federal lock-up that hosted the likes of Al Capone and Machine Gun Kelly, it's now part of the Golden Gate National Recreation Area. The once unapproachable "Rock" is one of the city's most popular visitor attractions.

What the wharf has lost in character, it has gained in shopping complexes, with scores of stores offering things unique and useless. Old brick warehouses have been re-born as the handsome **Cannery** and **Ghirardelli Square**. **Cost Plus** is northern California's largest import store and the **Anchorage** offers a collection of souvenir and specialty shops. **Pier 39** is an extension of the wharf's trend to tackiness, with carnival gimmicks as well as specialty shops.

The area's newest—and perhaps most unexpected—attraction is a troupe of sea lions that has annexed part of Pier 39's marina. Management called in the highly regarded California Marine Mammal Center to gently evict these aquatic squatters. When their efforts failed, pier officials shrugged, grinned and printed a brochure calling the invaders "Pier 39's Natural Attraction." Odds are that they'll still be there when you visit, yapping happily away and sunning themselves on the boat docks.

Just beyond Pier 39 is the city's **passenger ship terminal**, Pier 35. You might see a gleaming white ship in port, tempting you with the lure of far-away shores. Boarding passes are hard to come by, but it's fun to watch their departures under a cheerful rain of confetti and streamers. Arrivals and departures are listed in the shipping section of city newspapers.

The Wharf area is rather compact, so we won't suggest a specific walking tour. Wander at will, sniffing the crab pots and sampling its sundry attractions. If you need more guidance than our map offers, pick up a **Fisherman's Wharf walking tour** brochure from the convention and visitor's bureau.

As you wander about, do these things, or you won't have done Fisherman's Wharf:

● Start your outing with an Irish coffee (or breakfast, or both) at the city's penultimate tourist pub, the **Buena Vista Cafe** at Hyde and Beach.

● Watch old gentlemen of Italy play **bocce ball** at the courts at Van Ness and Beach.

● Stroll about the **Boat Basin**, then cross over to **Pier 45**, with its still-active fish packing plants and large seagoing trawlers tied up alongside the dock. You might see a glittering cargo being hauled ashore.

● Buy a walk-away **seafood cocktail** and have lunch on the hoof while shouldering past the steaming crab pots in the covered walkways of **Jefferson** and **Taylor streets**.

● Stroll the length of curving **Municipal Pier** and enjoy the view back at the city skyline.

● Indulge in a mid-afternoon hot fudge sundae at the Ghirardelli Square **Chocolate Factory**.

● Return after dark, when the crowds and clowns and street hawkers have left. Sit quietly on a wrought iron bench in **Aquatic Park** and listen to the silent echoes of old Fisherman's Wharf. Watch the evening mist caress the masts of the weathered boats, and pretend that there are no wax museum or fake cable cars down there.

WHAT TO SEE & DO

Alcatraz ● △△△△ ☺

Reached by Red and White Fleet sightseeing boats from Pier 41; frequent departures from 8:45 to 5 (shorter hours in the off-season). Adults $5, over 54, $4.50, kids 5-11, $3; audio-tape tour $2.50. For advance reservations: Ticketron, P.O. Box 26340, San Francisco, CA 94126; (415) 392-7469. The Isle of the Pelicans (*La Isla de los Alcatraces*) has been occupied since 1858, first as a mid-bay fort, then as a military prison. Its tenure as the infamous federal lock-up spanned only thirty years—from 1933 until 1963. Tape-recorded tours take visitors through the main cell block, messhall with tables still set and concrete-walled exercise yard.

Aquatic Park ● △△ ☺

Corner of Hyde and Beach Streets. This pretty little park offers a nice retreat from the wharf's carny atmosphere, with wrought iron benches and oldstyle lamps. The Hyde and Beach cable car terminus is here, along with information kiosks and a gazebo. Street musicians generally are on hand to entertain folks queuing up for the next car.

Bay cruises: see box

The Cannery ● △△

Beach and Leavenworth; 771-3112. This themed center offers about 50 shops and restaurants tucked into three floors of the 1894 brick Del Monte Fruit Cannery. Its focal point is the Courtyard, an appealing, tree-shaded gathering of benches and sidewalk cafes. Street artists perform on an outdoor stage here in summers.

Cost Plus ● △△

Taylor and North Point; 928-6200. What began as an import shop housed in an old warehouse has

---

SPEND A DAY
ON THE GLORIOUS BAY

This city born on a peninsula is best seen from the water that cradles it. An assortment of passenger boats play upon the bay, offering scenic tours and dinner cruises. Since the bridges that replaced the old ferryboats are jammed, commuter ferries now link San Francisco with its trans-bay neighbors. They're popular with visitors as well.

Operating from the Fisherman's Wharf area and from slips near the Ferry Building, these companies offer water transit to tourists and commuters:

Golden Gate Ferries shuttle commuters between the Ferry Building and the Marin communities of Sausalito and Larkspur. Both runs are popular with sightseers, particularly on weekends. They're best avoided during crowded commute hours; you'll have a long wait for your Marin-bound martini. The terminal is just south of the Ferry Building. Call 332-6600 for rates and schedules.

Red and White Fleet's ambitious schedule includes Bay sightseeing cruises, shuttles to Alcatraz and Angel Island State Park and high-speed catamaran trips to Tiburon and Vallejo's Marine World-Africa USA. These operate out of piers 41 and 43 1/2, near Fisherman's Wharf. Commuter trips to Vallejo, Oakland and Alameda run from Pier 1, just north of the Ferry Building. Red and White also has weekend dinner cruises. Call (800) 445-8880 (California only) or locally 546-BOAT for details.

Blue and Gold Fleet sails from the west marina of Pier 39, offering year-around scenic Bay cruises and weekend dinner cruises from spring until late fall. Call 781-7877.

Hornblower Dining Yachts feature dinner-dances nightly and lunch cruises on Fridays, casting off from Pier 33. Call 394-8900, extension 7. (See dining listing in Chapter 6.)

grown into a complex of several stores. They sell everything from decorator coffee mugs to Tijuana taxi horns.

Ghirardelli Square ● △△△

Beach and Larkin streets; 775-5500. The area's most attractive themed shopping center was fashioned from 1864 brick structures that housed a woolen mill, spice factory and the Ghirardelli Chocolate Manufactory. A touristy version of the chocolate factory remains, serving the best hot fudge sundaes west of the Hudson. The complex offers about 50 shops, a dozen restaurants and nice bay views.

Guinness Museum of World Records ● △△ ☺

235 Jefferson St. (Taylor); 771-9890. Daily 9 to midnight; shorter hours in the off-season. Adults $5.95, seniors $4.95, kids 5 to 12, $2.75. MC/VISA, AMEX. A collection of the world's tallest, smallest, fattest, fastest and skinniest people are portrayed in videos, photos and models, along with interesting footage of assorted world's records being set. Like the great domino topple, for instance. For reasons unclear, there's a waxen figure of Michael Jackson out front.

Haunted Gold Mine ● △ ☺

Jefferson near Mason; 885-4975 or (800) 439-4305. Sunday-Thursday 10 to 10, Friday-Saturday 10 to 11. Adults $4.95, kids 4 to 12, $2.25 (or combo ticket; see Wax Museum listing). MC/VISA. Designers of this scruffy exhibit couldn't decide whether to make it funny or scary, so they failed at both. It's basically a mirror maze mixed in with mining tableaux and an occasional head that drops from someplace and screams at you. After paying five dollars, I was ready to scream right back.

Hyde Street Pier Historic Ships ● △△△△ ☺

Foot of Hyde Street; 556-6435. Daily 10 to 6 May-October and 10 to 5 November-April; ranger-led tours hourly from 11 to 4. Adults $3; seniors and kids under 16 free. Walk about the decks and crawl through the holds of ships that made maritime history. The collection includes the *Balclutha*, an 1886 square-rigger; the 1895 sail-rigged cargo ship, *C.A. Thayer*; the 1890 sidewheel ferry *Eureka*; the 1904 paddle-wheel steam tug *Eppleton Hall*, the *Alma*, an

The 1886 square-rigged Balclutha is one of several historic ships at Hyde Street Pier; the city skyline rises beyond.

1891 scow schooner; and the *Wapama*, a steam schooner built in 1915. Some of the boats are undergoing restoration and may be withdrawn temporarily from the display. The pier was built in 1922 as the terminal for the Golden Gate Ferry Company.

Medieval Dungeon ● △△

Jefferson St. (Mason); 885-4975 or (800) 439-4305. Sunday-Thursday 10 to 10, Friday-Saturday 10 to 11. Adults $5.95, kids 4 to 12, $2.95 (or combo ticket; see Wax Museum listing). MC/VISA. If you're amused by torture chambers, spiked coffins, guillotines, skull crushers and waxen figures dripping simulated blood and guts, then go for the gore. But not before lunch. This is a display of man's inhumanity to man, carried to primeval—or we should say medieval—extreme. Some exhibits are hands-on; you can pull a lever and propel a hanging victim through a gallows trap door. Fun!

National Maritime Museum of San Francisco
● ΔΔΔΔ ☺

Beach and Polk streets; 556-3002. Free. Daily 10 to 5. Housed in a building resembling the superstructure of an Art Deco ship, the museum preserves a century of Bay Area maritime history. Exhibits are thematic, covering river boating, ferryboats, fishing and sailors' arts such as scrimshaw, knot-tying and—surprisingly—macrame. On display are fine examples of model ships, figureheads, historic photos and pieces of historic ships. This excellent museum fills two floors, and the second deck provides fine bay views as well as things nautical.

Pier 39 ● ΔΔ ☺

Off the Embarcadero, east of Fisherman's Wharf; 981-7437. This pier-based complex is a blend of shopping center and amusement park. Video games blink and bong in a huge game hall, kids ride plastic horses on a two-deck merry-go-round and acrobats perform aboard wobbly unicycles. Shoppers will enjoy specialty boutiques, such as stores for left-handers only, shops selling only chocolates, an all-year Christmas store and—our favorite—a Disney store. Pier 39 also has several seafood restaurants and fast food places.

Ripley's Believe It or Not Museum ● ΔΔ ☺

175 Jefferson St. (Taylor); 771-6188. Daily 9 to midnight; shorter hours in the off-season. Adults $6.50, seniors and teens $5.50, kids 5 to 12, $3.75. MC/VISA, AMEX. Robert L. Ripley, a man with an overbite and a great curiosity, traveled to nearly 200 countries to collect the world's oddest oddities. Models, photos, wax figures and stuffed versions of his grotesque gatherings are on display here, along with some of the misshapen people we met at the Guinness Museum of World Records.

San Francisco Experience ● ΔΔ

Pier 39, second level; 982-7550. Daily 10 a.m. to 10 p.m., shows every half hour. Adults $6, seniors and military $5, kids 6 to 16, $3. MC/VISA. This show gives you the shakes. A 4,000-watt "surround sound" jiggles your seats while computer-driven projectors and strobe lights simulate the earthquakes of 1906 and 1989. The Experience is an interesting quick study of the city's history and personality, with images flashed onto a 50-foot screen. However, it's not as awesome as the brochure suggests.

San Francisco International Toy Museum ● ΔΔ ☺

In the Cannery, second level (2801 Leavenworth); 441-8697. Tuesday-Friday 10:30 to 5, weekends 11 to 5; $2. Kids can play with modern toys in a special play area in this small museum, or admire antique ones from around the world. A gift shop offers present-day playthings for sale.

San Francisco Maritime National Historical Park ●

The park comes in several pieces. See individual listings for the **San Francisco Maritime Museum**, *U.S.S. Pampanito* submarine, and **Hyde Street Pier's** historic ships.

U.S.S Jeremiah O'Brien ● *See Chapter 14.*

U.S.S. Pampanito ● ΔΔΔ ☺

Pier 45; 929-0202. Adults $4, kids 12 to 18, $2; kids 6 to 11 and seniors, $1. Daily 9 to 9 (shorter hours in the off-season). A self-guiding taped tour takes you through the cozy confines of this submarine that sunk six enemy ships during World War II. Learn about the daring men of the "silent service," who scored more kills—and had a higher mortality rate—than any other branch of the military. Kids will be fascinated by the myriad of knobs, dials and levers and the gleaming torpedoes—disarmed, of course—still sitting in their cradles.

Wax Museum at Fisherman's Wharf ● ΔΔ ☺

145 Jefferson St. (Mason); 885-4975 or (800) 439-4305. Sunday-Thursday 10 to 10, Friday-Saturday 10 to 11. Adults $7.95, seniors and teens, $5.55; kids 6-12, $3.95. Combination tickets that include the Haunted Gold Mine, Medieval Dungeon and Laser Maze are available, saving about $2. MC/VISA. If the idea of stuffed people appeals to you, this place may be worth its hefty admission price. But it lacks focus, being a waxy mix of "patriots, pacifists and poets." Labels offer little background information, so this is hardly a learning experience. A Last Supper Tableau is well done, however. Naturally, the museum has a yucky "Chamber of Horrors" with a bloodied victim hanging from a meat hook and other upbeat exhibits. The brochure insults the museum even better than we can: "This is the human zoo.

WHERE TO DINE

Buena Vista ● △△△ $

2675 Hyde St. (Beach); 474-5044. American; meals $5 to $9; full bar. Weekends 8 a.m. to 2 a.m., weekdays 9 to 2. No reservations; casual. No credit cards. Most folks think of the "BV" as the landmark tourist bar that introduced Irish coffee to America. This Victorian pub also serves tasty breakfasts and light entrees. Pull up a chair (tables are expected to be shared) and enjoy a light bite, an "Irish" and a view of the waterfront.

Gaylord ● △△△△ $$$

Ghirardelli Square (North Point); 771-8822. Indian; dinners $15 to $25; full bar. Daily noon to 2 and 5 to 11. Reservations advised; dressy to informal. Major credit cards. The East Indian decor is exquisite and so are the bay views from Gaylord's high perch in Ghirardelli. It features lightly seasoned northern India dishes cooked in the round clay *tandoor*, accompanied by *kulcha* bread, steaming hot from the oven. Typically spicy curries are served as well.

Little Rio Cafe and Pizzeria ● △△ $$

2721 Hyde St. (Beach); 441-3344. Italian-Brazilian; meals $5 to $12; wine and beer. Sunday-Thursday noon to 10, Friday-Saturday noon to 11. MC/VISA. This cute little place with white nappery and blonde bentwood chairs offers cross-cultural oddities such as pizza with Brazilian-style spices and Brazilian-Italian pastas. The *feijoda* (black bean and meat stew) is quite tasty.

Neptune's Palace ● △△△ $$$ Ø

Far end of Pier 39; 434-2260. Seafood; dinners $20 to $30; full bar. Sunday-Thursday 11:30 to 9:30, Friday-Saturday 11:30 to 10. Reservations accepted; informal. Major credit cards. Early San Francisco decor provides an opulent setting, and the end-of-pier position provides nice bay views. Although large,

Neptune's is divided into intimate dining rooms; some are smoke-free.

Paprika's Fono ● △△△ $$

Ghirardelli Square (North Point); 441-1223. Hungarian; dinners $11 to $15; full bar. Daily 11 a.m. to 10 p.m. Reservations accepted; informal. MC/VISA, DIN. Paprika's is a delightfully cheerful place with hand-painted chairs and white nappery, sitting under a greenhouse roof with a bay view. The fare is spicy mid-European; try the paprika chicken or lamb *tokany* seasoned with tarragon.

Pizzeria Uno ● △△△ $

2323 Powell St. (Bay); 788-4055. Pizza; meals $7 to $10; full bar service. Daily 11 a.m. to midnight. No reservations; casual. MC/VISA, AMEX. It's simply the city's best pizza—a deep-dish Chicago style that arrives piping hot in its own personal skillet. Salads, sandwiches and soups are peddled as well, and we like the five-minute $4.50 "Express Lunch" of pizza and soup or salad. There's a second Uno on Lombard Street, listed in Chapter 15. Both places have attractive oldstyle decor.

Pompei's Grotto ● △△ $$

340 Jefferson St. (Jones); 776-9265. Seafood and pasta; dinners $8 to $15; full bar. Daily 8 a.m. to 11 p.m. Reservations accepted; informal. Major credit cards. Smaller and cozier than the other wharf fish parlors, Pompei's offers a large seafood and pasta menu. We like its red-checkered tables and old-fashioned ceiling fans; it has outside seating as well. A soup and salad lunch with excellent chowder and a slab of sourdough bread is a good buy at $5.95.

Spada ● △△△ $$$

1250 Columbus Ave. (in the Marriott Fisherman's Wharf, at Bay); 775-7555. American-Italian; dinners $12 to $25; full bar. Daily 6:30 a.m. to 10:30 p.m. Reservations accepted; informal. Major credit cards. This classy place with an Italian moderne look specializes in fresh seafood, pasta and prime rib.

Tarantino's ● △△△ $$

206 Jefferson St. (Taylor); 775-5600. Seafood-Italian; dinners $9 to $16; full bar. Daily 11 to 11. Reservations accepted; informal. Major credit cards.

Founded by Irishmen, not Italians, this venerable place is popular with visitors, yet it doesn't display a tourist mentality. Service is friendly and efficient, fish is properly cooked and it brews up a fine cioppino. Views over the boat basin and across the bay are nice. It's our Fisherman's Wharf favorite.

Vicolo Pizzeria ● ∆∆ $

Ghirardelli Square (North Point); 776-1331. Pizza, focaccia; meals $5 to $10; wine and beer. Monday-Saturday 11:30 to 11:30, Sunday 2 to 10. Casual; no reservations or cards. Designer pizzas are a specialty. Try salsa, mozzarella, feta, roasted sweet and hot peppers on a cornbread-olive oil crust, for instance. The look is bare-bones Art Deco. On a sunny day, sit outside and enjoy bay views. There's a second Vicolo at 201 Ivy Street, off Van Ness in the Civic Center (863-2382).

WHAT TO DO AFTER DARK

Cobb's Comedy Club ● ∆∆

In the Cannery (Leavenworth); 928-4320. Shows nightly at 9; doors open at 7:45. Most shows have an $8 cover and two-drink minimum. MC/VISA. Stand-up comics reach for your funny bone every night in this club just off the Cannery Courtyard.

WHERE TO SLEEP
(Detailed listings in Chapter 16)

Rooms for $100 and up

Holiday Inn ● *1300 Columbus Ave. (North Point)*
Hyde Park Suites ● *2655 Hyde St. (North Point)*
Marriott Hotel ● *1250 Columbus Ave. (Bay)*
Travelodge ● *250 Beach St. (Powell)*

Rooms for $50 to $99

San Remo Hotel ● *2237 Mason St. (Chestnut)*

"Boat" & breakfast

Bayside Boat & Breakfast ● *Pier 39 Marina*

SOUTH OF MARKET

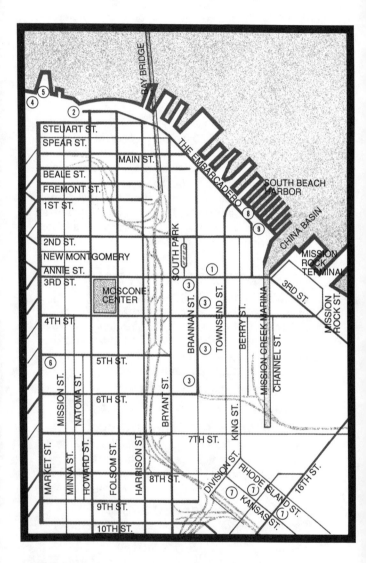

STEUART ST.
SPEAR ST.
MAIN ST.
BEALE ST.
FREMONT ST.
1ST ST.
2ND ST.
NEW MONTGOMERY
ANNIE ST.
3RD ST.
MOSCONE CENTER
4TH ST.
5TH ST.
6TH ST.
MISSION ST.
NATOMA ST.
BRYANT ST.
MARKET ST.
MINNA ST.
HOWARD ST.
FOLSOM ST.
HARRISON ST.
7TH ST.
8TH ST.
9TH ST.
10TH ST.
BRANNAN ST.
TOWNSEND ST.
SOUTH PARK
BERRY ST.
KING ST.
DIVISION ST.
RHODE ISLAND ST.
KANSAS ST.
16TH ST.
MISSION CREEK MARINA
CHANNEL ST.
3RD ST.
MISSION ROCK ST.
MISSION ROCK TERMINAL
CHINA BASIN
SOUTH BEACH HARBOR
THE EMBARCADERO
BAY BRIDGE

DIRECTORY

1. CARTOON ARTS MUSEUM
2. EMBARCADERO PROMENADE
3. FACTORY OUTLETS
4. FERRY BUILDING
5. FERRY PLAZA
6. OLD MINT MUSEUM
7. MERCHANDISE SHOWROOMS
8. SAILING SHIP DOLPH REMPP
9. SOUTH BEACH HARBOR PARK

Eight

SOUTH OF MARKET

Picadilly was never like this

A QUICK LOOK: Primarily a shipping, warehousing and industrial district, South of Market is emerging as a nightlife and discount shopping area. The region we cover runs from the western waterfront south to South Van Ness Avenue.

SOME GUIDEBOOKS have compared South of Market, or SoMa, with London's SOHO nightlife and theater area. But there's little similarity. The area's original nickname, "South of the slot" is probably more appropriate, referring to cable car tracks that once ran down Market Street.

Several supper clubs and discos have cropped up here, but they're scattered and not concentrated as they are in London's SOHO. Also, they tend to open and shut and change names frequently, so we list only a few of the more durable ones at the end of this chapter.

Much of SoMa is a collection of weathered warehouses and dim alleys where you may be reluctant to venture afoot and alone after sunset. However, with its rising popularity as a nightlife center, the area is looking more secure and less shabby these days. The southern waterfront is undergoing a residential renaissance, with an upcropping of apartments and condos.

SoMa also offers pleasantly seedy pier cafes, an occasional museum and factory outlets featuring discount clothing, accessories and jewelry. Several **discount showrooms** are along Brannan between Third and Sixth. Large **merchandise marts** are grouped around Kansas and Townsend streets. Most are for wholesale trade only, but you'll find a few discount centers and factory showrooms here as well. And some trade shows are open to the public.

Since SoMa's lures are dispersed, we suggest a driving tour instead of a walkabout. Start at the **Ferry Building** and head southeast on the Embarcadero. You'll note that this is more of a working waterfront with tugs and barges and such, unlike the tourist-oriented western side. However, it isn't very busy, since Oakland has stolen most of the cargo action.

Smart new condos and apartments rim the waterfront for the first mile. Sea gulls perch insolently on the hoods of BMWs. Residents jog along the Embarcadero, while their aquatic toys sit in slips in **South Beach Harbor.** An attractive promenade borders the harbor and a public pier wraps around it. Note the high-and-dry ship which houses the **Dolph Rempp** restaurant (reviewed below).

At this point, the Embarcadero blends into Berry Street. Turn left onto Third Street and cross the **China Basin** inlet, spanned by an old steel drawbridge named for local baseball hero Lefty O'Doul. Take an immediate left onto China Basin Street and continue along the waterfront. After a couple of miles, you bump into Islais Creek Channel. Go right a block to Third Street, take another right and start heading back.

After about a mile, turn left onto Mariposa Street and follow it thirteen blocks to Kansas, which puts you in the heart of the **merchandise showrooms**. Go right on Kansas, then half-right onto Townsend. Follow it back to Third and turn left toward the city skyline. After two blocks, swing right into **South Park,** a collection of oldstyle brick buildings and a few Victorians around an patch of green. Dating from 1850, it was the city's first planned development, with tree-lined streets rimming an oval park. It's emerging as a trendy professional center for attorneys, graphic artists and such. **South Park Cafe**, a small country-style French restaurant, serves affordable tasty continental fare (reviewed below).

Emerging from South Park, follow Third past the **Moscone Convention Center** to Market Street.

WHAT TO SEE & DO

Cartoon Art Museum ● △△ ☺

665 Third St., fifth floor (Brannan); 546-3922. Adults $2.50, seniors $1.25, kids $1. Wednesday-Friday 11 to 5, Saturday 10 to 5. A history of chuckles is preserved here, with original cels, sketches, toys, dolls, videos and other samples of cartoon art. The **Printing Museum of Northern California** (495-8242) occupies the foyer outside, tracing the history of paper and printing. It's open Monday-Saturday from 9 to 5 and it's free.

Factory outlets

The "Style" section of the Sunday *Chronicle-Examiner* lists factory outlets and discount centers. They include—but are not limited to—South of Market outlets.

The Old Mint Museum ● △△△△ ☺

Fifth and Mission streets; 744-6830. Free. Weekdays 10 to 4; historic movies on the hour and tours on the half hour. The only Federal Greek revival structure in California, this granite edifice housed the San Francisco mint from 1874 to 1937. It's now one of the city's finest museums, with coins, coin-making equipment, California Gold Rush memorabilia, period furnishings and thick-walled vaults that once protected fortunes in gold. In fact, a fortune is still on display: a stack of 28 gold bars weighing more than 10,000 ounces. Multiply *that* by the current market rate!

South Beach Harbor Park ● △△

Embarcadero at Second Street. This small park has a promenade, fishing and sitting pier, lawn with picnic tables and public potties.

WHERE TO DINE

If you like funkily rustic waterfront grub, try **Red's Java House** at Pier 30 (788-9747) or **The Java House** (495-7260) at Pier 40. Both look ready to topple into the bay but they've stood for generations. They serve simple, hearty fare and take no credit cards. Red's Java is open from 6 a.m. to 4 p.m. weekdays only; *the* Java's hours are 6 to 6 weekdays and 7 to 6 weekends. Two other waterside restaurants, **Mission Rock Resort** and **Olive Oil's**—not quite as scruffy—are listed below.

Cadillac Bar and Grill ● △△△ $$

One Holland Court (off Howard, between Fourth and Fifth, downtown), 543-8226. Mexican bistro; dinners $8 to $16; full bar service. Monday-Thursday 11 to 11, Friday 11 to midnight and Saturday 5 to midnight. Casual; no reservations. Major credit cards. Although it's better known as chaotic, Corona-wielding yuppie bar, the Cadillac also generates excellent *fajitas*, pork *carnitas* and seafood from its mesquite grill.

Hamburger Mary's ● △ $

1582 Folsom (12th); 626-5767. American bistro; meals $5 to $9; full bar service. Daily 11 a.m. to 1:15 a.m. Reservations accepted; totally casual. Major credit cards. This place, which looks thrown together with surplus lumber and decorated by Goodwill Industries, has been dishing up thick, squishy 'burgers for years. I don't care for the chaos and blaring jukebox, but it's a fun joint for slumming.

Julie's Supper Club ● △△△ $$ Ø

1123 Folsom (Seventh); 861-0707. California cuisine; meals $7 to $14; full bar service. Tuesday-Thursday 5:30 to 10:30, Friday-Saturday 5:30 to 11:30. Reservations essential on weekends; casual. MC/VISA. Julie's is a jivin' 1950s style supper club and lounge with music to match. The food is good for the price, but don't plan to carry on a whispered conversation between bites.

Mission Rock Resort ● △△ $

817 China Basin (Mariposa); 771-6363. American; meals $5.50 to $10; full bar service. Weekdays 10 to 3, weekends 8 to 4. No reservations; casual. MC/VISA, AMEX. Don't look for a mission, a rock or a resort. This popular cafe/pub perched on a weathered pier draws a mixed blue and white collar luncheon crowd. They come for the sunny outdoor tables and the

The city is filtered through a forest of masts at South Beach Marina, part of the newly-developing South of Market area.

excellent hamburgers served on soft French rolls. The place also peddles soups, salads and seafoods, along with hefty weekend breakfasts.

Olive Oil's ● △△ $$

295 China Basin Way (Pier 50); 495-3099. American; meals $6 to $14; full bar service. Lunch weekdays 11 to 3, brunch weekends 10 to 3. Casual; no reservations or credit cards. Nautically rustic Olive Oil's has indoor dining and outdoor seating around old cable reels. The menu ranges from sandwiches to seafood entrees.

Sailing Ship Dolph Rempp ● △△△△ $$$$ Ø

Pier 42 (Embarcadero at Berry); 777-5771. California-French; dinners $27.50 to $55; full bar service. Tuesday-Saturday from 6 p.m. Reservations advised;

informal to dressy. Major credit cards. Although it's built into an old three-masted schooner, the Dolph Rempp is too classy to be a tourist gimmick. Artfully prepared meals are served in stylish 19th century glass-enclosed dining rooms. In previous lives, the Dolph was an 1800s Barbary Coast cargo ship, and then a star in *Hawaii, Mutiny on the Bounty* and other films.

South Park Cafe ● △△△ $$

108 South Park (between Second and Third); 495-7275. Country French; dinners $10 to $14; wine and beer. Lunch Monday-Friday 11:30 to 3, dinner Monday-Saturday 6 to 10. Reservations accepted for dinner only; informal to casual. MC/VISA. This cozy little place reminiscent of a Paris side street cafe serves excellent continental fare, backed up by a small, select California wine list. Seafood specials are particularly tasty.

WHAT TO DO AFTER DARK

Club DV8 ● △△ (disco)

540 Howard St. (First); 777-1419. Double dance floors vibrate with seventies-style disco music and occasional equally-loud live groups.

DNA Lounge ● △△△ (dance club)

375 11th St. (Harrison); 626-1409. Live groups and deejays alternate at this popular warehouse-sized disco.

Firehouse7 ● △△△ (live music, disco)

3160 16th St. (Mission); 621-1617. A recent arrival, Firehouse mixes live rock groups with disco dancing.

Paradise Lounge ● △△ (live music, disco)

1501 Folsom St. (Eleventh); 861-6906. This properly funky SoMa pub features a mixed bag of live jazz, rock and pop, alternating with disco dancing.

Slim's ● △△△ (nightclub, disco)

333 11th St. (Folsom); 621-3330. The classiest of the SoMa night spots with a New Orleans motif, this place owned by Boz Skaggs offers a mix of jazz, rock, blues and other American-roots music. It also has a rather fine cafe.

Nine

CIVIC CENTER/POLK GULCH

Architecture, artistry and leather

A QUICK LOOK: City, state and federal office buildings are clustered around Civic Center Plaza, in a wedge between upper Market Street and Van Ness Avenue. It's also the city's performing arts and fine arts center. Boutiques, leather shops and cafes of Polk Street extend north from there. You can reach the Civic Center by BART or Muni, running under Market Street. Take the California cable car to Van Ness and you're in the heart of Polk Gulch.

THE CIVIC CENTER is certainly appropriate to San Francisco's status as a world-class city. Granite and marble French Renaissance buildings house the City Hall, War Memorial Opera House and Veteran's Memorial. Built in stages early in this century, the complex was designed by architect Daniel Burnham, also responsible for Washington's Union Station and the Manila Hotel in the Philippines. Burnham had a master plan for the entire city, with monumental structures and Parisian-style boulevard, but it was shelved in the haste to rebuild after the 1906 earthquake.

City Hall at Van Ness and Grove is the crown jewel of this complex—a regal green copper-domed edifice patterned after the Nation's Capitol. Its spired

CIVIC CENTER AREA

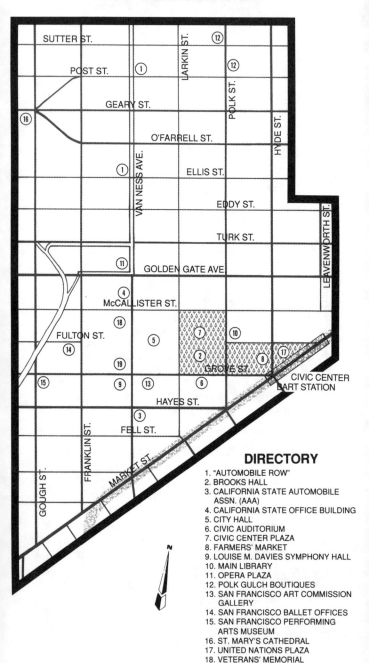

DIRECTORY

1. "AUTOMOBILE ROW"
2. BROOKS HALL
3. CALIFORNIA STATE AUTOMOBILE ASSN. (AAA)
4. CALIFORNIA STATE OFFICE BUILDING
5. CITY HALL
6. CIVIC AUDITORIUM
7. CIVIC CENTER PLAZA
8. FARMERS' MARKET
9. LOUISE M. DAVIES SYMPHONY HALL
10. MAIN LIBRARY
11. OPERA PLAZA
12. POLK GULCH BOUTIQUES
13. SAN FRANCISCO ART COMMISSION GALLERY
14. SAN FRANCISCO BALLET OFFICES
15. SAN FRANCISCO PERFORMING ARTS MUSEUM
16. ST. MARY'S CATHEDRAL
17. UNITED NATIONS PLAZA
18. VETERANS' MEMORIAL (MODERN ART MUSEUM)
19. WAR MEMORIAL OPERA HOUSE (OPERA & BALLET)

dome is higher, in fact: sixteen feet, three inches, to be precise.

This grand edifice was host to one of the city's blackest days. On November 27, 1978, ex-supervisor Dan White killed Mayor George Moscone and gay supervisor Harvey Milk. He gunned them down in their offices after the mayor had refused to re-instate White in his supervisorial seat. The ultra-conservative ex- policeman received a light sentence after his attorney blamed his antics on a sugar rush; it was the famous "Twinkie defense." The last chapter in this grim tale was written several years later. White, freed from prison but not from guilt, committed suicide.

The **War Memorial Opera House** and **Veterans Memorial Building** opposite City Hall are twins, except for the opera house's high fly loft. The third and fourth floors of the Veterans Memorial houses the **San Francisco Museum of Modern Art,** whose collections include Picasso, Matisse, Diego Rivera and Calder. The museum also operates a cozy little cafe on the fourth floor and a fine book and art shop in the lobby. The opera house—obviously—is home to the world-renowned San Francisco Opera, as well as the city's equally-acclaimed ballet company.

Architects attempted to maintain the Civic Center's timeless look with the classic-modern **Louise M. Davies Symphony Hall** and the **Edmund G. Brown California Office Building.** But they look more like the work of the Michelen tire man. The symphony hall at Van Ness and Hayes has a rounded front, resulting in an odd, bread-dough look. The interior, however, is architecturally stunning: a study in chandeliers, lush carpeting and grand stairways. The new state office building at Van Ness and McAllister also has a circular puffy look, but with an attractive inner courtyard. A huge state seal is mounted on the facade like a monster coin.

The turquoise glass cereal box building at Van Ness and Hayes is headquarters of AAA's **California State Automobile Association.** The glasswork shields an older Spanish-California facade. The Latin look is still evident on the main floor, worth a brief peek. AAA produces the best maps of the city and surrounds, but you have to be a member to get one.

Hiking west on Hayes, you'll encounter something of a **restaurant row** and several **art galleries**. In fact, three dozen restaurants are in the Civic Center area; several are recommended at the end of this chapter. As you stroll along Hayes, note the ornate facade of the **San Francisco Schools building** between Van Ness and Franklin. There's a nice mural on its rear.

Civic Center Plaza, across Polk from City Hall, forms a landscaped roof over the **Brooks Hall** exhibit center and parking garage. It's also haven to many of the unwashed and washed-up of society, who doze on its benches and camp under its manicured trees. **Civic Auditorium** to the right of the plaza is a combined performance hall and exhibit center. Across the plaza and to the left is the Baroque **San Francisco City Library,** which soon will move to newer quarters. Check out the library's **San Francisco Room,** a mini-museum to the city's lively past.

Continuing downhill, Civic Center Plaza merges into brick- surfaced **United Nations Plaza,** which hosts an old-fashioned **farmers' market** every Sunday and Wednesday.

POLK GULCH

If you're still in a walking mood, head north from the Civic Center to explore Polk Gulch, with its boutiques, antique shops, *avant garde* clothing stores and ethnic cafes. Polk Street was one of the city's first gay enclaves. Most of that community has since shifted up Market to the Castro.

You begin encountering the gulch's shop-and-cafe district at Polk and Post, about seven blocks up from the Civic Center. Note that Polk is relatively level, although paralleling Van Ness climbs more steeply. That's because it follows the course of an old stream bed—the source of its Polk Gulch nickname.

At Clay Street, you crest Russian Hill and begin traveling down toward Fisherman's Wharf. The shopping district ends around Polk and Broadway, blending into a residential area. Since you're in the neighborhood, you might enjoy strolling—or driv-

POLK GULCH

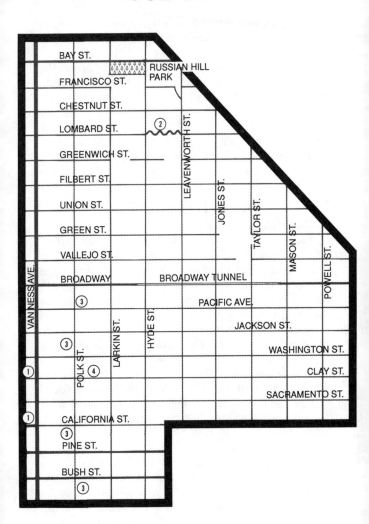

BAY ST.

RUSSIAN HILL PARK

FRANCISCO ST.

CHESTNUT ST.

LOMBARD ST. ②

LEAVENWORTH ST.

GREENWICH ST.

FILBERT ST.

JONES ST.

UNION ST.

TAYLOR ST.

GREEN ST.

VALLEJO ST.

MASON ST.

BROADWAY   BROADWAY TUNNEL

POWELL ST.

③   PACIFIC AVE.

VAN NESS AVE.

LARKIN ST.   HYDE ST.   JACKSON ST.

③   POLK ST.   WASHINGTON ST.

①   ④   CLAY ST.

SACRAMENTO ST.

①   CALIFORNIA ST.

③
PINE ST.

BUSH ST.

③

DIRECTORY

1. "AUTOMOBILE ROW"
2. "CROOKEDEST STREET" (LOMBARD)
3. POLK GULCH BOUTIQUES
4. RUSSIAN HILL CREST

ing—down the **crookedest street in the world**. Turn east onto Lombard from Polk; the squiggle begins a block away at Lombard and Hyde.

Return along Van Ness, the city's **Automobile Row.** We aren't suggesting that car lots are interesting, but some of the grand old auto showrooms—dating back to the Thirties—are quite impressive. As you stroll, veer two blocks uphill on Geary to **St. Mary's Cathedral** at Geary and Gough. With a tapered, winged roof reaching skyward—presumably toward heaven—it's the city's most dramatic religious structure.

WHAT TO SEE & DO

City Hall ● △△△△

Polk between Grove and McAllister. San Francisco's City Hall may be the most opulent public building west of the Mississippi—a showplace worthy of the grand city it represents. The interior is resplendent in marble columns, statuary in ornate niches and a sweeping marble grand stairway.

Cultural shopping

San Francisco Ballet Shop *in the ballet office at 455 Franklin St. (861-5600);* ***San Francisco Opera Shop***, *199 Grove St. (565-6414);* ***Museum Book Shop***, *ground floor of Veteran's Memorial (863-2890)*. Need a tutu, *Le Figaro* videocassette or a scholarly volume on Picasso? These cultural boutiques offer a wide range of hard-to-find cultural items. Call for hours.

Heart of the City Farmers' Market ● △△

United Nations Plaza between Market and Larkin; 647-9423. Sunday 8 to 5, Wednesday 8 to 5:30. An urban farmers' market? Certainly. Dozens of turnip farmers, peach pickers and even fishmongers set up stalls under bright blue awnings two days a week.

St. Mary's Cathedral ● △△△ ☺

1111 Gough St. (Geary); 567-2020. Free; daily 9 to 5. Covering two city blocks, this striking example of modern church architecture is fashioned in the form of a giant, fluted cross 200 feet high. Within this great space, a geodesic-waffled ceiling is set off by four sparkling seams of leaded glass converging in the center of the dome. An *art nouveau* sculpture of thin steel rods hangs over the sanctuary like a surrealistic cascade of angel dust.

San Francisco Art Commission Gallery ● △△
155 Grove (Van Ness); 554-9682. Free; donations accepted. Tuesday-Friday 11 to 5, Saturday noon to 5. This small gallery's exhibits by local artists lean toward the wonderful lunatic fringe of art impressionism.

San Francisco Museum of Modern Art ● △△△
Veteran's Memorial Building, Van Ness at McAllister; 863-8800. Adults $4, seniors and kids under 16, $1.50; Tuesday is free day. Tuesday, Wednesday, Friday 10 to 5, Thursday 10 to 9, weekends 11 to 5, closed Monday. Some exhibits here stretch your definition of art, and well they should. SFMMA is one of America's leading museums on the leading edge of the art world.

San Francisco Performing Arts Library & Museum ● △△
399 Grove St. (Gough); 255-4800. Free; donations accepted. Weekdays noon to 5. This museum has collected hundreds of thousands of artifacts, costumes, videotapes, periodicals, press clippings and playbills of Western America's music, dance, opera and theatre companies. Fortunately, they're not all displayed at once.

Civic Center area tours
Civic Center, City Hall, and city tours
Departing from the main library; 558-3981; free. City Guides, volunteers of the Friends of the Library, conduct a series of walking tours through the Civic Center, Japantown and elsewhere in the city, lasting about an hour and a half.

Performing arts tours
Meet at the Grove Street entrance to Davies Hall; 552-8338. Adults $3, seniors and students $2. Tours of various performing arts structures are conducted every half hour on Mondays from 10 to 2:30. Davies Symphony Hall tours are Wednesdays at 1:30 and 2:30 and Saturdays at 12:30 and 1:30.

WHERE TO DINE
Civic Center area

Act IV ● △△△ $$$$ Ø

333 Fulton St. (Inn at the Opera, off Franklin); 863-8400. Mediterranean; dinners $23 to $28; full bar service. Breakfast 7 to 10 daily, lunch weekdays 11:30 to 2, dinner Sunday-Thursday 5:30 to 9, Friday-Saturday 5:30 to 10:30. Reservations advised; dressy to informal. MC/VISA, AMEX. There's a touch of class in this elegant little dining room, with its paneled columns and flowered wall covering. The menu, sort of spicy continental, offers creative *nouveau* entrees that change weekly.

California Culinary Academy ● △△△ $ to $$$$

625 Polk St. (Turk). Varied menus; meals $6 to $44; full bar service. Various hours, reservation policies; informal to casual. Major credit cards. Try the fare of budding young chefs in the academy's three restaurants: the Francisco-style **Academy Grill** buffet (771-1655); the **Careme Room** (771-3536) with glass-enclosed kitchens were students are busily brewing your dinner; and **Cyril's** (771- 3500), with a spicy Mediterranean menu.

City Picnic ● △ $

384-A Hayes St. (Franklin); 431-8814. Deli; meals $2 to $5. Weekdays 8 to 4. Casual; no reservations or credit cards. Ample, tasty focaccia sandwiches are a specialty at this popular Civic Center luncheon spot. There's a sunny patio out back.

Enoteca Lanzone ● △△△△ $$$$ Ø

601 Van Ness Ave. (in Opera Plaza at Golden Gate); 928-0400. Upscale Italian; dinners $20 to $50; full bar service. Lunch weekdays 11:30 to 2:30, dinner Monday-Saturday from 5. Reservations advised; informal to dressy. Major credit cards. This stylish restaurant serves creative northern Italian fare in a setting of quiet elegance. The cozy dining rooms are virtual galleries of the modern art collection of founder Modesto Lanzone.

Ivy's ● △△△ $$$$

398 Hayes St. (Gough); 626-3930. American regional; dinners $20 to $35; full bar service. Lunch

San Francisco's City Hall was patterned after the nation's capitol; its dome is more than 16 feet higher.

weekdays 11:30 to 2:30, dinner Sunday-Thursday 5:30 to 10:30, Friday-Saturday 5:30 to 11:30, brunch Sunday 11 to 2. Reservations advised; informal. MC/VISA. This trimly modern restaurant has a changing menu with a *nouveau* thrust; things like fried calamari with tomato coulis and corn-chili relish. Walls are draped with works of rising local artists.

Hayes Street Grill ● △△△ $$$ Ø

320 Hayes St. (Franklin); 863-5545. Seafood; dinners $17 to $21; full bar service. Lunch weekdays 11:30 to 2, dinners Monday-Thursday 5 to 10, Friday 5 to 11, Saturday 6 to 11. Reservations advised; informal. MC/VISA, DSC. This busy bistro is the city's best seafood restaurant. Not only is the fish unfailingly fresh and properly cooked, it's offered with a variety of sauces, such as herb shallot butter, Szechuan peanut and *beurre blanc.* This is a popular if somewhat noisy business lunch spot.

Kimball's Restaurant ● △△△ $$$ Ø

300 Grove St. (Franklin); 861-5555. California cuisine, meals $11 to $20; full bar service. Tuesday-Saturday 5 p.m. to 1 a.m. Reservations accepted; informal. MC/VISA, AMEX. This restaurant-jazz club in a handsome brick building with cheerful natural wood decor is a popular dinner stop for theater-goers.

Stars ● △△△△ $$$$

150 Redwood Alley (between McAllister and Golden Gate); 861-7827. Contemporary American; dinners $20 to $30; full bar service. Weekdays from 11:30 a.m., weekends from 12:30 p.m., oyster bar service to midnight. Reservations essential; informal. Major credit cards. One of the Bay Area's early California *nouveau* restaurants, this noisy, barn-like bistro is decorated with awards immodestly posted by its founder, Jeremiah Tower. It's the city's yuppie social center and power lunch haven. The daily-changing menu is excellent, based on whatever Jeremiah's young chefs find that's fresh.

Zola's ● △△△△ $$$$ Ø

395 Hayes Street (Gough); 864-4824. Mediterranean; dinners $25 to $35; full bar service. Monday-Saturday 5:30 to 10:30 p.m. Reservations advised; informal. Major credit cards. One of the city's rare—and welcome—smoke-free restaurants, Zola's has a stylish continental look and a definite *nouveau* tilt to its menu. With tasty entrees such as roast guinea hen with apple and chestnuts and grilled venison with chanterelles, it has earned rave reviews from local food critics.

Zuni Cafe ● △△ $$$$ Ø

1658 Market (Franklin); 552-2522. Continental nouveau; dinners $15 to $45; full bar service. Tuesday-Saturday 7:30 a.m. to midnight, Sunday 7:30 to 11. Reservations advised; casual. MC/VISA, AMEX. The daily-changing menu seems to be American *nouveau*, although the owners call it "Italian-French country." The look is airy and bright Southwestern and the fare is exceptional. However, we down-rate it because it's overpriced and the straight-backed seating is uncomfortable.

Polk Gulch

Adriatic ● △△△ $$
1755 Polk St. (Washington); 771-4035. Seafood; dinners $10 to $15; wine and beer. Lunch Tuesday-Saturday 11:30 to 2:30, dinner 5:30 to 9:30. Reservations accepted; informal. MC/VISA, AMEX. This cheery little country-style cafe with bentwood, wicker and lace offers excellent fare at modest prices. It's one of the city's better dining buys.

The Bagel Restaurant ● △△ $
1300 Polk Street (Bush); 441-2212. Jewish deli; meals $4.50 to $7.50; wine and beer. Daily 8 a.m. to 10 p.m. Casual; no reservations or credit cards. You don't have to travel east to find a good neighborhood Jewish deli. For decades, the Bagel has been dispensing hearty portions of corned beef, pastrami, lox and—of course—matzo ball soup.

Hahn's Hibachi ● △ $
1710 Polk St. (Clay); 776-1095. Korean barbecue; meals $5 to $6.50; wine and beer. Monday-Saturday 11 to 9:30. Casual; no reservations or credit cards. Ignore the early Formica decor and enjoy hearty dishes of spareribs or stir-fried seafood or meat and veggies. Ample meals are served with mouth-sizzling *kim chee*—peppered pickled cabbage.

Harris' ● △△△△ $$$$ Ø
2100 Van Ness Ave. (Pacific); 673-1888. American; dinners $30 to $40; full bar service. Lunch Wednesday 11:30 to 2, dinner 5 to 10 week nights and 5 to 10:30 weekends. Reservations advised; dressy. Major credit cards. Harris serves the city's best steaks and prime rib in a luxuriant setting. High ceilings, deep booths and paneled walls give it a genteel men's club feel.

Hard Rock Cafe ● △△ $
1699 Van Ness Ave. (Sacramento); 885-1699. American, meals from $5; full bar service. Daily 11:30 to 11:30. No reservations; laid back. MC/VISA, AMEX. Teen-agers desperate to mimic the Fifties and Sixties no longer queue up outside the various cafes Hard Rock. Although the novelty has worn thin, San Francisco's version still does quite well, serving generous portions of nostalgia and baby back ribs with cloying sweet sauce. The decor is visual fun: football helmets,

guitars, a candy apple red Cadillac emerging from one wall. We've said it before: they should charge admission and give away the food.

Mayes Italian/Seafood Restaurant ● △△△ $$

1233 Polk St. (Bush); 474-7674. Italian, seafood; dinners $10 to $15; full bar service. Monday-Saturday from 11:30, various closing hours. Reservations accepted; casual. MC/VISA, AMEX. In business since 1867, Mayes offers some of best dinner prices in the city, especially for its tasty seafood entrees. The look is early San Francisco, brightened by a recent face-lift.

Polk Street Beans ● △ $ Ø

1733 Polk St. (Clay); 776-9292. American; dinners under $10; wine and beer. Monday-Tuesday 8 a.m. to 6:30 p.m., Wednesday-Saturday 8 a.m. to 10 p.m., Sunday 9 to 6. No reservations; casual. MC/VISA. This European-style coffee house serves soups, sandwiches, pastries, espresso and such. Its atmosphere is invitingly funky, and it's all smoke-free.

Tommy's Joynt ● △△ $

1101 Geary Blvd. (Van Ness); 775-4216. Hofbrau; meals $5 to $15; full bar service. Daily 10 a.m. to 2 a.m. No reservations; casual. No credit cards. Decorated with a maniacal jungle of brik-a-brak, Tommy's is the penultimate San Francisco hofbrau. Corned beef and pastrami sandwiches are excellent, the buffalo stew is more curious than tasty and 90 beers are available for washing it all down. Splendidly garish early San Francisco murals cover the outer walls of this landmark.

Thai Spice Restaurant ● △△△ $$

1730 Polk St. (Clay); 775-4777. Thai; dinners $10 to $15; wine and beer. Daily 11:30 to 10. Reservations advised for weekends; casual. Major credit cards. Lace curtains and a pink interior accented by white nappery brighten this little place. Unlike most small Thai cafes, it has a remarkably large menu, with dishes not found elsewhere in the city. Try the salmon with red curry and coconut milk or prawn and calamari with basil and garlic.

WHAT TO DO AFTER DARK

Great American Music Hall ● △△△ (supper club)

859 O'Farrell St. (Polk); 885-0750. This small supper club offers a G-rated blend of live entertainers, ranging from folk and rock to comedy and jazz.

Kimball's Restaurant ● ΔΔ (jazz club)
300 Grove St. (Franklin); 861-5555. Local jazz artists and some with national stature convene several nights a week a this popular club-restaurant.

San Francisco Ballet ● ΔΔΔ
War Memorial Opera House, Van Ness at Grove; 621- 3838. The season begins in mid-December with *The Nutcracker* and runs through spring with several beautifully-presented ballets.

San Francisco Opera ● ΔΔΔ
War Memorial Opera House, Van Ness at Grove; 621-3838. The fall opening of the opera is the city's major gala. This world-noted company has two seasons: September-December and May-June. Do your opera shopping early; tickets are scarce.

San Francisco Symphony ● ΔΔΔΔ ☺
Davies Symphony Hall, Van Ness at Grove; 431-5400 for tickets or write San Francisco Symphony, Davies Hall, SF 94102 for a list of upcoming performances. The world-acclaimed symphony offers a busy, innovative season of classics, pops and youth concerts, under the skilled baton of Herbert Blomstedt. Its 200 or more performances are presented from September through June.

WHERE TO SLEEP
(Detailed listings in Chapter 16)
Rooms for $100 and up
Holiday Inn ● *50 Eighth St. (Market)*

Rooms from $50 to $99
Atherton Hotel ● *685 Ellis St. (Hyde)*
Phoenix Inn ● *601 Eddy St. (Larkin)*
Valu Inn ● *900 Franklin St. (Eddy)*

Rooms under $50
Essex Hotel ● *684 Ellis St. (Larkin)*

Bed & breakfast inns
Albion House ● *135 Gough St. (Oak)*

MISSION DISTRICT

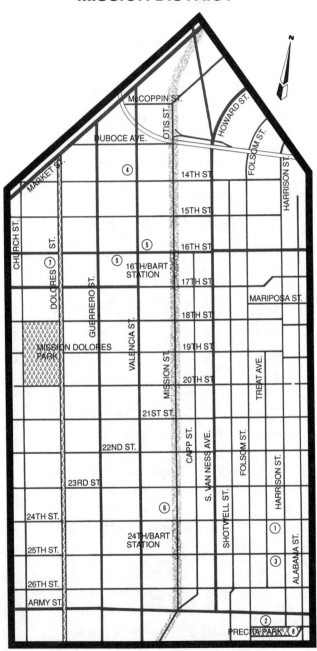

DIRECTORY

1. BALMY ALLEY (MURALS)
2. FLYNN ELEMENTARY SCHOOL (MURALS)
3. GARFIELD POOL (MURALS)
4. LEVI STRAUSS FACTORY
5. "LITTLE BOHEMIA"
6. MEXICAN CULTURAL CENTER
7. MISSION DOLORES
8. PRECITA EYES MURAL CENTER

Ten

THE MISSION DISTRICT
Making a run for the border

A QUICK LOOK: The Mission District extends south from the Civic Center to Army Street. Roughly, it's cradled between Dolores Street to the west and Alabama to the east. Mission Street is the main drag and BART runs beneath it for several miles, with stations at 16th and 24th streets. Primary lures are scores of Latin murals and the city's founding church.

LOCALS CALL IT, simply, "The Mission." It's a reference not to the adobe church that spawned the city, but to a working class neighborhood that's heavily Hispanic, with a generous mix of Filipinos, blacks and a scatter of honkeys.

Mission San Francisco de Asis is located here, on the district's outer edge at Dolores and 16th streets. It's better known as Mission Dolores, from the creek where it was established, *Arroyo de los Dolores,* "the stream of sorrows."

The Hispanic heart of the district is focused along 24th Street, between Valencia and Alabama. Don't expect cute little pastel adobes, curio shops and *senoritas* in flaring skirts. The Mission is an honest, blue-collar neighborhood that's a bit scruffy around the edges. However, you'll find Latin flavor in family-owned cafes, small grocery stores with *pinatas* hanging from the ceiling and Mexican bakeries that issue such delights as deep-fried, sugar-frosted *churros* and chewy coconut macaroons called *cocadas*.

The best reason for marching into the Mission is to view its 200 or more murals. Artists—mostly Hispanic—have splashed political statements and ethnic pride throughout the neighborhood in bright fall colors. Murals range from garage door panels to monumental works that cover the sides of large buildings.

"They are colors that exaggerate the essence of life," said one of the muralists.

Unfortunately, many have been marred by graffiti, which must be terribly frustrating to those trying to create beauty in this neighborhood of decent working folk.

These outdoor artworks are nurtured by a remarkable organization called the **Precita Eyes Mural Center**. The non-profit group fosters and encourages muralists; many of the Mission's artists are members. Precita Eyes conducts **guided mural walks** on the first and third Saturday of the month. (See the listing below.)

To see many of the murals and sample other Hispanic lures of the Mission, take BART to the **24th Street Station**. Our suggested "stroll" covers about 30 blocks, so you may prefer to drive.

At the 24th Street Station, look for Michael Rios' vivid example of BART art—a mural depicting humanoid columns uplifting the rail tracks. The **Mexican Cultural Center**, on Mission near 24th, glitters with a large impressionistic mural; inside is **Galleria Museo,** with changing Hispanic art exhibits.

Travel eight blocks east on 24th, then turn right into **Balmy Alley**. This scruffy little corridor glitters with 28 murals, painted on garage doors and fences.

Return to 24th and stop for a snack at the large self-service **La Victoria Bakery** at Alabama Street. Continue along 24th to Harrison and turn right. You'll see brilliant murals on the **Garfield Swimming Pool** building at Harrison and 25th, and an impressive collection on the **Leonard R. Flynn Elementary School** at Harrison and Precita Avenue.

The Mission District's murals range from provocatively heroic to social and political; this one is at 24th Street and Alabama.

Precita Park, opposite the school, is a pleasant little wedge of green with a playground and benches. **Precita Eyes Mural Center** is across the way, at 348 Precita Ave. Stop in to see its murals and other folk art and pick up a map that will direct you to more outdoor paintings. This also is the meeting spot for the twice-monthly mural walks.

Head west through Precita Park, turn right on Folsom, then left onto 26th Street. Follow it about ten blocks to **Dolores Street** and turn right. Dolores is one of the city's prettiest boulevards, with a grassy, palm-shaded center strip. It's lined with Victorian homes; many are undergoing restoration.

Cruise along Dolores for about a mile and you'll encounter the city's roots—**Mission San Francisco de Asis.** No, it isn't the grand edifice with ornate baroque towers. That's the **Basilica of San Francisco,** completed in 1926. The humble, white-washed adobe mission kneels in the basilica's shadow. It's the city's most venerated building and one of the oldest, completed in 1791.

Walk through the little chapel, with its curious green and brown chevron ceiling beams and simple altar with saints stuck in their saintly niches. Then step into the basilica and admire its lofty vaulted arch ceiling, domed altar and glittering tapestry of leaded glass. Return to the mission to view relics in a small museum, then step into the quiet little cemetery-garden. Here, heroes, saints and a few sinners lie in the shadow of the church that nurtured a city.

From the mission, turn right onto 16th street and follow it to Valencia. Although you're still in the Mission District, this area is tilting toward Bohemia. Places like the **New Dawn Cafe** and **Cafe Picaro,** both on 16th, are right out of 1960s North Beach.

Turn left onto Valencia and look for an oldstyle yellow wooden building on your left, at the corner of Clinton Park. This is history of another sort—the oldest surviving factory of the apparel giant, **Levi Strauss & Co.** It was built in 1906 after the earthquake destroyed the company headquarters near the waterfront. Plant tours are conducted on Wednesdays (see below).

You'll shortly encounter Market Street. Turn left and into the next chapter of our San Francisco adventure.

WHAT TO SEE & DO

Levi's Tour ● △△ ☺
Levi Strauss & Co., 250 Valencia St. (Clinton Park); 565-9153. Tours Wednesday at 10:30 and 2; free. Reservations required. See box for details.

Mexican Cultural Center ● △
Mission near 24th Street; 863-7058. Museum open Tuesday-Friday 10 to 6 and Saturday 11 to 4. The political-social-cultural center for Mission Hispanics, it also houses a little theater group and **Galleria Museo** with Mexican-American art and folkloric exhibits.

Mission San Francisco de Asis ● △△△△
Dolores at 16th Street; 621-8203. Daily 9 to 4; $1 donation. Self-guiding tours take you into the sanctuary of this historic mission, then through a small museum and cemetery-garden. The next-door basilica also is open to visitors, except during services.

Precita Eyes Mural Center and mural walks ●
△△△ ☺

348 Precita Ave. (Folsom); 285-2287. Monday 10 to 4 and 7:30 to 10, Tuesday and Thursday 10 to 5 (closed at noon) and 7:30 to 10, Wednesday 1 to 4 and 7:30 to 10, Friday 1 to 4; Free. Mural walks first and third Saturdays at 1:30, $3 adults and $1 students and seniors. Saturday mural walks start at this cheerful storefront gallery. They last two hours, covering eight blocks and about 40 murals; outings are preceded by a slide show. Phone reservations are accepted, but they aren't necessary.

WHERE TO DINE
Several Mexican mom and pop restaurants are scattered through the Mission. Most are basic smashed beans and rice places that will fill you up for less than $10. They're all pretty much the same, so we have no specific recommendations. Here are a few other places of note:

Cafe Nidal ● △ $
2491 Mission (21st); 285-4334. Mideastern; dinners $5 to $10; wine and beer. Monday-Friday 7 a.m. to 8 p.m., Saturday 8 to 5. Casual; no reservations or credit cards. Serving *falafels* and other light Mideastern fare, Nidal has a casually pleasant coffee house look.

Cafe Picaro ● △ $
3120 16th Street (Valencia); 431-4089. American-Bohemian; dinners $5 to $7; wine and beer. Sunday-Thursday 9 a.m. to midnight, Friday-Saturday 9 to 1 a.m. Exceedingly casual, no reservations or credit cards. It's a funky blend of Bohemian cafe and used bookstore. Buy 'em or read 'em here. The atmosphere is more interesting than the seafood and pasta entrees.

Don Quijote Restaurant ● △△ $$
2351 Mission St. (20th); 550-8325. Mexican; dinners $6 to $12; wine and beer. Daily 11 a.m. to 7 p.m. Casual, no reservations or credit cards. With flowers on the tables and photos of old Spain on the walls, Quijote's look is a cut above the standard Mexican formica beanery. It features the usual rellenos, tacos, burritos and such.

LEVI'S 501's: A RIVETING STORY

They captured the fancy of James Dean and Marlon Brando, spurring a casual, free-thinking style of dress that has spread worldwide. Russian students scrape rubles together to buy them on the black market; Japanese snap them up at $90 a pair.

All this fuss over a pair of jeans called Levi's 501's.

When 24-year-old Bavarian immigrant Levi Strauss hit San Francisco in 1853, he found a city raging with gold fever. He'd brought tent and sail canvas, planning to join his brother-in-law in the dry goods business. "What we need is britches that won't bust their seams," the miners told him.

So Levi used his canvas to sew pants instead of tents. When that ran out, he switched to a brown cotton fabric made in Nimes, France. This sturdy *serge de Nimes* earned the nickname of "denim."

In 1873, he was contacted by Nevada tailor Jacob Davis, who'd hit on the idea of riveting pants pockets for added strength. He financed Davis' patent and brought him into the firm. Later, with the development of indigo dye, the familiar blue denims took form. By the 1880s, lot number 501 of "those pants of Levi's" were the company's best seller.

Levi's 501's are now the *apparel apparent* of film stars, cowboys real and imagined, hippies and yuppies, starving artists, sassy lasses and an occasional President. This cult-like denim adoration has made Levi Strauss & Co., the world's largest apparel manufacturer, with annual sales topping $2.5 billion. The firm is still owned by descendants of the founder.

You can see these historic britches being made during free tours of the company's oldest existing plant. It's housed in a 1906 yellow wooden structure at 250 Valencia Street, two blocks south of upper Market. Hour and a half tours are conducted on Wednesdays only, at 10:30 a.m. and 1 p.m. Reservations are required and should be made well in advance; call (415) 565-9153.

Most of the firm's factories are highly automated, even computerized. But here, skilled cutters and seamstresses still build the britches manually. Levi's clothing line is extensive, but this plant produces only button-fly 501's. Unfortunately, you can't buy a pair of these hand-made classics. The factory's entire output is shipped to Japan, where Nippon yuppies pay triple-price for a fabric of American history.

Los Guitarras ● ΔΔ $$

3200 24th St. (South Van Ness); 285-2684. Mexican; dinners $8 to $14; full bar service. Monday-Friday 11 a.m. to 10:30 p.m., Sunday 10 to 10:30. Reservations accepted, casual. Major credit cards. Stylized Mexican paintings, serapes and wrought iron create a cute and cozy atmosphere, and guitarists provide dinner melodies. The enchilada-burrito fare is better than average.

New Dawn Cafe ● ΔΔ $

3170 16th Street (Valencia); 533-8888. American-Bohemian; dinners $4 to $8; wine and beer. Daily 8 to 3:30. Casual; no reservations or credit cards. Like Picaro, New Dawn is deliberately funky. The gimmick here is used furniture and nick-knacks. It's like eating in a second-hand store.

WHERE TO SLEEP
(Detailed listings in Chapter 16)
Bed & breakfast inns

Dolores Park Inn ● *3641 17th St. (Dolores)*
Inn San Francisco ● *943 S. Van Ness (Twentieth)*

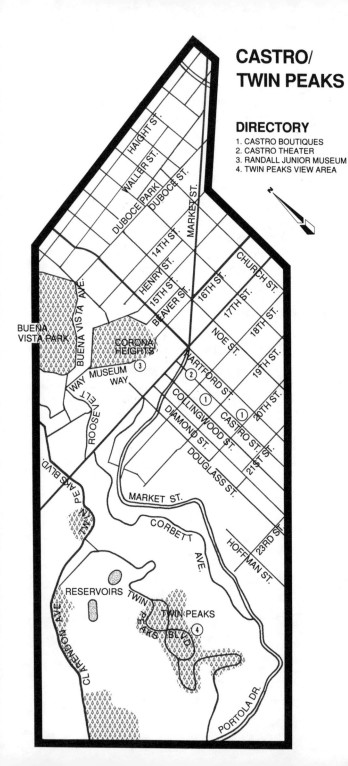

CASTRO/ TWIN PEAKS

DIRECTORY
1. CASTRO BOUTIQUES
2. CASTRO THEATER
3. RANDALL JUNIOR MUSEUM
4. TWIN PEAKS VIEW AREA

Eleven

CASTRO/TWIN PEAKS
Different points of view

A QUICK LOOK: The Castro District, off upper
Market Street, is the city's largest gay community,
which doesn't make it a tourist attraction. What does
is its collection of boutiques and some noteworthy
restaurants. Continuing up Market, you can reach
Twin Peaks, offering dramatic city vistas.

UNDERSTANDABLY, the awful specter of AIDS
has taken much of the vitality out of the Castro. The
streets are quieter now and posters warn residents to
be wary of gay-bashers. Still, a startling number of
leather bars draw crowds of slender young men and
an occasional bewildered tourist.

If you enjoy exploring boutiques, galleries and a
few antique shops, take a brief stroll through this
well-kept neighborhood. Many firms occupy refurbished Victorians. The business district is quite small,
running three blocks along Castro between Market
and Nineteenth, then extending a block or so in each
direction from Eighteenth and Castro.

Note the handsome old **Castro Theater** at Castro and Market, an Art Deco survivor that features
movie classics and themed film festivals. No, the
Twin Peaks bar next door wasn't inspired by that
awful television show. It's named for the two noted
landmarks visible through its windowed walls.

The Castro offers several interesting restaurants. We particularly like the sunny open space of the **Patio Cafe**, and cozy little **Ryan's**, tucked into a Victorian. Another dining cluster huddles around Market and Church streets, four blocks below the Castro. Two are interesting for different reasons. Art Deco moderne **Le Piano Zinc** and **Sparky's** Fifties style diner are listed at the end of this chapter.

Parking is difficult around the Castro, so you might take Metro Muni to the Castro Street station and explore afoot. If you're into tunnels (pun intended), you can re-board the train and trundle through the long **Twin Peaks Tunnel**. You'll next see daylight at West Portal, an attractive little shopping area set in a small, sheltered valley.

TWIN PEAKS CLIMB

Eventually, you'll want to retrieve your car to finish this chapter, which invites you on a long haul up Market Street to the **Twin Peaks vista point**. It's a required stop on every tour bus route. That awful red and white steel structure beside the peaks is **Sutro Tower**. It improves local TV reception but raises havoc with the area's esthetics.

Indians occupying the hilly San Francisco peninsula were more imaginative in naming the twin promontories; they called them "Maidens' Breasts."

To reach them, follow Market as it curves upward and changes its name to Portola Drive. Just over the crest, turn right onto Twin Peaks Boulevard and follow it past a forest of transmission towers to the vista point. The road does a figure-eight around the dual mounds—creating a bra effect, if you think like an Indian.

From here, the Bay Area fans out at your feet like a living diorama. The sweep is awesome—from the East Bay on your right to the Golden Gate Bridge and Marin Headlands to the left. On a clear day, you can glimpse the Farallon Islands, thirty-two miles at sea, and Point Reyes Peninsula, thirty-five miles north. Signs at the view area identify the features spread out before you.

The viewpoint often gets crowded and idling tour buses may foul the air. (Why do drivers leave the engines running?) We prefer to achieve a loftier vantage point by climbing the peaks themselves. Railroad tie steps have been set in their flanks, so the hike isn't difficult. From there, your panorama becomes circle-rama, with a view down the San Mateo County coast and the southern East Bay.

Incidentally, the city lights are stunning from the viewpoint at night, but be wary of dark shapes. Occasional nocturnal muggings have been reported.

From the peaks, we take you to a lesser but more craggy promontory and to an unusual museum for kids. Continue north on Twin Peaks Boulevard, following **49-mile Scenic Drive** signs. They'll direct you to Roosevelt Way; follow this to Museum Way and turn right. This deposits you in the parking lot of the **Josephine D. Randall Junior Museum.**

The museum is interesting both for its youth-oriented exhibits and for its vantage point. It's cleaved into the flanks of **Corona Heights**, offering lofty city vistas. You can follow a steep path from the museum to the craggy ramparts above. The view isn't as awesome as it is from Twin Peaks, but the red rock upcroppings should appeal to youngsters, who may want to play an urban version of King of the Mountain.

From the museum, follow Roosevelt downhill, go right on Fifteenth, then right again on Castro.

See? We've cleverly taken you in a loop.

WHAT TO SEE & DO

Castro Theater ● Δ

429 Castro St. (Market); 621-6120. Admire the Art Deco marquee and lobby, and perhaps buy a ticket to study its 1930s interior. The on-screen emphasis is movie classics and retrospective film festivals.

Randall Junior Museum ● ΔΔ ☺

Museum Way (Roosevelt); 863-1399. Tuesday-Saturday 10 to 5; free. The Randall is a youth-oriented center focusing on natural sciences and art, with live critters, mineral exhibits, a youth art gallery and such. It's also an activity center, offering woodworking, ceramic and other classes.

Twin Peaks ● △△△△ ☺
Rimmed by Twin Peaks Boulevard, off Portola Drive. At 922 and 904 feet, they're the city's second and third highest promontories, barely topped by 927-foot mount Davidson. But since Davidson is thatched with trees, the grassy dual peaks offer better city views.

WHERE TO DINE

El Toreador Fonda Mejicana ● △△ $
50 West Portal Ave. (Vicente); 556-8104. Mexican; dinners $7 to $9; wine and beer. Tuesday-Sunday 11 to 9:30. Reservations for six or more only; casual. Major credit cards. Cheerful Mexican decor and inexpensive "Fiesta dinners" elevate El Toreador above the city's dozens of smashed beans and rice places. And we like the selection of 75 beers. Suds are our beverage of choice with smashed beans and rice.

Le Piano Zinc ● △△△ $$$ Ø
708 14th Street (Market and Church); 431-5266. French-California; dinners $12 to $20; wine and beer. Daily 11 to 11. Reservations advised; informal. MC/VISA, AMEX. The look is Art Deco-California brasserie, which translates as an intimate, stylish little cafe with an innovative *nouveau* menu. The piano has been replaced by a take-out bar; every menu item—even *cassoulet* with duck *confit* and sausage—can be prepared to go. The dining room is smoke-free.

The Patio Cafe ● △△ $$
531 Castro St. (18th); 621-4640. American; dinners $9 to $14; full bar service. Daily 8 a.m. to 11 p.m. No reservations; very casual. MC/VISA, AMEX. Want to hang out in the Castro? Here's where you do it. Pick up a menu on the way in and find a seat in this multi-level patio surrounded by Victorian backsides. Try the eggs Benedict or other breakfasts; they're the best things on the menu. This is one of the city's best people-watching cafes, since the clientele is mixed—*very* mixed. Pay on the way out, please.

Ryan's ● △△△ $$$ Ø
4230 18th St. (Diamond); 621-6131. American nouveau; dinners $12 to $18; wine and beer. Monday-Saturday 6 p.m. to 10 p.m., weekend brunch 10 to 3.

Reservations advised; informal. MC/VISA. Coziness and innovative changing menus are the keys to Ryan's success. Portions are generous and tasty and prices are fair. It's one of our favorite cafes, with casually intimate dining rooms tucked into an old Victorian. The look is artistic as well, with artworks on the walls and votive candles on the tables.

Sparky's Diner ● △△ $

242 Church St. (Market); 626-5837. American diner; meals $5.50 to $12.95; wine and beer. Open 24 hours. No reservations; very casual. MC/VISA, AMEX. You'll be lost in the Fifties again in this all-American diner, done in bold black and white. The menu tilts toward burgers, pizzas, salads and breakfast omelets.

WESTERN ADDITION/JAPANTOWN

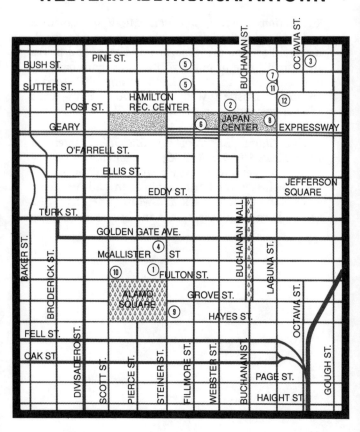

DIRECTORY

1. ARCHBISHOP'S MANSION
2. BUCHANAN SHOPPING MALL
3. BUDDHIST CHURCH OF S.F.
4. CHATEAU TIVOLI VICTORIAN
5. FILLMORE RESTAURANT ROW
6. KABUKI HOT SPRINGS
7. KONKO-KYO CHURCH
8. MIYAKO HOTEL
9. THE "PAINTED LADIES"
10. RUSSIAN CONSULATE VICTORIAN
11. SOTO ZEN BUDDHIST MISSION
12. TEA CEREMONY (NICHI BEI KAI)

Twelve

WESTERN ADDITION/ JAPANTOWN

Painted Ladies, sushi and boutiques

A QUICK LOOK: One of the city's most eclectic neighborhoods, the Western Addition stretches from Van Ness Avenue west toward Golden Gate Park. Its mixed offerings include hundreds of Victorians, a Japanese enclave and an emerging restaurant row.

WHEN THE CITY outgrew its waterfront roots, its limbs reached westward, toward a windblown area of sand dunes and scrub brush. This new residential area beyond Van Ness Avenue was simply called the Western Addition.

The name does not tell the tale of this eclectic enclave, then or now. Yesterday, it was an area filled with those overly-ornamented rowhouses described under the catch-all name of "Victorians." Today, it is the city's richest repository of these architectural relics, as well as the site of *Nihonmachi,* the Bay Area's largest Japanese settlement. Further, it harbors some fine restaurants and boutiques. Most are along Fillmore Street, a gentrified former slum area.

A few decades ago, the Western Addition was victimized by runaway redevelopment. Hundreds of aging Victorians that had become ragged rentals were

The "Russian Consulate" is one of several Victorian mansions rimming Alamo Square.

bulldozed into oblivion. They were replaced with apartment towers that the former occupants couldn't afford, and by faceless low rent housing projects that they could.

VICTORIANA DRIVE

We'll steer you through the more appealing areas of the Western Addition on a driving tour, starting from Castro and Market, where we abandoned you in the last chapter. Drive north up Castro past the large Davies Medical Center to Duboce, turn right and follow it downhill to Fillmore Street and turn left. You're in the heart of Victoriana.

Note the brilliant blue and green onion domed house on the left at Fillmore and Hayes. Cross Hayes on Fillmore, turn left up Fulton Street and you'll skim the edge of **Alamo Square.** You're in the heart of the Alamo Square Historic District, the city's richest repository of Victorians.

Find a place to park and walk the four perimeter streets of the square. You'll make new architectural discoveries at every turn of your head. Among the better visual delights are the French Empire style **Archbishop's Mansion,** a bed and breakfast at Fulton and Steiner, and the **Russian Consulate,** an elaborate four-story manor at Fulton and Scott streets that once housed the Czar's emissary to San Francisco.

The city's most-photographed painted ladies are six matched row-houses at Steiner near Pierce. They're best viewed—and photographed—from Alamo Square with the modern city skyline rising in the distance.

From the upper left-hand corner of the square, go one block north on Scott, then right on McAllister past a row of elaborate Italianate Victorians. Hang a left onto Steiner and watch for an incredible fairy castle conglomeration of witches' hat towers, friezes and cupolas at Steiner and Golden Gate. It's **Chateau Tivoli**, built in 1892 by an Oregon lumber baron and now a bed and breakfast inn. (See B&B listing in Chapter 16.)

Incidentally, two Victorian mansions are museums open to the public. They're just over the hill in Pacific Heights and we'll explore them in Chapter 15.

As you continue along Steiner, Victoriana soon gives way to contemporary housing. Turn right onto Geary Boulevard and start looking for a place to park. It's time for some sushi.

JAPANTOWN

When the first *issei*—Japanese immigrants— came to San Francisco in the 1860s, they settled near their Chinese cousins downtown. Both Asian ghettos fell victim to the 1906 earthquake and fire. The Chinese stayed to rebuild but the Japanese shifted to the Western Addition, where sturdy Victorian houses where spared by the disaster.

They suffered the awful humiliation of relocation during World War II, then they returned in the late 1940s, determined to rebuild their community. The task wasn't easy. Most of the internees had been ruined economically and many of the area's homes—

used to shelter wartime defense workers—had deteriorated.

Doggedly pushing back the encroaching slum, the Japanese-Americans created a cheerful ghetto of little cafes, communal baths and teahouses. When urban renewal reached the Western Addition, residents worked with officials to create a focal point for their community. The result was a cavernous covered mall called **Japan Center**, opened in 1968.

Today's *Nihonmachi* is a curious mix of *Dai Nippon* and Victoriana. Residents have restored many of the old homes, preserving the area's Western look. Some Victorians, in fact, were moved intact from other areas, which were being urbanly renewed with bulldozers. Japantown has few of the cutesy curled rooflines of Chinatown, yet it's rich with Asian flavor. Cloth *noren* hanging over shop doorways keep away evil spirits and temples draw Buddhist and Shinto faithful into meditation. Several of these temples are open to visitors; see listings below.

An ideal time to visit *Nihonmachi* is during the April **Cherry Blossom Festival**, when the community comes alive with floral decorations, traditional dances, parades and thumping *gion* drums.

Wrapped by Geary, Laguna, Post and Fillmore, Japan Center is the commercial heart of *Nihonmachi*. The exterior is rather austere, looking more like an extended gymnasium complex. The interior is much more attractive—a bright and cheerful Japan in a can. It consists of three enclosures—the Peace Plaza Mall, Kintetsu Building and Kinokuniya Building. An enclosed "shopping overpass"—the first of its kind in America—spans Webster Street, linking the Kintetsu and Kinokuniya buildings. An open-air **Peace Plaza** is dressed up by a 100-foot pagoda and reflection pools. It's undergoing a million-dollar face-lift, which may be accomplished by the time you read this.

Step inside the center and Japan comes alive before your eyes. It brims with restaurants, curio shops, folk craft shops, Oriental art galleries and kimono boutiques.

Some places of note: the large **Kinokuniya** book store with 100,000 titles in Japanese and English; **Murata Pearls**, where you can buy pearl-set jewelry

Picture pretty, these kimono-clad Japanese lasses are all dressed up for a Cherry Blossom Festival dance.
—photo courtesy Louise Hanford Agency

or a handful of loose pearls; and the **Ikebana Society of America** gallery, with its striking floral arrangements. **Galerie Voyage** sells Japanese prints and paintings, and you might see its artist-manager Yoshitsugu Yoshii working on one of his unusual *hiaku* prints using acrylic and glue. If you're in the market for a century-old merchant's chest, drop into **Mashiko Folk Craft**.

When you grow weary of walking and shopping, you can be rubbed the right way with a shiatsu massage at **Kabuki Hot Springs**. It's one of the few authentic Japanese bath houses in this country, offering saunas and traditional hot tubs in addition to massages.

May's Coffee Shop in the Kintetsu building is more Japanese than its sounds. It's a walk-up place

offering noodle soups and other inexpensive luncheons that can be consumed at nearby tables. Try a
taiyaki, a fish-shaped waffle-batter pastry filled with
sweet bean paste, served hot off the griddle.

Kintetsu Restaurant Mall, suggestive of a
Japanese village street, is lined with places to dine.
They range from the budget **Mifune** noodle house
and unusual **Isobune** sushi restaurant where diners
pluck morsels off little boats, to the large **Benihana,**
with an impressive Shogunate Japan decor.

The Japanese-modern **Miyako Hotel** anchors
one end of Japan Center, offering both Eastern and
Western style rooms. (See listing in Chapter 16.) Its
Asuka Brasserie is a mix of Japan and California,
both in its decor and menu. Holding down the center's other end are the earlier-mentioned Kabuki Hot
Springs, and the multi-screen **AMC Kabuki 8 Theaters**.

Buchanan Street Mall is an Asian *shopping-
strauss* that T-bones into Japan Center, running between Post and Sutter. It's handsomely landscaped
with paving blocks, fountains, sculptures and
benches. More Japanese shops and restaurants, and
a few Korean cafes, rim the mall and spill onto nearby
Post and Sutter streets. Like their Japan counterparts,
some cafes display realistic plastic models of their
dishes. No, they don't look good enough to eat, but
you get a visual image of the strange dishes you'll be
ordering.

Strolling the rough paving stones of the mall, you
can smell the fresh sushi and frying *tempura.* Asian
mom and pop cafes with *tatami* floors and rice paper
shoji screens offer inviting retreats. It's easy to pretend that you're in Japan.

But who on earth let that Denny's restaurant in
here?

GENTRIFIED FILLMORE

Nearby Fillmore Street also is experiencing a renewal. But look for oysters on the half shell, not sushi.
In comfortable coexistence with *Nihonmachi*, it has
become the city's newest yuppie dining and shopping
area.

Upscale cafes, boutiques and designer shops occupy refurbished Victorians along Fillmore. The shopping-dining area extends from Post north to Jackson Street, on the edge of affluent **Pacific Heights.**

This nine-block stretch invites strolling and window-shopping. Browse through the boutiques and plan lunch at one of the many cafes. **Oritalia Restaurant**, 1915 Fillmore, is tucked into an upscale alley near Bush Street. **Pacific Heights Bar and Grill** at 2001 Fillmore (Pine) is a stylish oak and brass place offering a dozen raw shellfish and an extensive seafood menu. Across the street, **Harry's Bar** is a trendy pub done in mahogany, brass and mirrored walls. Old New Orleans decor and Cajun-Creole fare have put **The Elite Cafe** on the culinary map at 2049 Fillmore (California).

Vivande Porta Via at 2125 Fillmore (California) is the city's classiest cafe-deli and **Spinelli Coffee Company** at 2455 Fillmore (Jackson) is a good place to stop for a cup—or a pound—of designer coffee.

If you were to continue up Fillmore, you'd wind up in Pacific Heights, and then the Marina District, another trendy shopping and supping area. But that comes three chapters from now. We must first visit the land of the flower children.

WHAT TO SEE & DO

Alamo Square Historic District ● △△△
Bounded by Hayes, Steiner, Fulton and Scott streets. The city's best collection of Victorian homes—and a few lavishly-done mansions—rim the square. It's the site of the "Painted Ladies," six matched Victorians often seen on postcards and posters.

Buddhist Church of San Francisco ● △△
1881 Pine St. (Octavia); 776-3158. Monday-Friday 10 to 5, Sunday services at 11. This is a curious blend of Asian Buddhist temple and American church, with oak pews and an ornate lacquered gold and red altar. If you ring a bell at the doorway, someone will show you around. Our you're welcome at Sunday services.

Japan Center ● △△△△ ☺
Bounded by Geary, Laguna, Post and Fillmore. Most shops open from 9 to 6; 922-6776. This collection of

restaurants and shops is an enclosed slice of Japan, transported to San Francisco. The Peace Plaza is its focal point.

Japantown tours ● △△
Departing from the main library, Larkin at Fulton in the Civic Center; 558-3981; call for times; free. City Guides, volunteers of the Friends of the Library, conduct periodic walking tours through Japantown and elsewhere in the city.

Konko-Kyo Church of San Francisco ● △△
1909 Bush St. (Laguna); 931-0453. Open 8 to 5 weekdays, various weekend hours and services. This handsome wooden gabled structure is typical of a Japanese *Shinto* temple with an attractive, simple altar—less ornate than the one at the Buddhist church. The Shinto faith is a blend of nature worship and ancestor veneration.

Soto Zen Buddhist Mission ● △△
1691 Laguna St. (Sutter); 346-7540. Open most days from 7 to 5. The chapel with a simple wooden altar can be reached by entering through a basement side door via a parking lot and walking upstairs. Quiet please; meditations often are being conducted downstairs.

Tea ceremonies ● △△
Nichi Bei Kai Cultural Center, 1759 Sutter St. (Laguna); 751-9676. First and third Saturdays, 2 p.m.; Make advance reservations to experience a traditional tea ceremony, held in an attractive little Japanese-style building.

WHERE TO DINE
Nihonmachi
Asuka Brasserie ● △△△ $$$ Ø
In the Miyako Hotel (1625 Post St.); 922-3200, ext. 7223. Japanese-California nouveau; dinners $11 to $30; full bar service. Daily 6:30 a.m. to 10 p.m. Reservations advised; informal. Major credit cards. East and West meet in this airy restaurant with its stylish Japanese-California decor of polished woods and framed Oriental prints. The menu ranges from *fettuccine* Alfredo with smoked salmon to Spicy Oriental Chicken.

Benihana of Tokyo ● △△ $$ Ø

In Japan Center (Kintetsu Restaurant Mall); 563-4844. Japanese; dinners $10 to $18; full bar service. Lunch Monday-Friday 11:30 to 2 and Saturday noon to 3; dinner Monday-Thursday 5 to 10, Friday-Saturday 5:30 to 11 and Sunday 4:30 to 10. Reservations accepted; informal. Major credit cards. The decor is impressive in this large restaurant: old world Japan with lacquered rough beams, statues of warlords and decorative folk arts. The service is a gimmick, best reserved for party gatherings. Our "Japanese" chef, named Tony, stood before our table and chopped our food with flashing flourishes of his knife and fried it before our eyes. Think of it as high speed culinary *tai chi*. Think of the food—stir-fry veggies with chicken, steak, fish or shrimp—as high-priced chop suey.

Iroha Restaurant ● △△ $$

1728 Buchanan Mall (Post); 922-0321. Japanese; dinners $6 to $14; wine and beer. Daily 11:30 to 9:30. No reservations; informal. Major credit cards. Owned by an Osaka restaurant family, the Iroha specializes in noodle dishes, along with traditional yakitori, tempura and other Japanese fare. The interior is simple but pleasing: wooden booths accented by modern Japanese lanterns, all done in red, black and orange.

Mifune ● △△ $

In Japan Center (Kintetsu Restaurant Mall); 922-0337. Japanese; dinners $5 to $10; wine and beer. Daily 11 to 9:30. No reservations. MC/VISA. "It's okay to slurp your noodles," says the menu at this cozy-boothed little place. Tasty, inexpensive meals are built around huge bowls of noodles—either thick white *udon* or skinny buckwheat *soba*. They're great on a chilly day. It's run by the same folks who brought you Iroha (above).

Fillmore & elsewhere

The Elite Cafe ● △△△ $$$

2049 Fillmore St. (California); 346-8668. Cajun-Creole; dinners $20 to $25; full bar service. Monday-Saturday 5 to 11, Sunday 10 to 3 and 5 to 10. No reservations; informal. Major credit cards. Cajun and Creole fare tilts toward American regional in the

Elite's creative kitchen, with offerings like Iowa pork chops. But you can get redfish and other things blackened. The look is classy New Orleans bistro.

May Sun Restaurant ● ∆∆∆ $

1740 Fillmore St. (Post); 567-7789. Teriyaki-Mandarin; dinners $5.50 to $9.50; wine and beer. Monday-Saturday 11:30 to 9. No reservations; informal. Major credit cards. It's our favorite small cafe in the city—an attractive little place that serves remarkably good food at remarkably low prices. The menu is a mix of Japanese and Mandarin; try the Kung-Pao prawns, or the teriyaki dinner, a bargain at $6.50.

Pacific Heights Bar and Grill ● ∆∆∆ $$$ Ø

2001 Fillmore (Pine); 567-3337. Seafood; dinners $15 to $20; full bar service. Dinner nightly from 5:30, Sunday brunch 10:30 to 2:30. Reservations advised; informal. MC/VISA, AMEX. The look is trendy-modern with pastel colors, oak trim and a copper-topped bar. The fare is fish, properly done, along with the West Coast's largest raw bar. If you're ready for New Zealand green-lipped mussels, this is the place.

Ten-Ichi Japanese Restaurant ● ∆∆ $$

2235 Fillmore St. (Sacramento); 346-3477. Japanese; dinners $12 to $25; wine and beer. Weekdays 11:30 to 10, weekends 5 to 10. No reservations; casual. MC/VISA. The look is rural Japan, with bamboo furniture and earthenware bud vases. A backroom sushi bar has more of a Tokyoesque modern look. The Japanese menu offers interesting variations, such as thin-sliced, pan-fried "Butter-yaki" steak and a mixed-seafood tempura.

Thep Phanom Restaurant ● ∆∆ $

400 Waller (Fillmore); 431-2526. Thai; dinners $4 to $10; wine and beer. Daily 5:30 to 10:30. Reservations accepted; casual. Major credit cards. Cute, cozy and inexpensive, Thep Phanom serves tastily spicy Thailand creations done with lemon grass, peanut sauce and curry.

THOSE SASSY "PAINTED LADIES"

"Nobody seems to think of building a sober house. Of all the efflorescent, floriated bulbousness and flamboyant craziness that ever decorated a city, I think San Francisco may carry off the prize."

These words by a *New York Times* reporter described the city's Victorian architecture in 1883.

Why is this architectural style called "Victorian?" It hardly seems inspired by 19th Century England. The houses are overdone with sunbursts, friezes, fans, pediments, teardrops, rosettes and other geegaws. Some have paint jobs that would pale a peacock. They're hardly the sort of thing that staid old Queen Victoria would sanction. @BOX 9 = They were called Victorians merely because most were built when the good queen was on the throne. This "Victorian" craze reached its peak in the second half of the last century. Circumstance dictated the architectural style. Land was limited on this narrow peninsula, so homes were built tall and skinny. Most shared common walls. To avoid a monotonous rowhouse look, builders used ornate decorations. Teardrops, friezes and sunbursts could be ordered from catalogues.

Redwood—sturdy, plentiful and easily milled— was the wood of choice. Bay windows, destined to become a San Francisco landmark, invited more light into these slender structures. Some builders erected gaudy matched sets of these "painted ladies." Others sought—and certainly achieved—architectural individuality.

By the time the fad had died down around 1915, the city brimmed with more than 45,000 of these structures. Since the fire caused by the 1906 earthquake was stopped at Van Ness Avenue, about 14,000 survive. Many have been sheathed in faceless stucco or paneling. But hundreds of these painted ladies now wear bright new make-up that probably outshines their original efflorescent, floriated bulbousness.

To learn more about these distinctive dwellings, check area bookstores for a series of brightly-photographed *Painted Ladies* books by Elizabeth Pomada and Michael Larsen.

WHERE TO SLEEP
(Detailed listings in Chapter 16)

Rooms for $100 and up
Archbishop's Mansion • *1000 Fulton (Steiner)*
The Miyako Hotel • *1625 Post St. (Japan Center)*

Rooms from $50 to $99
Miyako Inn • *1088 Sutter St. (Buchanan)*

Bed & breakfast inns
Alamo Square Inn • *719 Scott St. (Fulton)*
Chateau Tivoli • *1057 Steiner St. (Golden Gate)*

Thirteen

HAIGHT/PARKSIDE

"Hashbury," Golden Gate Park, the Sunset & Richmond

A QUICK LOOK: The Haight-Ashbury borders the southern edge of Golden Gate Park's panhandle. The park—one of America's finest—continues westward to the ocean. The Sunset, a large residential district, is on the park's southern flank. It's a nice place to live, but of little interest to visitors, except for its ocean beach. The Richmond District on the park's north side offers a wealth of small ethnic cafes.

WHO CAN FORGET the "Summer of Love"—1967?

Thousands of teen-agers—disillusioned by parents, convention and the evil Vietnam War—descended on the Haight-Ashbury, seeking some sort of urban nirvana. Tolerated by an indulgent city, they were part of a gentle, psychedelic society of free thinking, free love and cheap dope. Tie-dyed T-shirts, shaggy hair and peace beads were uniform of the day.

"When you come to San Francisco," advised the song, "wear flowers in your hair."

Acid rock was born here and acid was the drug of choice. When police were called to quell student protests at nearby universities, these "peaceniks" thrust their flowers in the barrels of riot guns. The kids of the Hashbury became regulars on the six o'clock news. *Time Magazine* called the area "the

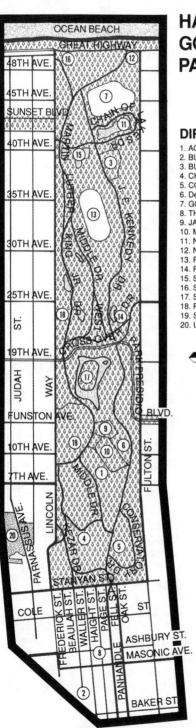

HAIGHT-ASHBURY/ GOLDEN GATE PARK

DIRECTORY

1. ACADEMY OF SCIENCES
2. BUENA VISTA PARK
3. BUFFALO PADDOCK
4. CHILDREN'S PLAYGROUND/CAROUSEL
5. CONSERVATORY OF FLOWERS
6. DeYOUNG/ASIAN MUSEUMS
7. GOLF COURSE
8. THE "HAIGHT"
9. JAPANESE TEA GARDEN
10. MUSIC CONCOURSE
11. NORTH LAKE
12. NORTH WINDMILL
13. POLO FIELD
14. PORTALS OF THE PAST
15. SOUTH LAKE
16. SOUTH WINDMILL
17. STOW LAKE
18. REDWOOD GROVE
19. STRYBING ARBORETUM
20. U.C. MEDICAL CENTER

vibrant epicenter of America's hippie movement." It was even on the tour bus route.

The Flower Children are gone, probably putting their well-mannered kids through UC Berkeley and tending their flower gardens in Hayward.

The old neighborhood, now simply The Haight, is dressier these days. Victorian crash-pads, where rebellious youths gathered to smoke dope and exchange vacant stares, are being refurbished by post-yuppie families.

It isn't really gentrified, however. Cafes still lean toward funk and there are more budget-priced junk shops and used clothing stores than boutiques. The famed intersection of **Haight and Ashbury** is marked by a clothing store, an ice cream parlor and a collectibles shop. A few long-haired youths still hang out in the Haight, but they're more likely to be indolent punks begging quarters than idealists seeking a psychedelic nirvana.

We liked yesterday's kids better. We were drawn here, in fact, as sort of weekend hippies during the Haight's heyday.

The area's best lure is its fine collection of Victorian homes. Scores line the streets, and some function as bed and breakfast inns. **Spencer House** at 1080 Haight (Baker), is a stylish Queen Ann converted to a B&B. **The Red Victorian B&B** at 1665 Haight (Belvedere) retains some of the earthy charm of the hippie era.

Nearby **Buena Vista Park,** a hillside slope of evergreens and eucalyptus, is rimmed by 19th century homes, including several mansions. Noteworthy among them is the **Spreckles Mansion,** a Colonial-style manor at 737 Buena Vista West (Masonic). After you've admired the homes, stroll about the park's wooded paths and admire views of the city.

Hints of hippie history linger about some Haight-Ashbury houses, although no signs mark their significance. Once known as the "Dead House," the Victorian at **710 Ashbury** vibrated to the acid sounds of the Grateful Dead. Some distance away, Jefferson Airplane's crash pad was at **2400 Fulton Street.** On the dark side of history, **636 Cole Street** was occupied by Charles Manson—ironically, during the Summer of Love.

When you've finished studying the painted ladies, save some time for a Haight Street stroll. It's worth it for the cutesy shop names, if nothing else: **Taming of the Shoe, Out of the Closet** (clothing), **Dinostore** (clothing), **All You Knead** (restaurant) and **Bound Together** (books).

Achilles Heel at Haight and Clayton is the area's most interesting pub; its decor is a blend of Victorian and Hashbury funk. **Global Village,** under the Red Victorian, is an environmentally proper store selling "save the rainforests" T-shirts and endangered animal figurines.

Hell's Kitchen cafe at 1793 Haight (Shrader) appears to be a cluttered leftover from yesterday, but it's actually an imitation, opened late in 1990. The closest thing to a head shop is **Smokeart** at 1340 Haight (Central). Stop by for your Janice Joplin poster and ZigZag cigarette papers.

GOLDEN GATE PARK

It's a short walk or bike ride from the Haight to the city's splendid Golden Gate Park. Indeed, the park's tree-sheltered paths are quite bike-able and you can rent one at a nearby bike shop. (See listing below.)

One of the world's largest manmade parks, Golden Gate is much more than a grassy expanse dotted by trees, lakes and statues of people no one remembers. Its 1,017 acres shelter world-class museums, an outstanding science center and planetarium, a pair of Dutch windmills, a buffalo paddock, tennis courts, playgrounds, an outdoor band shell, ten gardens, a golf course and even a polo field.

San Franciscans love to play in their park, particularly on weekends when the main road, **John F. Kennedy Drive**, is closed to vehicles. They hike, run, power-walk, roller-skate, skateboard and cycle over its roadways and miles of trails. On a sunny summer Sunday, you'll be hard pressed to find a place to park.

Remarkably, this expanse of lawn, forests and gardens once was a wasteland of windblown sand dunes. When it was set aside for public use in 1870, the press laughingly called it "The Great Sand Park.

A 24-year-old surveyor named William Hammond Hall designed the complex park and began anchoring down the sand with special imported grasses, lupine and even barley. In 1887, Scottish gardener John McLaren took over the task; he kept at it until his death in 1943 at the age of ninety-six.

You could spend days—indeed your entire vacation—exploring the park's lures. Use the map on these pages and the listings under "What to see and do" to plan your time.

Start your visit with a stop at ivy-entwined **McLaren Lodge** just inside the park at Stanyan and Fell. You can pick up maps and other park information; it's open weekdays from 9 to 5; phone 750-3659.

Include in your "must see list" the combined **de Young and Asian Art** museums, the wonderful **California Academy of Sciences,** the **Conservatory of Flowers** and the **Japanese Tea Garden**.

SUNSET, ZOO & BEACH

After you've done the park, drive south along landscaped Sunset Boulevard, which passes through the Sunset District with its monotonous rows of small stucco houses.

Then head west on Sloat Boulevard (via an underpass) and talk to the animals at the **San Francisco Zoo**. It offers a goodly collection of a thousand or more critters. Some of the newer exhibits, such as the **Primate Discovery Center** and **Gorilla World** with America's only true zoo gorilla family, are state of the zoological art.

Having learned what's new at the zoo, continue west on Sloat to the **Great Highway**, where you're greeted by the scalloped breakers of the Pacific Ocean.

This great stretch of strand, known simply as **Ocean Beach,** extends from the San Mateo County line ten miles north to the Golden Gate. Much of it is rimmed by sea cliffs and sand dunes anchored by ice plant. It's more of a bundling beach than a swimming shore. The currents are treacherous, the weather's often chilly and the water's always so. Sea lions and wet-suited surfers are the only regular participants.

San Francisco's ocean shore is part of the **Golden Gate National Recreation Area**, which we will discuss at length in the next chapter. But since you're in the neighborhood, you might want to explore the Sunset District's portion of the strand.

Drive south on the Great Highway until it hits Skyline Boulevard at **Lake Merced.** This freshwater lagoon has a boat house with rentals, picnic areas and a hiking-biking trail around the lake perimeter. **San Francisco State University** is just beyond. Four golf courses surround the lake: **Harding Park, Olympic, Lake Merced** and **San Francisco Golf Club.**

From Lake Merced, follow Skyline less than a mile south to **Fort Funston**, on a sand dune bluff overlooking the Pacific. Only a few concrete bunkers remain from the old fort, which is now part of the GGNRA. With 200-foot cliffs and a fairly constant wind, it's a popular hangout for **hang gliders.** You may see them doing their Icarus thing, gliding gracefully over the surf like giant fix-winged butterflies.

A short trail leads to **Battery Davis,** a graffiti-scrawled gun emplacement once armed with 16-inch rifles capable of hurling shells 25 miles to sea. If you're wearing your Nikes, you can continue 9.1 miles along the Coastal Trail to the Golden Gate Bridge.

Otherwise, retrace your route up Skyline—perhaps with a scenic loop around Lake Merced Boulevard—and pick up the Great Highway again. It'll take you across Golden Gate Park's ocean front and into the Richmond.

RICHMOND DISTRICT

The highway becomes Point Lobos Avenue, which swings inland and dissolves into Geary Boulevard. Geary and Clement, a block to the north, are lined with ethnic cafes; we list several of them below.

You may want to park and walk several blocks of **Clement**—particularly between 25th and Fifth avenues. It's lined with these ethnic cafes, along with several antique shops and boutiques.

There's also a surprising selection of Irish pubs in the Richmond. If there's a bit of Erin in your soul, take a pint at **The Plough and the Stars** at 116 Clement St. (Second Avenue), **Rocky Sullivan's** at 4737 Geary (12th Avenue) or **Ireland's 32** at 3290 Geary Blvd. (Third Avenue). Rocky's and Ireland's serve passable Irish fare.

Yes, we did skim the edge of the legendary Cliff House back there at Point Lobos Avenue. We're about to get to it—in the next chapter.

WHAT TO SEE & DO
Golden Gate Park attractions
California Academy of Sciences ● ΔΔΔΔ
Off the Music Concourse; 750-7145 or 750-7111; 750-7141 for planetarium/laserium. Daily 10 to 5 (to 7 from July 4 to Labor Day). Adults $4, kids 12-17 and seniors $2, kids 6-11, $1. Planetarium: adults $2.50, seniors and kids $1.25; Laserium shows: adults $6, kids 6 to 12 and seniors $4. One of America's premiere science centers, the academy includes Steinhart Aquarium and Laserium, Morrison Planetarium and outstanding science, wildlife and anthropology exhibits. Graphics, lasers, videos and computers help this lively place come to life. Plan on several hours here. Founded in 1853, it's a leading research center as well as an extraordinary museum of things scientific.

Children's Playground and Carousel ● Δ ☺
Kezar Drive (Arguello); 558-4249. Daily 10 to 5 in summer, Wednesday-Sunday 10 to 4 the rest of the year. Free; carousel rides $1 for adults, 25 cents for kids. A handsomely restored 1912 Hershel-Spillman carousel is the centerpiece of this play area. There's also a gift shop and kiosk with park information.

Conservatory of Flowers ● ΔΔΔ
John F. Kennedy Drive (just beyond McLaren Lodge); 558-3973. Daily 9 to 5 (until 6 from March through September). Adults $1.50, kids and seniors free. Fashioned after London's Kew Garden Conservatory, this grand Victorian greenhouse shelters a lush jungle of orchids and other tropical plants. Striking pictorial flower beds out front are changed periodically to reflect seasonal themes.

Golden Gate Park's Japanese Tea Garden offers quiet retreat from the busy city.

M.H. de Young Memorial Museum ● (750-3659) ∆∆∆
Asian Art Museum ● (668-8921) ∆∆∆

Tea Garden Drive, near the Music Concourse. Wednesday-Sunday 11 to 5. Adults $4, kids 12 to 17 and seniors $2. Although they're separate entities, de Young and Asian Art museums share the same building and the same admission ticket. It's also good for the **Palace of the Legion of Honor** art museum in Lincoln Park (Chapter 14). De Young features American art—primarily paintings, sculpture and furnishings, as well as material from England (as America's mother country) and artifacts from Pacific cultures. The Asian Museum has an outstanding collection of artifacts, statuary and scrolls from China, Japan, Buddhist India and Tibet. **Cafe de Young** serves light fare cafeteria-style from 10 to 4.

Japanese Tea Garden ● ΔΔ ☺
Tea Garden Drive (just beyond de Young); 558-4268. Daily 8:30 to 5:30. Adults $2, kids and seniors $1. Walk the cobbled paths of this lushly landscaped formal garden, then pause for a spot of Japanese tea and cookies in the teahouse for $1.20. A gift shop sells things Japanese.

Strybing Arboretum ● ΔΔ
Martin Luther King Jr. Drive (Lincoln Way); 661-1316. Weekdays 8 to 4:30, weekends 10 to 5; free. This large botanical garden with 6,000 plants features a redwood walk, succulents, California native plants and a "Fragrance Garden" for the blind.

Outside the park

Bicycle Rentals are available from **Lincoln Cyclery**, 722 Stanyan Street (Haight), 221-2415; and **Park Avenue Cyclery**, 1269 Ninth Ave. (Lincoln Way), 665-1394.

Buena Vista Park ● ΔΔ
Off Haight, rimmed by Buena Vista Avenue. Often overlooked by visitors, Buena Vista is a large, attractive forested park offering impressive city views, walking paths and a children's playground. Several Victorians stand along its perimeter.

Fort Funston ● ΔΔ ☺
Off Skyline Drive; 556-8371. Open 6 a.m. to 9 p.m.; free. Enjoy views of city and sea from coastal bluffs and hike about the remnants of this fort. It was a coastal defensive battery through World War II, then a NIKE missile installation. Facilities include a beach, potties, picnic places, hiking trails and a hang gliding area.

Lake Merced ● ΔΔ ☺
Skyline and Lake Merced boulevards. Boathouse, 753-1101; golf course, 664-4690. Rent a rowboat or sailboat, picnic along the shore, hike or bike the perimeter path or play a round at one of four nearby golf courses.

San Francisco Zoological Gardens ● ΔΔΔ ☺
One Zoo Road (Sloat); 753-7172. Daily 10 to 5. Adults $6, kids 12 to 15 and seniors $3; 30-minute Zebra Train ride $2 for adults and $1 for kids and

seniors; Children's Zoo $1; carousel rides 75 cents. Stare quizzically at your ancestral cousins, then learn about them with hands-on exhibits at the **Primate Discovery Center.** It's the zoo's best feature. Other major attractions are **Gorilla World,** housing America's only zoo gorilla family, and the old-fashioned **Lion House,** where the big cats are fed from 2 to 3 daily. With several state-of-the-zoological-art enclosures, the once-scruffy zoo is rapidly getting some respect.

WHERE TO DINE
Haight Ashbury/Parkside
Dish ● △△ $$
1398 Haight St. (Masonic); 431-3534. American regional; dinners $10 to $15; wine and beer. Weekdays 8 to 2:30 and 6 to 10, weekends 8 to 10. Casual; MC/VISA, AMEX. It's probably the Haight's most reliable restaurant, serving tasty chicken, chops and fish dishes. A simple 19th century look is accented by collector plates perched above the wainscoting, and bentwood chairs.

Hell's Kitchen ● △ $
1793 Haight St. (Shrader); 255-7170. American; meals $5 to $10; wine and beer. Daily 7 to 4 and 5 to 10. No reservations; casual; no credit cards. Trying to recapture the Haight's days of yore, the Kitchen is decorated with antique shop clutter. The menu is eclectic, too, ranging from chorizo and egg breakfasts to lunch burgers to Southwestern entrees for dinner.

House of Piroshki ● △ $
1231 Ninth Ave. (Lincoln); 661-1696. Russian-Mideastern deli; meals $4 to $8; wine and beer. Tuesday-Saturday 11 to 5. No reservations or credit cards; casual. A piroshki—should you wonder—is a large fried dumpling stuffed with spiced chicken, pork, beef and/or cheese and veggies. The city's best are made here, to be consumed on the premises or taken away. This unadorned little place also sells other deli items, pastries and truffles. It's a handy lunch stop, within a short walk of Golden Gate Park's major museums and Academy of Sciences.

Pork Store ● Δ $
1451 Haight St. (Masonic); 864-6981. American; meals $5 to $10. Daily 7 a.m. to 2 p.m. No reservations; casual. MC/VISA. Comic piggy art brightens this otherwise formica-funky breakfast and lunch diner. Omelets, sandwiches and salads emerge from the kitchen.

Richmond District

Alejandro's Sociedad Gastronomica ● ΔΔΔΔ $$$ Ø
1840 Clement St. (19th Avenue); 668-1184. Latin mix; dinners $10 to $19; full bar service. Monday-Saturday 5 to 11, Sunday 4 to 11. Reservations accepted; informal. Major credit cards. The lengthy title adds up to a stylishly decorated restaurant serving creative Spanish, Peruvian and Mexican fare. It's one of the city's nicest dining habitats, with ceramic tile trim, pre-Columbian artifacts and post-Columbian strolling guitarists.

Bali Restaurant ● ΔΔ $
3727 Geary Blvd. (Arguello); 221-9811. Indonesian; dinners $8 to $10; wine and beer. Tuesday-Thursday 11:30 to 10, Friday-Saturday 11:30 to 10:30, Sunday 11:30 to 10. Informal; MC/VISA. The fare is Indonesian with a strong Chinese accent, since the owners are Chinese from Bali. Spicy dishes such as *sambal udang* (shrimp with hot chili and coconut milk) and crispy sesame chicken are delicious. The decor is simple but cute: bamboo trim on the walls and framed batik prints.

Bill's Place ● ΔΔ $
2315 Clement St. (25th Avenue); 221-5262. American; mostly hamburgers; meals $6 to $10; wine and beer. Sunday-Thursday 11 to 10, Friday-Saturday 11 to 11. No reservations; casual. No credit cards. Bill names his hamburgers for local celebrities and they're quite good (the burgers, not the celebrities). The decor is curiously fun: chandeliers, formica tables and presidential portraits. There's a Japanese-style patio garden out back.

THE RICHMOND

45TH AVE.

40TH AVE.

35TH AVE.

ANZA ST.

GEARY BLVD.

30TH AVE.

CLEMENT ST.

25TH AVE.

CALIFORNIA ST.

20TH AVE.

15TH AVE.

PARK PRESIDIO BLVD.

BALBOA ST.

10TH AVE.

MOUNTAIN LAKE PARK

ARGUELLO PARK

CABRILLO ST.

5TH AVE.

LAKE ST.

ARGUELLO ST.

COMMONWEALTH ST.

U.C.S.F.

MASONIC AVE.

PRESIDIO AVE.

O'FARRELL ST.

LYON ST.

BAKER ST.

Cafe Riggio ● △△△ $$
4112 Geary Blvd. (Fifth Avenue); 221-2114. Regional Italian; dinners $10 to $20; full bar service. Monday-Saturday 5 to 11, Sunday 4:30 to 10. Reservations for eight or more only; casual. MC/VISA. Hidden in the hinterlands, this attractive restaurant serves some of the city's best Italian food. It *definitely* serves the city's best calamari. Fresh fish, veal and chicken dishes are specialties.

Clement Street Bar & Grill ● △△ $$
708 Clement St. (Eighth Avenue); 386-2200. California cuisine; dinners $10 to $17; full bar service. Lunch Tuesday-Saturday 11:30 to 3, dinner Tuesday-Sunday 5 to 10:30, Sunday brunch 10:30 to 3. Reservations accepted; casual. Major credit cards. A crackling fireplace adds cheer to this oldstyle dining room. The chef creates tasty grilled seafoods, California pastas and vegetarian dishes.

The Grapeleaf ● △△△ $$
4031 Balboa St. (41st Avenue); 668-1515. Mediterranean-Lebanese; dinners $12 to $15; full bar service. Wednesday-Saturday from 6 and Sunday from 5. Reservations advised on weekends; casual. Major credit cards. Gabe Michael's Mideastern fare is spicy and so is the belly dancer who wriggles several nights a week. Enjoy your lamb kebabs and *dolmas* in a charming Lebanese village atmosphere. We'll forgive the dancer's calling card, which invites you to the Grapeleaf "when you care to send the belly best."

Kasra Persian Cuisine ● △△ $$
349 Clement St. (Fifth Avenue); 752-1101. Persian; dinners $7 to $15; full bar service. Monday-Thursday 11 a.m. to 10 p.m., Friday 11:30 to 10, Saturday-Sunday 6 to 11. Reservations advised on weekends; casual. MC/VISA, AMEX. Assorted Persian shish kabobs are featured in this cute little place with pink nappery and brass trim. Try the *fesenjun,* a spicy dish with chicken, walnuts and pomegranate paste.

Khan Toke Thai House ● △△△△ $
5937 Geary Blvd. (23rd Avenue); 668-6654. Thai; dinners $5 to $11; wine and beer. Daily 5 to 10. Reservations accepted; casual. MC/VISA, AMEX. It's simply the best Southeast Asian restaurant in the city,

with charming Thailand village decor, an outstanding menu and attentive service. The dishes—spiced
with curry, peanut sauce and ginger—are excellent
and the prices are amazingly modest.

Pacific Cafe ● △△△ $$ Ø
*7000 Geary Blvd. (34th Avenue); 387-7091. Sea-
food; dinners $10.98 to $20; wine and beer. Daily 5 to
10. No reservations; casual. MC/VISA, AMEX.* One of
several cafes Pacific in the Bay Area, it serves fresh
seafood at remarkably modest prices in a pleasant
environment. Although the Pacifics don't take reservations, they offer a free glass of wine at the bar if
you have to wait for a table.

Pat O'Shea's Mad Hatter ● △△ $
*3754 Geary Blvd. (Third Avenue); 752-3148.
American; meals $5 to $12; full bar service. Monday-
Saturday 11:30 to 9, Sunday 11 to 3. Casual; no
reservations or credit cards.* What's the city's best
sports bar doing in the restaurant section? It earned
its niche by serving remarkably tasty and inexpensive
fish and chops, along with filling hamburgers and
other sandwiches. Although this is no couch potato
place, a dozen videos broadcast every TV sports event
they can snatch from the satellites.

Singapore-Malaysian Restaurant ● △△ $
*836 Clement St. (Ninth Avenue); 750-9518. Malay-
sian; dinners $7.50 to $10; wine and beer. Daily 11:30
to 10. Casual; MC/VISA.* This simply-attired little cafe
features the cooking styles of Chinese who migrated
to the Malay peninsula. It's a mix of stir-fry meats and
veggies with coconut milk, pepper and peanut sauce
flavors. Another specialty is *rojak,* a cold salad of fresh
fruits and vegetables with a chili, shrimp and sesame
dressing. Try the coconut or ginger flavored steamed
rice with your meal.

Taiwan Restaurant ● △△ $
*445 Clement St. (Sixth Avenue); 387-1789. Tai-
wanese-Chinese; dinners $6 to $10; wine and beer.
Monday-Saturday 11 to midnight. Reservations for
groups only; casual. MC/VISA, AMEX.* Chinese emi-
grants to Taiwan brought a broad mix of ethnic fare,
from lightly-spiced Cantonese to peppy Hunan and
Szechuan. This simply-decorated little place reflects

this heritage. The over-sized menu ranges from Tai-wanese fish ball soup to spicy Szechuan prawns to Cantonese vegetarian dishes.

Tia Margarita ● △△ $$

300 19th Ave. (Clement); 752-9274. Mexican; dinners $7.50 to $13; full bar service. Tuesday-Thursday 4 to 10, Friday-Saturday 4 to 11, Sunday 3 to 10. Reservations accepted; casual. MC/VISA. It's a long-established family cafe with a pleasing Mexican decor. Specialties include *carne asada, pollo asada* and other dishes that are a step beyond burritos (although you can get them as well).

WHAT TO DO AFTER DARK

I-Beam ● △ (heavy metal disco)

1748 Haight St. (Cole); 668-6006. The harsh sounds of hard rock bellow from speakers the size of mini-vans in this joint. Deejays and live bands alternate.

Holy City Zoo ● △△ (stand-up comedy)

408 Clement St. (15th Avenue); 386-4243. One of the city's senior comic clubs, the Zoo is a training ground for newcomers and a platform for established locals.

The Plough and the Stars ● △△ (Irish music)

116 Clement St. (Second Avenue); 751-1122. This pub with the curious name features dancing and live Irish music nightly.

Rockin' Robbin's ● △△ (disco)

1840 Haight St. (Shrader); 221-1960. A 1950s-style disco, it's decorated mostly with hubcaps, offering a mix of Moetown, soul and generic rock.

WHERE TO SLEEP
(Detailed listings in Chapter 16)

Rooms for $50 to $99

Day's Inn ● *2600 Sloat Blvd. (Great Highway)*
Great Highway Motor Inn ● *1234 Great Highway (Lincoln)*
Seal Rock Inn ● *545 Point Lobos Ave. (48th)*

Bed & breakfast inns

The Red Victorian ● *1665 Haight St. (Cole)*
Spencer House ● *1080 Haight St. (Baker)*
Victorian Inn on the Park ● *301 Lyon St. (Fell)*

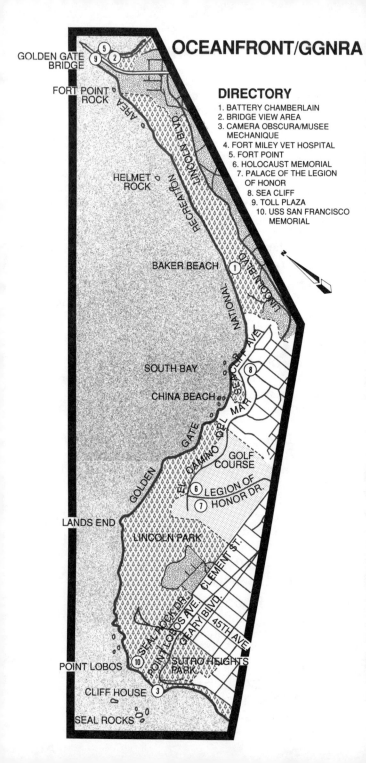

OCEANFRONT/GGNRA

DIRECTORY

1. BATTERY CHAMBERLAIN
2. BRIDGE VIEW AREA
3. CAMERA OBSCURA/MUSEE MECHANIQUE
4. FORT MILEY VET HOSPITAL
5. FORT POINT
6. HOLOCAUST MEMORIAL
7. PALACE OF THE LEGION OF HONOR
8. SEA CLIFF
9. TOLL PLAZA
10. USS SAN FRANCISCO MEMORIAL

GOLDEN GATE BRIDGE

FORT POINT ROCK

AREA

HELMET ROCK

RECREATION LINCOLN BLVD.

LINCOLN BLVD.

BAKER BEACH ①

SOUTH BAY

CHINA BEACH

SEA CLIFF AVE

⑧

DEL MAR

GOLDEN GATE NATIONAL

GOLF COURSE

EL CAMINO

⑥ LEGION OF
⑦ HONOR DR.

LANDS END

LINCOLN PARK

CLEMENT ST.

SEAL ROCK DR.

POINT LOBOS AVE.

GEARY BLVD.

45TH AVE.

POINT LOBOS ⑩

SUTRO HEIGHTS PARK

CLIFF HOUSE ③

SEAL ROCKS

⑤ ②
⑨

Fourteen

THE GGNRA & THE GOLDEN GATE

The Bridge and that amazing urban park

> **A QUICK LOOK:** That famous bridge sits at the city's northern tip, linking—with a majestic arc of steel—the headlands of San Francisco and Marin. Around it, riding off in all directions, are lures of the Golden Gate National Recreation Area.

IT MAY BE THE MOST UNUSUAL national parkland in America. It's certainly the most versatile. Imagine a federal reserve that contains miles of beaches and hiking trails, a sea lion sanctuary, a redwood forest, a famous prison, old army forts, historic ships, several museums and a cliff-side restaurant!

Conceived in the mind of the late Congressman Phillip Burton, the Golden Gate National Recreation Area was created in 1972. It preserves much of the city's shoreline, the headlands and hinterlands of Marin County and several military historic sites. It also includes **Muir Woods National Monument** in Marin County, **Alcatraz** and **Angel Island State Park** (within GGNRA's boundaries but administered by the state).

A patchwork of 114 square miles, it's the world's largest urban park and the most visited unit of the national park system, drawing 20 million people a year. It's destined to become even larger when the historic Presidio army base is decommissioned and turned over to the park service. The transfer is set for Sept. 30, 1995. Much of the Presidio's beachfront is already a part of the GGNRA.

The national recreation area is headquartered at Fort Mason, a former World War II cargo and troop staging center west of Fishmerman's Wharf.

To properly sample this complex park, we'll suggest a scenic-historic drive, with frequent stops for browsing and hiking. Although most of our route is within the park, we'll step outside occasionally to take in other lures. We'll pass some of the city's prettiest vistas—wild, broken shorelines and lush green headlands framed through Monterey cypress

We begin at the **Cliff House,** as much a part of the city's historic fabric as the Golden Gate Bridge. And it's considerably older. Poised precariously over crashing breakers off Point Lobos Avenue, it dates back to 1863. The present structure, housing restaurants and the **Phineas T. Barnacle Pub** (see listing), was built in 1909. The bar, incidentally, is a great place to watch the sun sizzle into the Pacific. But get there early if you want a window seat.

A **GGNRA Visitor Center** sits behind the Cliff House, with an equally impressive view. It's a good starting point for area exploration, since it offers assorted brochures, maps and guidebooks. An on-duty ranger can answer your questions about this complex urban park.

Next door is **Musee Mechanique,** a somewhat dusty but intriguing collection of old coin-fed music boxes and penny arcade machines. Not surprisingly, they now require a quarter. Also nearby is the **Camera Obscura**, with a slowly-revolving lens reflecting images of the area onto a parabolic screen. The sunset effect borders on awesome. Ole Sol casts its shattered glass beam across the screen, then flashes a mysterious crown of green as it melts into the sea.

Just offshore stand **Seal Rocks,** jagged sea stacks painted antique white by centuries of sea bird visitations. Yapping sea lions are regular visitors, too, but you can see more of them at Pier 39.

From the Cliff House, follow Point Lobos Avenue inland briefly, then turn left onto El Camino del Mar. You soon draw up at the **Point Lobos** overlook, the city's westernmost thrust. This lush promontory is little changed from the days when only Indians occupied the San Francisco peninsula. Paths snake between wind-bent cypress and thick underbrush, leading to the beach a hundred feet below. The strand is popular with skinny-dippers on warm days. Take care on these steep trails. They're prone to landslides and you may arrive at the beach more quickly than you'd intended.

The overlook offers postcard glimpses of the Golden Gate Bridge. The great span—often filtered through cypress limbs—will appear and vanish frequently on your route. Nearby is the **U.S.S. San Francisco Memorial**—part of the shell-pocked bridge of the city's namesake ship. It survived—just barely—the 1942 battle of Guadalcanal.

You can pick up the **Coastal Trail** here and wander through cypress forests and over wild sea bluffs. It's easy to lose yourself in a make-believe wilderness, convinced that civilization is a world away. Then you round a bend, and the Golden Gate Bridge stands in the distance. This may be the most stunning urban hike in America. After about a mile and a half, you'll emerge onto Camino Del Mar, just short of the upscale enclave of **Sea Cliff.**

Return to your car, drive from the Point Lobos parking lot and take a quick left onto Seal Rock Drive. The route becomes Clement Street as you pass the large Fort Miley Veterans Medical Center. Turn left onto Legion of Honor Drive (34th Avenue) into **Lincoln Park Golf Course,** as velvety as a lumpy billiard table.

Within the park is the city's finest art museum, the **Palace of the Legion of Honor**, with world-class exhibits of European art. It's dramatic in both stature and setting, a marble columned mirror-image of the Legion of Honor in Paris, sitting atop a green knoll. Even if you aren't museum-prone, take time to stroll through skylighted galleries of this architectural jewel.

Sculptor George Segal's stark **Holocaust** monument is at the northeast corner of the Legion of Honor parking lot. It recalls the horror of the Jewish death camps in World War II.

As you leave the parking area, turn right onto El Camino Del Mar and follow it into Sea Cliff, the carefully landscaped lair of the city's super rich. Their cliff-hanging mansions create the only break in the GGNRA shoreline from Fort Funston to Fisherman's Wharf. **China Beach,** a cliff-rimmed thumbnail of sand below the posh homes, is part of the reserve, however. To reach it, take a sharp left onto Seacliff Drive and follow it to its end. You'll see a small parking area and a path to the sheltered beach, which is named for a yesteryear Chinese fishing camp.

The China Beach access is a bit hard to find, but no matter. You probably won't mind following all of those curving streets past Sea Cliff's palaces of prosperity.

When you've finished, emerge onto Lincoln Boulevard and follow signs down to **Baker Beach**. This wide corridor of sand is popular with locals. Expect to see many bikini-clad bodies on warm days. Farther up the beach, toward the Golden Gate, you'll see all body; no bikini. Most are slender young men. Park rangers have asked skinny-dippers to stay in rock-rimmed coves out of sight of mom and pop and the ogling kids.

Battery Lowell A. Chamberlin, a gun emplacement turned into a mini-museum, is a short walk from the Baker Beach parking lot. You'll see an unusual six-inch disappearing rifle that could fold out of sight after firing.

Beyond the battery, during low tide, you can hike through a series of little crescent beaches all the way to the Golden Gate. It requires some careful rock-climbing and perhaps a bit of surf-slogging. The visual rewards are worth the effort. Take your camera; these are beach-to-bridge views that less adventurous souls will never see. Don't try it at high tide; you'll be forced up dangerous slopes. A safe trail follows the crest of the headlands, along the edge of Lincoln Boulevard.

Driving north from Baker Beach on Lincoln, you enter the green, cypress and eucalyptus realm of the **Presidio of San Francisco**. It dates from 1776, established as a Spanish garrison to protect the new mission a few miles away. It is currently headquarters for the U.S. Sixth Army, although it is scheduled for decommissioning.

Whenever we explore this lush, park-like base, we're struck by a wonderful irony. The military, in arming San Francisco's shoreline to the teeth, preserved it—by default—from commercial development. Without this saber-rattling presence, the glorious seacoast would be dotted with condos instead of conifers.

Here's more irony: The scores of cannons and mortars that once bristled from these shores never fired a mean shot. Legions of soldiers spent decades huddled behind cold concrete, waiting for an enemy who never came.

Several turnouts along Lincoln Boulevard invite you to stop for assorted views of the golden bridge. As you near that grand span, watch for small Merchant Road, veering off to the left. It'll take you to **Battery Godfrey** and **Battery Marcus Miller**, two rather elaborate gun emplacements that are missed by most visitors.

Back on Lincoln, you'll pass under Doyle Drive, the elevated highway leading to the bridge. The popular Golden Gate viewpoint is just to your left, after you cross under the highway. Parking spaces here are metered and they're often full. Continue along Lincoln Boulevard to **Fort Point** turnoff and park down there. Space is usually more plentiful—and it's unmetered. You can first explore the fort, then hike up to the bridge. It's steep but take your time; the views are nice.

This massive brick citadel, officially called Fort Winfield Scott, sits under a steel arch of the bridge. Modeled after Fort Sumner, it was completed in 1861 to forestall possible Confederate sea attacks during the Civil War. An historical twist: Sumner received a thorough Rebel shelling; Fort Point has never been touched by hostile fire.

National Park Rangers in period costume conduct cannon-loading drills and other military functions of the day. You can explore the fort's long, echoing hallways and step inside cold brick rooms to view historic exhibits. The view of the bridge and the city skyline from the fort's top deck is awesome.

Now, climb the path to the **Golden Gate Bridge,** that engineering miracle that has become the city's trademark. It's not enough to stand among the viewpoint crowds and stare in wonder. You should walk this slender span. The bridge sidewalk is open daily from 5 a.m. to 9 p.m. The round trip is more than three miles, so if you haven't the time or energy, at least go to mid-bridge.

Feel its strength shudder beneath your feet. Admire the distant cityscape, looking now like a model in a blue diorama of sky and bay. Stare dizzily down to the restless Pacific, more than 200 feet below; watch toy ships pass.

Having done this, retrieve your car, drive across the bridge, take the Alexander Avenue exit, then go left under the **U.S. 101 freeway**. Veer right and climb Conzelman Road to the ramparts of the **Marin Headlands**. The view is superb, with the golden span below and the city cradled in its graceful inverse arch.

You can poke about more fortifications here, including **Battery Spencer,** an elaborate set of bunkers just above the bridge. From Spencer, a downhill drive—or hike—takes you to **Kirby Beach** for yet another awesome view, with the city skyline beneath the span.

You could spend most of a day—actually, several days—visiting GGNRA elements of Marin Headlands and hidden valleys beyond. **Point Bonita Light, Rodeo Beach, Tennessee Valley** and miles of trails await your exploration. A ranger station near Rodeo Beach has maps, brochures and hiking guides.

When you return to the city, continue along Lincoln Boulevard through the Presidio. Plan a stop at the **Presidio Army Museum** at Lincoln and Funston. It offers a mix of military lore and San Francisco history, scattered through several rooms of the former station hospital.

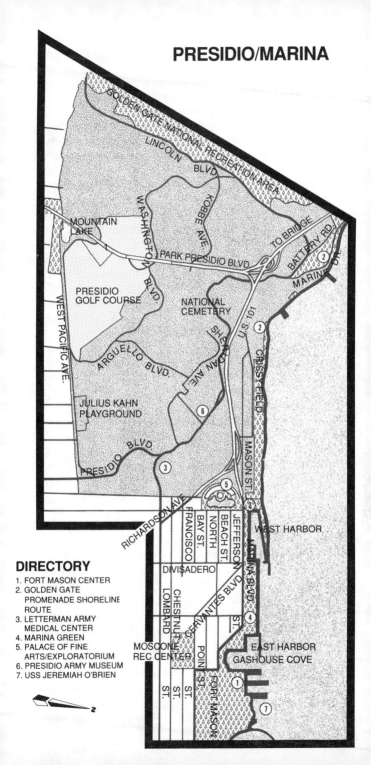

PRESIDIO/MARINA

GOLDEN GATE NATIONAL RECREATION AREA

LINCOLN BLVD

KOBBE AVE.

TO BRIDGE

BATTERY RD.

MARINA DR.

MOUNTAIN LAKE

WASHINGTON BLVD.

PARK PRESIDIO BLVD.

U.S. 101

PRESIDIO GOLF COURSE

NATIONAL CEMETERY

SHERIDAN AVE.

CRISSY FIELD

WEST PACIFIC AVE.

ARGUELLO BLVD.

JULIUS KAHN PLAYGROUND

MASON ST.

PRESIDIO BLVD

RICHARDSON AVE.

WEST HARBOR

FRANCISCO

BAY ST.

NORTH

BEACH ST.

JEFFERSON

MARINA BLVD.

DIVISADERO

CHESTNUT

LOMBARD

CERVANTES BLVD.

ST.

POINT ST.

EAST HARBOR
GASHOUSE COVE

MOSCONE REC CENTER

FORT MASON

ST.

ST.

ST.

ST.

DIRECTORY
1. FORT MASON CENTER
2. GOLDEN GATE PROMENADE SHORELINE ROUTE
3. LETTERMAN ARMY MEDICAL CENTER
4. MARINA GREEN
5. PALACE OF FINE ARTS/EXPLORATORIUM
6. PRESIDIO ARMY MUSEUM
7. USS JEREMIAH O'BRIEN

N

As you approach a fork in Lincoln Boulevard, veer left onto Lombard, pass through the Presidio gate and—after three blocks—turn left onto Divisadero. (Left turns aren't allowed during commute hours, so you'll have to loop around to the right.) Follow Divisadero four blocks to North Point and go left again.

You'll pull up shortly at the **Palace of Fine Arts,** a resplendent study in Beaux Arts architecture, mirrored in a reflection pool. It's neither a palace nor an art museum, but a re-constructed survivor of the 1915 Panama-Pacific International Exposition, which celebrated the opening of the Panama Canal. Thanks to the efforts of a 1990 fund drive, the architectural landmark is now floodlighted at night.

The **Exploratorium,** a youth-oriented wonderland of science, occupies one wing of the palace. Filled with 650 exhibits—most of them hands-on—it encourages kids to explore the wonders of science and nature. Typically, curious adults will step in for a brief look and—three hours later—they're still in there, twisting handles and knobs, punching computer keyboards and grinning.

From the Exploratorium, continue along Baker to the **Marina Green**, which rivals Golden Gate Park as a locally-favored place to play. Take a break here and watch kites, frisbees and footballs fly about. Enjoy views of the bay in front of you and the city behind, and stroll past masts of pleasure boats in three small craft harbors.

At any point along the green, you can pick up the **Golden Gate Promenade,** a shoreside hiking-biking trail. It extends three and a half miles between Aquatic Park and Fort Point, offering an unraveling panorama of bay and city views.

Just beyond the Marina is amazingly busy **Fort Mason Center**. Several former Army cargo sheds have been recycled into a nucleus of cultural-political-educational activity. These drab buildings shelter everything from museums to environmental protection groups to the latest liberal causes.

Among its tourist lures are the large **Mexican Museum** with an adjacent crafts and folkloric shop, the **San Francisco Craft and Folk Art Museum,**

Museo Italo Americano and the **African-American Cultural Society Museum.** Two historic vessels are parked here: the World War II liberty ship **U.S.S. Jeremiah O'Brien** and the old steam tug **Hercules.** The O'Brien is open for regular tours. Still undergoing restoration, the steam tug is accessible less frequently.

You can buy cheap books at the Friends of the Library **Book Bay Bookstore** and catch a play at the **Magic Theatre.** Purchase a whole-earth muffin and a healthy salad at **Cooks & Company** and devour them in the adjacent **Coffee Gallery,** with a mix of dining tables and works of local artists.

Greens, an notable vegetarian restaurant, occupies a soaring space in one of the cargo sheds. Its **Tassajara Bakery** sells wonderfully tasty yet terribly healthy multi-grain things.

A free monthly newsletter tells you what's happening in this simmering sociological center. On any given day, you can attend a class on the use of Mace, learn Microsoft Word, practice your yoga or *tai chi,* or see a travel film.

The main body of Fort Mason is on a low bluff above, housing the GGNRA headquarters, where you can obtain maps, brochures and advise. It's also home to the **San Francisco Youth Hostel**, in case you want to park your backpack and your body for a night.

WHAT TO SEE & DO

To begin, the **GGNRA information number** is 556-0560. You can write for a brochure to: Golden Gate National Recreation Area, Building 201, Fort Mason, San Francisco, CA 94123. Office hours are 9:30 to 4:30 weekdays. **Fort Mason Center's** number is 441-5705 or write: Fort Mason Foundation, Building A, Fort Mason Center, San Francisco, CA 94123.

African-American Cultural Society Museum ●
△△

Fort Mason Center Building C; 441-0640. Wednesday-Sunday noon to 5. Adults $1, kids 50 cents. This small combined museum and handicrafts shop features Black American arts and crafts as well as artifacts from Africa.

Angel Island State Park ● △△△ ☺

In San Francisco Bay; open sunup to sundown; round-trip fare $7.10, less for kids; call 546-2815 for ferry service. Administered by the state of California, Angel Island is an attractive forested island reached by passenger ferry from Fisherman's Wharf (see Chapter 7) or Tiburon. Miles of hiking and biking trails, picnic glens and relics of an old Chinese immigration station draw thousands of visitors annually. The ferryboat ride over is fun, too.

Battery Lowell A. Chamberlin ● △△ ☺

Baker Beach; 556-8371. Daily 11 to 4; free. An unusual "disappearing rifle" (actually an artillery piece) and historical exhibits of the area's beach fortification are featured in this small museum, housed in a coastal bunker.

California Palace of the Legion of Honor ● △△△△

Legion of Honor Drive (Lincoln Park); 750-3600. Wednesday-Sunday 10 to 5. Adults $4, youths 12 to 17 and seniors $2 (same-day tickets also good at de Young and Asian Arts museums). This colonnaded palace exhibits eight centuries of European art. Its collections include an exceptional Rodin sculpture retrospective, elegant porcelains and paintings by Van Gough, Renoir, Monet and other past masters. The imposing French neo-classical building was completed in 1920 as a monument to California's fallen heroes of World War I.

Camera Obscura ● △△ ☺

1090 Point Lobos Ave. (behind the Cliff House); 752-9422. Daily 10 to sunset; Adults $1, kids 50 cents. Images of the area are reflected onto a parabolic screen; several holographs also are on exhibit.

Cliff House ● See restaurant listing

Exploratorium/Palace of Fine Arts ● △△△△ ☺

3601 Lyon St. (Baker); 563-7337 or 561-0360 for recorded information. Wednesday 10 to 9:30, Thursday-Sunday 10 to 5. Adults $6, seniors $3, kids 6 to 17, $2 (all tickets good for six months). Occupying a wing of the palace, the Exploratorium invites you to make lightning, create color spectrums, fiddle with magnetism, check the latest weather satellite photo

Towers of the Golden Gate Bridge reach toward a canopy of fog; the great brick citadel of Fort Point sits under its massive arch.

and such. Its creators call it "the museum of science, art and human perception." The palace is a leftover from the 1915 Pan-Pacific Exposition, worth a look for its classic Beaux Arts rotunda and colonnade. Stop by at night, when it's bathed in floodlights and mirrored in a reflection pool.

Fort Point National Historic Site ● △△△△ ☺

Off Lincoln Boulevard; 556-1693. Daily 10 to 5; free. This grand brick edifice offers impressive views of the city and the Golden Gate Bridge that arches directly over it. Massive corridors and roof-top ramparts invite exploration. Features include cannon drills, guided tours, historic exhibits, videos and a bookstore.

"The Holocaust" memorial ● △△
Northeast corner of Palace of the Legion of Honor parking lot. This unsettling reminder of German wartime atrocities depicts a man standing before barbed wire, with victims of the death camps behind him.

Marin Headlands ● △△△△ ☺
Across the Golden Gate Bridge; take Alexander Avenue exit, then go left under the freeway and right up to the headlands. Rodeo Beach ranger station open daily 9:30 to 4:30; phone 331-1540. This promontory above the Golden Gate offers the area's best bridge-and-city views. Beyond are beaches, hiking trails, bunkers and hidden valleys. The area's **California Marine Mammal Center** (331-7325) is a non-profit organization that nurtures injured and orphaned sea lions and seals, then releases them back into the surf.

Mexican Museum ● △△
Fort Mason Center Building D; 441-0404. Wednesday-Sunday noon to 5. Adults $3, seniors and kids $2. The Mexican-American experience is reflect in folk art and fine art in this well-organized museum. A gift shop with Mexican art and handicrafts is adjacent.

Musee Mechanique ● △△ ☺
1090 Point Lobos Ave. (behind the Cliff House); 386-1170. Weekdays 11 to 6, weekends 10 to 7; free. It brims with dozens of early-day music boxes, Nickelodeons and Rube Goldberg devices.

Museo Italo Americano ● △△
Fort Mason Center Building C; 673-2200. Wednesday-Sunday noon to 5; free. This small museum features changing and permanent exhibits of Italian-American arts and artists.

Presidio Army Museum ● △△△ ☺
Lincoln Boulevard (Funston); 561-4115. Tuesday-Sunday 10 to 4; free. Two hundred years of Bay Area military and civilian history are on display. Exhibits include military uniforms and weapons, and an outstanding collection of 1906 San Francisco earthquake photos. Out back are displays of "earthquake cottages; 6,000 were built by the Army to house '06 quake refugees.

A BRIDGE SO FAR

It strides across the bay's narrow neck like a giant steel harp. Its moods change with the weather: proud and regal in sunlight; mystical and serene in a bridal veil of fog. Its towers sometimes disappear into the clouds, like fairy tale pathways to Oz.

The Golden Gate Bridge was conceived by a stubborn five-foot Chicago engineer named Joseph Baermann Strauss. Arriving in San Francisco in 1917, he spent years trying to convince people that the bay entrance could be spanned. Construction finally began in 1933. Although Strauss was the "father of the bridge," historians now credit consulting architect Irvin F. Morrow with the bridge's sweeping design and striking Art Deco towers. Further, Strauss' health failed during construction and most of the work was supervised by his chief assistant Clifford Paine. The diminutive engineer died a year after his dream became a reality.

Spanning the bay was an almost impossible task. The south pier had to be sunk offshore, where tidal surges swept through the narrow channel as fast as 60 miles an hour. Laboring on a floating trestle, workmen became seasick in 15-foot swells. When the towers were completed, workers had to span a mile of empty space, above water 318 feet deep.

Strauss was a stickler for safety and there were no casualties until the bridge was nearly finished. Nineteen men plummeted into a safety net strung beneath the span and formed the "Halfway to Hell Club" to celebrate their survival. Then, just weeks before the bridge was done, a scaffolding broke, ripped through the net and took nine men to their graves.

When it was completed, the Golden Gate boasted the world's longest single span and tallest bridge towers. More than 80,000 miles of wire were spun into its thick suspension cables and enough concrete was poured into its piers to pave a five-foot-wide sidewalk to New York.

The bridge was opened on May 27, 1937 and 202,000 people walked across its roadbed. Fifty years later, 800,000 surged across in a joyous anniversary celebration. I was among that sea of talking heads, taking part in history's first bridge love-in. Fortunately, I didn't learn until later that our immense weight had actually flattened the gentle arch of the mile-wide center span.

San Francisco Craft and Folk Art Museum ●
△△△

Fort Mason Center Building A; 775-0990. Tuesday-Sunday 11 to 5; adults $1. It's one of the city's better small museums. Changing shows range from American and foreign folk art to costume jewelry, furnishings and crafts. The entire museum often devotes itself to a particular theme. A small gift counter sells jewelry and artifacts, including items relating to current shows.

U.S.S. Jeremiah O'Brien Liberty Ship ● △△ ☺
Pier 3, Fort Mason; 441-3101. Weekdays 9 to 3, weekends 11 to 4. Adults $3, seniors and kids $1, families $6. Prowl the welded steel decks and engine room of America's only fully operational Liberty Ship. Three thousand were built to carry troops and supplies overseas during World War II.

WHERE TO DINE

Scores of restaurants are scattered through the Richmond District (last chapter) and Marina District (next chapter), which this chapter wraps around. In addition, here are two directly in your path:

The Cliff House ● △△△ $$$
1090 Point Lobos Ave.; 386-3330 or 387-5847. American, seafood, pasta; dinners $12 to $25; full bar service. Sunday-Thursday 9 a.m. to 10:30 p.m., Friday-Saturday 9 to 11. Reservations accepted upstairs. Informal to casual; major credit cards. The food's almost as good as the view at this historic cliff-side complex. It's actually three restaurants: the early San Francisco-style **Upstairs at the Cliff House,** the more casual **Seafood and Beverage Company** and the **Phineas T. Barnacle**, an oldstyle pub with libations and light fare.

Greens ● △△△△ $$$ Ø
Fort Mason Center (Building A); 771-6222. Vegetarian; meals from $12, Friday-Saturday prix fixe dinners $32; wine and beer. Lunch Tuesday-Saturday 11:30 to 2:15, dinner Tuesday-Saturday 6 to 9:30, Sunday brunch 10 to 2, bakery counter Tuesday-Saturday 10 to 4:30 and Sunday 10 to 3. Reservations advised; informal to casual. MC/VISA. Using mushroom magic, cheeses, polenta, creative pasta and

clever seasonings, Greens assembles entrees so hearty that you'll never ask: "Where's the beef?" The decor is mostly outside; this spacious, high-ceiling restaurant has picture windows on the bay.

UNION STREET/PACIFIC HEIGHTS

BAKER ST.
BRODERICK ST.
DIVISADERO ST.
SCOTT ST.
PIERCE ST.
①
STEINER ST.
FILLMORE ST.
WEBSTER ST.
BUCHANAN ST.
CHARLTON COURT
LAGUNA ST.
OCTAVIA ST.
④ GOUGH ST.
⑤
FRANKLIN ST.
VAN NESS AVE.

SUTTER ST.
BUSH ST.
PINE ST.
CALIFORNIA ST.
SACRAMENTO ST.
③
CLAY ST.
WASHINGTON ST.
②
JACKSON ST.
PACIFIC AVE.
BROADWAY
VALLEJO ST.
GREEN ST.
UNION ST.
FILBERT ST.
GREENWICH ST.
LOMBARD ST.
CHESTNUT ST.

DIRECTORY
1. ALTA PLAZA PARK
2. HAAS-LILIENTHAL HOUSE
3. LAFAYETTE PARK
4. OCTAGON HOUSE
5. WASHERWOMEN'S LAGOON SITE

N

Fifteen

UNION STREET/ PACIFIC HEIGHTS
The Marina & the mansions

A QUICK LOOK: The Marina District runs from the Marina Green to the steep slopes and upscale homes of Pacific Heights. Union Street—called Cow Hollow by locals—is the region's most popular shopping and dining area. You can find just about everything here but a parking place. Lombard Street is the city's motel row.

COW HOLLOW is a rather inelegant name for one of the city's classiest shopping and residential districts.

Put aside visions of boutiques and mansions for the moment and picture a green valley, ribboned by creeks running into the bay. It offered good pasturage and the first dairy was established here in 1861. A little freshwater lake near the present corner of Franklin and Lombard became known as Washerwoman's Lagoon, since women converged there to do their laundry.

The picture gets worse: Tanneries, slaughterhouses and sausage factories were built to process worn-out dairy cows. The lagoon was fouled by tannery waste and had be filled. Responding to complaints by affluent Pacific Heights residents, the Board of Health kicked out the cows and closed the tanneries near the end of the century.

Cow Hollow became an ordinary neighborhood of modest Victorians and clapboard homes. Union Street was lined with grocers, small stores and an occasional service station. Then in the 1950s, a few antique shops and decorator showrooms were attracted by cheap rents, and the **Union Street** renaissance was set into motion.

Today, the area features a goodly collection of boutiques, specialty shops, restaurants, French bakeries, art galleries, fashionable food stores, some first-rate saloons and charming bed and breakfast inns. And of course, those tasteful antique shops and decorator showrooms are still about. The look is a blend of Victorian and Edwardian.

A merchants' association publishes the *Union Street Shopping & Dining Guide,* listing most of the area's 200 businesses. It brims with perfectly logical reasons to mistreat your credit card. The group also encourages businesses to maintain the neighborhood's character by giving merit awards for architectural preservation.

Most of Cow Hollow's shopping/dining bounty lines Union for seven blocks between Franklin and Steiner. Some of the shops spill downhill toward Lombard.

This is a park-and-walk neighborhood, if you can find a place to park. The Number 41 bus that travels along Sacramento Street from the Financial District may be the best solution. On the other hand, if you can afford the prices at Union Street boutiques, you can afford a cab to get you there. (One designer dress shop, no longer in business, saw customers by appointment only.)

If you begin your walk at Franklin and Union, hike half a block up Gough Street to admire the unusual 1861 **Octagon House,** an eight-sided structure with a museum of early American furnishings and decorative arts.

As you stroll along Union, duck into shallow alleys to discover hidden gardens, Dutch-door shops, landscaped courtyards and postage stamp patios. A good example is Charlton Court, where two oldstyle homes have been converted into the city's first B&B, known simply as **The Bed and Breakfast Inn.**

Another pleasant shopping, dining and strolling area is **Chestnut Street** between Franklin and Baker. It's not as upscale as Union and therefore is more affordable.

PACIFIC HEIGHTS

Rising above all that Union-Chestnut street commerce—topographically, at least—is Pacific Heights, the city's largest arena of affluence. It's a gathering of mansions, manor houses, Victorians, Edwardians and an occasional consular residence. Danielle Steele and Robin Williams are among the notables occupying these slopes.

Like Cow Hollow, Pacific Heights had bucolic beginnings—as an area of vegetable farms and nurseries. Then folks who could afford homes with a view began building them on these ramparts.

The city's convention and visitors bureau publishes a **walking brochure** that takes you through twenty-two level and downhill blocks of this steeply tilted neighborhood. If you can't find a copy, here's an abridged version:

Begin at the **Haas-Lilienthal House**, a resplendent Victorian mansion-museum at 2007 Franklin St. (Washington). Stroll three blocks west along Washington, past **Lafayette Park** and the **Adolph Spreckles** mansion at 2080 Washington. Turn right onto Laguna for a block, then left onto Jackson and right onto Buchanan for two blocks. (Still with us?)

Go left onto Broadway and you'll see a classy **Georgian-style home** just off Broadway at 2550 Webster. Continuing through rows of opulent abodes, note the **Sacred Heart Convent**, built into three turn-of-the-century homes in the 2200 block of Broadway. From there, the guide suggests that you follow Fillmore down to Union street and walk along Cow Hollow to the **Octagon House** at Union and Gough.

Most of Pacific Heights is a bit hilly for walking. In fact, it contains many of the city's steepest streets. As a cruel joke on those of us who still drive stick-shifts, some of these streets have traffic signals or stop signs just short of their crests.

You can see scores of deluxe dwellings by driving

a meandering route through the neighborhood. Many of the more ornate ones are along **Jackson, Pacific** and **Broadway** going east and west. Traveling north and south (uphill and down dale), you'll see splendid examples along **Franklin, Gough, Octavia, Laguna** and **Buchanan**.

Then, check your brakes and start looking for a place to park.

WHAT TO SEE & DO

Union Street shopping ●
The *Union Street Shopping & Dining Guide* is available from various merchants, or contact: Union Street Association, 1685 Union St., San Francisco, CA 94124; phone 441-7055.

Haas-Lilienthal House ● △△△
2007 Franklin St. (Jackson); 441-3000. Tours Wednesday from noon to 4 and Sunday 11 to 4:30. Adults $4, seniors and kids under 13, $2. A wonderful assemblage of turrets, towers, cupolas and friezes, this busy 1886 Queen Anne beauty is home to the Foundation for San Francisco's Architectural Heritage. Tours are conducted through rooms furnished with period antiques. If you can't get there for a tour, the structure is still worth viewing from the outside.

Lafayette Park ● △△
Pacific Heights, corner of Washington and Gough. This four-block square of green offers respite from Pacific Heights hill-climbing. Occupying the highest point in the neighborhood, the park provides smashing views of the city.

The Octagon House ● △△
2645 Gough St. (Union); 441-7512. Second and fourth Thursdays and second Sundays noon to 3. Free; donations accepted. Looking like a misplaced lighthouse, this odd structure houses a museum of Colonial and Federal silver, pewter, furniture and documents. It's operated by the Colonial Dames of America.

WHERE TO DINE

Balboa Cafe ● △△ $$$
3199 Fillmore St. (Greenwich); 921-3944. California-American regional; dinners $12 to $20; full bar

service. Weekdays 11 a.m. to 11:30 p.m., Saturday 10:30 to 11:30, Sunday 10:30 to 10:30. Reservations for six or more only; informal. Major credit cards. The Balboa is a designer bistro with a turn-of-the-century look and a lively bar scene. The menu lists upscale hamburgers, pastas, regional dishes and complex salads.

Bepple's Pie Shop ● △△ $

1934 Union St. (Laguna) and 2142 Chestnut St. (Steiner); 459-7868. Desserts and light meals, $6 to $8; wine and beer. Monday-Wednesday 7 a.m. to 11:30 p.m., Thursday 7 to midnight, Friday 7 to 1 a.m., Saturday 9 to 1, Sunday 9 to 10. Casual; no reservations or credit cards. What's for dessert? How about tasty American-style deep-dish pies, served in a homey atmosphere of warm woods and wainscoting? Both locations also serve full "country breakfasts" and light meals of meat pies, quiche and such.

Bonta ● △△△ $$

2223 Union St. (Fillmore); 929-0407. Italian; dinners $10 to $18; wine and beer. Tuesday-Thursday 5:30 to 10:30, Friday-Saturday 5:30 to 11, Sunday 5 to 10. Informal to casual; reservations advised. MC/VISA. Highly regarded by local food critics, this tiny cafe serves generous portions of perfectly prepared pasta and other things Italian. Seafood dishes are exceptional; try the *fettuccine de mare* with assorted seafoods or the fried *calamari*. In-house desserts are wickedly tasty. With uncarpeted tile floors, the place gets a bit noisy, but most patrons seem too preoccupied with their pasta to fret about it.

Cafe Majestic ● △△△△ $$$

1500 Sutter St. (in the Majestic Hotel at Gough); 776-6400. California cuisine; dinners $15 to $24; full bar service. Breakfast weekdays 7 to 10:30, brunch weekends 8 to 2, lunch Tuesday-Friday 11:30 to 2, dinner daily 5:45 to 9:30. Reservations advised; dressy to informal. Major credit cards. The Majestic Hotel and its adjoining cafe are striking examples of turn-of-the-century opulence. The innovative menu offers interesting early San Francisco dishes, as well as *nouveau* low calorie/low cholesterol fare.

Chateau Suzanne ● △△△△ $$$$ Ø

1449 Lombard St. (Van Ness); 771-9326. French-Chinese; six-course dinners $25.50 to $32.50; full bar service. Tuesday-Saturday 5:30 to 9:30. Reservations suggested; dressy to informal. MC/VISA, AMEX. We're letting the culinary cat out of the bag. Overlooked by many, this is one of the city's most delightful restaurants. Entrees—French with Chinese accents—are as pretty as they taste, yet they're low-fat and low-cholesterol. The setting is one of simple elegance and the smiling man who takes your coat is the creator of all this—former busboy and Empress of China manager Stanley Toy.

Chestnut Street Grill ● △△ $

2231 Chestnut St. (Scott); 922-5558. Light American; meals $5 to $10; full bar service. Monday-Thursday 11 to 11, Friday 11 to midnight, Saturday 10 to midnight, Sunday 10 to 11. No reservations; casual. MC/VISA, AMEX. Scores of innovative sandwiches are named for regulars at this lively Marina District hangout. The place is decorated mostly with camaraderie.

Gelco's ● △△△ $$$

1450 Lombard St. (Van Ness); 928-1054. European; lamb specialties; dinners $12 to $20; full bar service. Daily 5:30 to 11:30. Reservations accepted; casual. Major credit cards. The look is European country inn and the specialty is baby lamb, served in a variety of ways with generous five-course dinners. *Mousaka,* steak, veal and fish also appear on the small menu.

L'Entrecote de Paris ● △△△ $$$ Ø

2032 Union St. (also at 230 California St., in the Financial District); 931-5006. French; dinners $12 to $18; full bar service. Monday-Thursday 11:30 to midnight, Friday-Saturday 11:30 to 2 a.m. Reservations suggested; informal. Major credit cards. Seemingly transported from Paris, this cute little bistro is totally French in decor, menu and friendly attitude. Try the cafe's namesake dish—Parisian-style steak with *pommes frites.* Live music is featured most nights.

L'Escargot ● △△△ $$$

1890 Union St. (Octavia); 567-0222. French-continental; dinners $13 to $20; wine and beer. Daily 5:30 to 10:30. *Reservations suggested; informal. Major credit cards.* Tucked under the eves of a Victorian, this charmingly French country-style restaurant with pink nappery is noted for its *escargot*, of course, as well as rack of lamb, *Dijon* veal and pork *Normandie*.

La Barca ● △△ $$

2036 Lombard St. (Fillmore); 921-2221. Mexican; dinners $6 to $14; full bar service. Daily 4 to 11. Reservations accepted, casual. MC/VISA, AMEX. Looking more Latin than necessary, La Barca is a study in Spanish tile, ornamental iron and even a waterfall. The menu swings from smashed beans and rice to savory Mexican seafood.

The Mansions Hotel Restaurant ● △△△△ $$$$

2220 Sacramento St. (Laguna), 929-9444. Continental; full bar service. Dinner shows Monday-Thursday at 6:45 for $35 prix fixe, Friday-Saturday at 6:15 for $40. Reservations essential; dressy. Major credit cards. Excellent dinners are served in an opulent Victorian dining room, but that's only the end. In the beginning, the meal is preceded by a magic show conducted by a friendly ghost or two. On weekends, owner Bob Pritikin entertains with his musical saw and performs such stunts as "The incredible Peking Snow Duck Double Transfer." That quiet hum you hear in the background comes from a Lawrence Welk bubble machine.

Marina Cafe ● △△△ $$

2417 Lombard St. (Scott); 929-7241. Italian-seafood; dinners $10 to $15; full bar service. Monday-Saturday 5 to 11, Sunday 4 to 10. Reservations accepted; casual. Major credit cards. Dressed in early San Francisco marble and mahogany, this attractive cafe peddles a tasty line of fresh seafood entrees and appetizing pasta. The *cioppino* is particularly noteworthy.

Olive's Gourmet Pizza ● △△ $ ∅

3249 Scott St. (Lombard); 567-4488. Pizza, pasta; meals $5.50 to $10.50; wine and beer. Sunday-Thursday 11:30 to 10:30, Friday-Saturday 11:30 to 11:30. Reservations for six or more only; casual. No credit cards. Is gourmet pizza a self-canceling phrase? Olive's comes close to gourmet; a hundred varieties are served, with imported cheeses and assorted toppings over a cornmeal crust.

Perry's ● △△△ $$ Ø
1944 Union St. (Laguna); 922-9022. American; dinners $10 to $25; full bar service. Daily 11 a.m. to 1 a.m. Reservations advised; informal. MC/VISA, AMEX. Perry Butler's San Francisco-style bistro has been a Union Street fixture since Christ was a corporal. It's a place-to-be-seen bar as well as a worthy restaurant. Honest American steaks, chops, fresh seafood and excellent hamburgers are served to the faithful. The folks are even remarkably nice to strangers.

Pietro's Ristorante ● △△△ $$
1851 Union St. (Laguna); 563-4157. Italian; dinners $13 to $18; full bar service. Daily 5:30 to 10:45. Reservations accepted; informal. MC/VISA, AMEX. Tucked into a cozy alley, Pietro's brims with oldstyle chianti-bottle ambiance. It serves a variety of homemade pastas, along with good *scaloppine, osso buco* and *pesce fresco.* (For you folks from Iowa, that's fresh fish.)

Pizzeria Uno ● △△△ $
2200 Lombard St. (Steiner); 563-3144. Pizza; meals $7 to $10; full bar service. Daily 11 a.m. to midnight. No reservations; casual. MC/VISA, AMEX. In case you missed it in the Fisherman's Wharf chapter, Uno serves the city's best pizza—a deep-dish Chicago style that arrives piping hot in its own personal skillet. Salads, sandwiches and soups are peddled as well. This and the Wharf place have attractive old-style decor.

Prego ● △△△ $$$ Ø
2000 Union St. (Buchanan); 563-3305. Italian; dinners $15 to $20; full bar service. Daily 11:30 to midnight. Reservations essential; informal. MC/VISA, AMEX. A culinary high-tech creation of Spectrum Foods, Prego peddles northern Italian fare seasoned with California *nouveau* accents. A recent dinner of shrimp-tomato-garlic-hot pepper pasta was rather memorable. The look is contemporary: drop lamps, white nappery and modern art. Try not to spoil your appetite with the wonderful skinny breadsticks.

Scott's Seafood ● ΔΔΔ $$$ Ø
2400 Lombard St. (Scott); 563-8988. Seafood; dinners $15 to $22; full bar service. Monday-Thursday 11:30 to 10:30, Friday-Saturday 11:30 to 11, Sunday 9:30 a.m. to 10:30 p.m. Informal to casual; major credit cards. The city's best seafoods aren't served at Fisherman's Wharf and Scott's is durable proof. A long-time Marina District favorite, this handsomely furnished fish parlor offers aquatic dishes from all over the world.

Vlasta's European Restaurant ● ΔΔΔ $$
2420 Lombard St. (Scott), 931-7533. Mid-European; dinners $10 to $15; full bar service. Tuesday-Sunday 5:30 to 11. Informal to casual; reservations accepted. MC/VISA, AMEX. This restaurant on Lombard's motel row features a tasty mix of Czechoslovakian, Hungarian and German fare—ranging from Bohemian duckling to *rouladin*. The decor is charmingly European, with wainscoting and dark woods and the prices are surprisingly modest.

WHAT TO DO AFTER DARK

Paul's Saloon ● ΔΔ (bluegrass/country)
3251 Scott St. (Lombard); 922-2456. This long-time favorite twangs out country and bluegrass music most nights, with an occasional stand-up comic for variety.

Pasand Restaurant & Lounge ● ΔΔ (jazz)
1875 Union St. (Laguna); 922-4498. It's a pleasant mix of East Indian food and good instrumental and vocal jazz, spiced with a little Latin music.

Pierce Street Annex ● ΔΔ (variety, open mike)
3138 Fillmore St. (Greenwich); 567-1400. A lively singles and sports bar, the annex offers musical and variety entertainment, including amateur "Starmaker" shows.

WHERE TO SLEEP
(Detailed listings in Chapter 16)
Rooms from $50 to $99
Buena Vista Motor Inn ● *1599 Lombard St. (Gough)*
Lombard Motor Inn ● *1475 Lombard St. (Franklin)*
Quality Hotel ● *2775 Van Ness Ave. (Lombard)*

The Queen Anne ● *1590 Sutter St. (Octavia)*
Star Motel ● *1727 Lombard St. (Laguna)*
Town House Motel ● *1650 Lombard St. (Gough)*
Lombard Plaza Motel ● *2026 Lombard St. (Fill-
more)*

Bed & breakfast inns

Art Center Bed & Breakfast ● *1902 Filbert St.
(Laguna)*
The Bed & Breakfast Inn ● *Four Charlton Court
(Union)*
Edward II Bed & Breakfast ● *3155 Scott St.
(Lombard)*
The Mansions Hotel ● *2220 Sacramento St.
(Laguna)*
Union Street Inn ● *2229 Union St. (Fillmore)*

Sixteen

PILLOW PLACES
Where to rest your head

LODGINGS ARE NOT INEXPENSIVE in San Francisco. An ordinary hotel room with a view of a brick wall across the alley can go for $100 and beyond. An eleven percent city room tax nudges it even higher.

However, you can get a suitable room for less than $50. We offer here a sampler of hotels, motels and inns listed by price range. Generally, lodgings outlying areas are less expensive. We list some examples at the end of this chapter.

If we were playing tourist, we'd find affordable lodging right in the city, so we could awaken to its sights, sounds and smells. Who wants to commute when they're on vacation? We also favor bed and breakfast inns and boutique hotels. They aren't necessarily cheaper than other lodgings, but they're often more charming and many are in restored Victorians. Several are included in this chapter.

For a more complete list of budget lodgings (and other things cheap), spend $6.95 for Louis E. Madison's **San Francisco on a Shoestring**. It's published by A.M. Zimmerman & Co., 2210 Jackson St., Suite 404, San Francisco, CA 94115; (415) 929-7577. We've never met the author and have no financial interest in this book. We're just trying to be helpful.

Although motels and hotels are scattered throughout the city, most are grouped in four areas: downtown/Financial District, Fisherman's Wharf, on Van Ness Avenue north of the Civic Center and along

Lombard Street—the city's motel row. Of course, there's the usual cluster of business-oriented hotels near San Francisco International Airport, in San Mateo County.

Price ranges shown are for a double room during the summer tourist season. They were current at press time but—obviously—are subject to change. Before we begin, we'll repeat our pricing and rating systems from the introduction:

$ ● a standard double for under $50

$$ ● $50 to $74

$$$ ● $75 to $99

$$$$ ● $100 to $149

$$$$$ ● $150 or more

◻ **Adequate** ● A clean place that meets minimum standards.

◻◻ **Good** ● A well-run establishment with most essentials, such as room phones, color TV and oversized beds.

◻◻◻ **Very Good** ● Substantially above average, generally with a pool, restaurant and other amenities.

◻◻◻◻ **Excellent** ● An exceptional property with elegant rooms; most such places will have extensive facilities.

◻◻◻◻◻ **Awesome** ● Outstanding by every measure; one of the best hotels in the country.

Ø non-smoking rooms available

ROOMS FOR $100 AND UP

Archbishop's Mansion ● ◻◻◻◻◻ **$$$$** Ø **(Alamo Square)**

1000 Fulton St. (Steiner), SF 94117; (415) 563-7872. Doubles and singles $100 to $285, suites $189 to $285. MC/VISA, AMEX. The city's most beautifully-restored mansion; Victorian-French style with 15 elegantly done rooms. TV and phones; some rooms with fireplaces and spas. Full breakfast, hot beverage and wine service. Beautifully furnished sitting rooms, sweeping grand staircase. Once the home of San Francisco Archbishop Patrick Riordan.

Campton Place ● △△△△ **$$$$$** Ø (downtown)

340 Stockton St. (Post), SF 94108; (800) 235-4300 or (415) 781-5555. Doubles and singles $180 to $300. Major credit cards. Understated elegance best describes this 126-room hotel. Features include TV, room phones, terry robes, free newspapers and Financial District limo service. Equally noted is **Campton Place Restaurant,** serving from 7 a.m. to 10 p.m. daily; American cuisine; dinners $30 to $70.

The Donatello ● △△△△ **$$$$$** (downtown)

501 Post St. (Mason), SF 94102; (800) 792-9837 in California, (800) 227-3184 outside, (415) 441-7100. Doubles $155 to $165, singles $140 to $160, suites $200 to $375. Major credit cards. The decor in its 140 rooms might be described as elegantly modern Italian. TV movies, room phones, morning newspaper, other amenities; some refrigerators. Locally-acclaimed **Ristorante Donatello** serves from 7 to 10:30 a.m. and 5:30 to 11 p.m., Northern Italian, dinners $35 to $65; see listing in Chapter 3.

The Fairmont ● △△△△△ **$$$$$** Ø (Nob Hill)

950 Mason St. (California); (800) 527-4727 or (415) 772-5000. Doubles $175 to $265, singles $145 to $235, suites $450 to $2,000. Major credit cards. We rate the Fairmont and Westin St. Francis as the city's leading world-class hotels. Built at the turn of the century by silver magnate William Fair, the Fairmont is rich in history and opulence. Its 595 rooms and suites have TV movies, room phones and all other amenities; shopping arcade, several bars including a sky room lounge; **five restaurants** including locally popular Squire and Mason's; dinners from $15 to $40.

Four Seasons Clift ● △△△△△ **$$$$$** Ø (downtown)

495 Geary St. (Taylor), SF 94102; (800) 332-3442 or (415) 775-4700. Doubles $180 to $290, singles $180 to $270, suites $305 to $1,200. Major credit cards. One of the city's finest mid-sized hotels, with 180 rooms. TV movies, room phones, bathrobes, other amenities; limo service to the Financial District. **The French Room** serves 6:30 a.m. to 10:30 p.m., California cuisine; dinners from $30.

Galleria Park Hotel ● △△△ $$$$ Ø (downtown)

191 Sutter St. (Montgomery), SF 94111; (800) 792-9639 or (415) 781-3060. Doubles and singles $120 to $130, suites $139 to $250. Major credit cards. A 177-room hotel adjacent to Galleria Shopping Center. Nicely-appointed rooms with TV movies, phones, honor bars; running track and mini-park; atrium lobby with fireplace. **Bentley's Seafood Grill** open weekdays 11:30 a.m. to 10 p.m., Saturdays 5 to 10; dinners $16 to $30. See listing in Chapter 3.

Grand Hyatt ● △△△ $$$$$ Ø (downtown)

345 Stockton St. (Post), SF 94108; (800) 233-1234 or (415) 398-1234. Doubles $205 to $260, singles $175 to $230, suites $350 to $1,550. Major credit cards. Formerly Hyatt Union Square; 693-room luxury hotel with TV movies, room phones, refrigerators, health club and other amenities. **Plaza Restaurant** serves from 6:30 a.m. to 11:30 p.m., American-continental; dinner $20 to $25.

Handlery Union Square ● △△△ $$$$ Ø (downtown)

351 Geary St. (Powell), SF 94102; (800) 223-0888 or (415) 781-7800. Doubles $109 to $145, singles $99 to $130. Major credit cards. Older refurbished hotel with 377 rooms. TV movies, room phones, coffee and tea makers; outdoor pool, sauna. **New Joe's** restaurant serves 7 a.m. to 10:30 p.m., American-Italian; dinners $12 to $25.

Holiday Inn ● △△△ $$$$ Ø (Civic Center)

50 Eighth St. (Market), SF 94103; (800) HOLIDAY or (415) 626-6103. Doubles $114 to $145, singles $99 to $130. Major credit cards. Free guest parking; 389 rooms. TV movies, room phones; outdoor pool. **Jubilee Restaurant** serves 6 a.m. to 10 p.m.; American; dinners $11 to $14.

Holiday Inn ● △△△ $$$$ Ø (Financial District/Chinatown)

750 Kearny St. (Washington), SF 94108; (800) HOLIDAY or (415) 433-6600. Doubles $114 to $150, singles $99 to $139, suites $350 to $450. Major credit cards. Free guest parking; 566 rooms. TV movies, room phones, outdoor pool; free Financial District limo service. **Lotus Blossom Restaurant** serves

6:30 a.m. to 2 p.m. and 5:30 to 10; California and Oriental fare; dinners $7 to $16.

Holiday Inn ● △△△ $$$$ Ø **(Fisherman's Wharf)**

1300 Columbus Ave. (North Point), SF 94133; (800) HOLIDAY or (415) 771-9000. Doubles and singles $106 to $205, suites $250 to $450. Major credit cards. Free guest parking; 580 rooms. TV movies, room phones; small swimming pool. **Charlie's** restaurant serves from 6:30 a.m. to 10 p.m.; American-continental; dinners $11.75 to $17.25.

Holiday Inn ● △△△ $$$$$ Ø **(Union Square)**

480 Sutter St. (Powell), SF 94108; (800) HOLIDAY or (415) 398-8900. Doubles $157 to $175, singles $137 to $155, suites $350 to $650. Major credit cards. Located on Union Square, the downtown Holiday Inn has 401 rooms. TV movies, room phones; health club. **White Elephant** restaurant open daily 6:30 a.m. to 10 p.m.; continental; dinners $15 to $25.

The Huntington ● △△△△ $$$$$ **(Nob Hill)**

1075 California St. (Taylor), SF 94108; (800) 652-1539 in California, (800) 227-4683 outside, (415) 474-5400. Doubles $180 to $230, singles $160 to $210, suites $245 to $640. Major credit cards. An outstanding small hotel with 140 rooms and suites, individually decorated with antiques and artworks. Its quiet elegance is often sought by visiting celebrities. TV movies, room phones, luxury amenities, tea and sherry, limo service. **Big Four** restaurant open daily 7 a.m. to 10:30 p.m.; contemporary cuisine; dinners $22 to $32. See listing in Chapter 3.

Hyatt Regency ● △△△△ $$$$$ Ø **(waterfront)**

Five Embarcadero Center (Market), SF 94111; (800) 233-1234 or (415) 788-1234. Doubles from $238, singles from $218, suites from $315. Curiously typewriter-shaped from the outside, it has the city's most striking lobby—a 17-story atrium with a spill-over fountain; 803 rooms. TV movies, room phones, self-service bar, other amenities. **Mrs. Candy's, The Market Place** and rotating roof-top **Equinox** restaurants serve from 6 a.m. to 1 a.m.; American and California cuisine; dinners $12 to $25.

Hyde Park Suites ● △△△ $$$$$ Ø (Fisherman's Wharf)

2655 Hyde St. (North Point), SF 94109; (800) 227-3608 or (415) 771-0200. All suites with full kitchens, $165 to $220. Major credit cards. Small suite hotel with 24 kitchen units. TV, room phones, free newspaper; continental breakfast, nightly wine, morning limo drop-off.

Mandarin Oriental ● △△△△△ $$$$$ Ø (Financial District)

222 Sansome St. (California), SF 94104; (800) 622-0404 or (415) 885-0999. Doubles $280 to $390, singles $245 to $355, suites $475 to $975. Major credit cards. The Mandarin is one of the city's premier mid-sized hotels, with 160 exquisitely furnished rooms. Tucked into eleven upper floors of the new 48-story First Interstate Center, all rooms have city views. Amenities include remote TV with movies, room phones, mini-bar refrigerators and—oh, my— bathtubs with a view. Locally popular **Silks** restaurant serves weekdays from 11:30 a.m. to 2 p.m. and nightly from 6 to 10 p.m., Sunday brunch 8 to 2; California-Asian cuisine, dinners $25 to $35. See listing in Chapter 3.

Mark Hopkins ● △△△△ $$$$$ Ø (Nob Hill)

One Nob Hill (Mason at California), SF 94108; (800) 327-0200 or (415) 392-3434. Doubles $200 to $305, singles $180 to $275, suites $375 to $1,400. Major credit cards. Old California refinement is preserved in this elegantly coiffed 391-room hotel. Its Top of the Mark sky room is a long-time San Francisco landmark. TV movies, room phones, mini bars, free newspapers, other amenities. **Nob Hill Restaurant** open daily 6:30 a.m. to 10:30 p.m.; French-California cuisine, dinners $19 to $27.

Marriott ● △△△ $$$$$ Ø (Fisherman's Wharf)

1250 Columbus Ave. (Bay), SF 94133; (800) 228-9290 or (415) 775-7555. Doubles $184 to $212, singles $164 to $192, suites $235 to $495. Major credit cards. Attractive low-rise hotel with 255 rooms. TV movies, room phones, mini-bars; exercise facility. **Spada** restaurant serves from 6:30 a.m. to 10:30

p.m.; American-Italian-seafood; dinners $12 to $25. See listing in Chapter 7.

Miyako Hotel ● △△△△ **$$$$** Ø **(Japan Center)**

1625 Post St. (Laguna), SF 94115; (800) 533-4567 or (415) 922-3200. Doubles $115 to $180, singles $95 to $160, suites $130 to $180. Major credit cards. This stylish 223-room hotel offers a choice of of traditional Japanese or Western style units or distinctive East-West rooms with both beds and *futons*. TV movies, room phones and other amenities; some rooms with private saunas and spa tubs. Japanese decor in rooms and public areas. **Asuka Brasserie** serves 6:30 a.m. to 10 p.m.; dinners $16 to $30. See listing in Chapter 12.

Monticello Inn ● △△△ **$$$$** Ø **(downtown)**

127 Ellis St. (Powell), SF 94102; (800) 669-7777 or (415) 392-8800. Doubles and singles $119 to $159, suites $139 to $159. Major credit cards. Early American style inn with 91 rooms. TV movies, room phones, mini-bars; continental breakfast and wine service; nearby workout facilities and pool. **Corona Bar & Grill** open from 11 to 11; Mexican-Southwestern fare, dinner $15 to $26. See listing in Chapter 3.

Pan Pacific Hotel ● △△△△ **$$$$$** Ø **(downtown)**

500 Post St. (Mason), SF 94102; (800) 533-6465 or (415) 771-8600. Doubles and singles $175 to $350. Major credit cards. Formerly the Portman, this 330-room hotel has a sleekly modern look. TV movies, room phones, other amenities; personal valets, Rolls Royce shuttle to Financial District. **Pacific Grill** serves from 7:30 a.m. to 10:30 p.m., Pacific Rim cuisine; dinners from $10.

Parc Fifty Five ● △△△△ **$$$$$** Ø **(downtown)**

55 Cyril Magnin St. (Eddy), SF 94012; (800) 338-1338 or (415) 392-8000. Doubles $190 to $235, singles $160 to $205, suites $340 to $1,100. Major credit cards. Formerly the Ramada Renaissance, this luxury hotel has San Francisco-style bay windows on its 1,003 rooms. TV movies, room phones, free breakfast and newspaper, wet bar; health club and business service center. **Corintia Ristorante** serves from 5:30 to 11 p.m. daily; upscale Italian. The more casual **Veranda Restaurant** is open from 6:30 a.m. to 10:30 p.m.

Park Hyatt ● △△△△ $$$$$ Ø (Financial District)

333 Battery St. (Clay), SF 94111; (800) 233-1234 or (415) 392-1234. Doubles $265 to $295, singles $235 to $265, suites $295 to $1,500. Major credit cards. Luxurious 360-room hotel with all amenities, opened in 1989. Remote TV, room phones, terry robes, mini-bars, writing desks, fruit bowl and candies; Mercedes courtesy cars. **Park Grill** open 6:30 a.m. to 10 p.m.; international menu; dinners from $15; Sunday "jazz brunch" from 10 to 2. Adjacent to Embarcadero Center.

San Francisco Hilton ● △△△△ $$$$$ Ø (downtown)

333 O'Farrell St. (Mason), SF 94102; (800) HIL-TONS or (415) 771-1400. Doubles $185 to $245, singles $160 to $220, suites $275 to $2,100. Major credit cards. City's largest hotel with 1,891 rooms. Luxury furnishings with TV movies, room phones, mini-bars, other amenities; pool, health club, shops. **Cafe on the Square, Kiku of Tokyo, Cityscape** sky room and **Lehr's Steakery** restaurants serve from 6 a.m. to 2 a.m.; dinners $12 to $29.

Shannon Court Hotel ● △△△ $$$$ Ø (downtown)

550 Geary St. (Taylor), SF 94102; (800) 821-0493 or (415) 775-5000. Doubles $100 to $125, singles $90 to $115, suites $200 to $275. Major credit cards. With 173 attractively-furnished rooms, this small hotel features continental breakfast, afternoon tea and other amenities. TV, room phones, some refrigerators. **La Mere Dusquene** serves from 5 to 10 p.m.; French; dinners $15 to $25.

Sheraton Palace ● △△△△ $$$$$ Ø (Financial District)

Two Montgomery St. (Market), SF 94103; (800) 325-3535 or (415) 392-8600. Doubles $200 to $260, singles $180 to $240, suites $350 to $1,500. Major credit cards. Sparkling new after a complete renovation, the legendary Sheraton has 550 stylishly-furnished rooms. TV movies, room phones, refrigerators, free newspapers; health club, spa and business center. The **Garden Court** with its elegant 1800s atrium skylight is a focal point, noted for its Sunday brunches.

Sir Francis Drake ● △△△ **$$$$ Ø (downtown)**

450 Powell St. (Sutter), SF 94102; (800) 652-1668 in California, (800) 227-5480 outside, (415) 392-7755. Doubles $140 to $210, singles $120 to $190. Major credit cards. Many of the venerable Drake's 417 rooms have been refurbished. TV movies, room phones, some refrigerators; exercise room. **Crusty's Sourdough Cafe** serves from 6:30 a.m. to 10:30 p.m.; American; dinners $11 to $17.

Stanford Court ● △△△△ **$$$$$ Ø (Nob Hill)**

905 California St. (Powell), SF 94108; (800) HO-TELS-1 or (415) 989-3500. Doubles $215 to $265, singles $185 to $235. Major credit cards. Upscale 392-room hotel with carriage entry; European decor. TV movies, room phones, complimentary coffee and newspapers, all amenities. **Fournou's Oven** serves from 6:30 a.m. to 2 p.m. and 5:30 to 11 p.m.; American cuisine; dinners $25 to $45.

Travelodge ● △△△ **$$$$ Ø (Fisherman's Wharf)**

250 Beach St. (Powell), SF 94133; (800) 255-3050 or (415) 392-6700. Doubles $107 to $175, singles $95 to $175, suites $225 to $300. Major credit cards. Many of its 250 rooms have bay or city views. TV movies, room phones, morning coffee and newspaper; free parking. Adjacent to Pier 39. **Angellinia's Cafe** features American fare and seafood, open from 7 a.m.

Villa Florence ● △△△ **$$$$ Ø (downtown)**

225 Powell St. (O'Farrell), SF 94102; (800) 553-4411 or (415) 397-7700. Doubles and singles from $129, suites $139 to $189. Major credit cards. Handsomely redone hotel with 177 rooms. TV movies, room phones, honor bar-refrigerators; free coffee in lobby. **Kuleto's** restaurant serves 7 to 11 p.m. Monday-Friday and 8 to 11 Saturday; northern Italian; dinners $18 to $25. See listing in Chapter 3.

Westin St. Francis ● △△△△△ $$$$$ Ø (downtown)

335 Powell St. (Geary), SF 94102; (800) 228-3000 or (415) 397-7000. Doubles $195 to $315, singles $160 to $280, suites $300 to $1,575. Major credit cards. One of San Francisco's two great world class hotels; 1,200 rooms; elegant lobby; shopping arcade. TV movies, room phones, refreshment centers, all luxury amenities. **Five restaurants** serve seafood, California, continental and American cuisine, various hours, dinners $7 to $30. See **Victor's** restaurant listing in Chapter 3.

ROOMS FROM $50 TO $99

Atherton Hotel ● △△ $$ (Civic Center)

685 Ellis St. (Hyde), SF 94109; (800) 227-3608 or (415) 474-5720. Doubles and singles $49 to $79. Major credit cards. Older refurbished hotel with 75 rooms; TV movies, room phones; complimentary snacks and wines; **Atherton Grille** serves from 7 a.m. to 2 weekdays and 8 to 1 weekends; American; full bar service.

Amsterdam Hotel ● △△ $$ (downtown/Nob Hill)

749 Taylor St. (Sutter), SF 94108; (800) 637-3444 or (415) 673-3277. Doubles $49 to $70, singles $44 to $65. MC/VISA, AMEX. Pension-style hotel with 34 rooms; TV, room phones, free breakfast.

Beresford Arms ● △△ $$$ (downtown)

701 Post St. (Jones), SF 94109; (800) 533-6533 or (415) 673-2600. Doubles $79 to $120, singles $69 to $120, kitchenettes $95 to $120, suites $120. Major credit cards. Redecorated older hotel with 96 rooms; TV, room phones, honor bars; free morning coffee, tea and pastries.

Buena Vista Motor Inn ● △△ $$ Ø (Marina)

1599 Lombard St. (Gough), SF 94123; (800) 835-4980 or (415) 923-9600. Doubles $71 to $84, singles $62 to $68. Major credit cards. Fifty rooms; TV movies, room phones, free coffee; sun deck; free parking.

Canterbury Hotel ● △△ $$$ Ø (downtown)

740 Sutter St. (Taylor), SF 94109; (800) 652-1614 or (415) 474-6464. Doubles $85 to $129, singles $79 to $109, suites $125 to $250. Major credit cards. Older, well-kept hotel with 250 rooms. TV movies, room phones, refrigerators; exercise room. **Lehr's Greenhouse Restaurant** serves from 6:30 to 11 p.m., Sunday brunch from 10 to 2; American; see listing in Chapter 3.

Cartwright Hotel ● △△ $$$ Ø **(downtown)**
524 Sutter St. (Powell); SF 94102; (800) 227-3844 or (415) 421-2865. Doubles $99, singles $90, suites $140 to $160. Major credit cards. This refurbished 114-room hotel features TV movies and room phones; refrigerators and hair dryers available. **Teddy's Restaurant** serves breakfast daily, 7 to 11:30.

Chancellor Hotel ● △△△ $$$ Ø **(downtown)**
433 Powell St. (Post), SF 94102; (800) 428-4748 or (415) 362-2004. Doubles $97 to $107, singles $87 to $92, suites $155. Major credit cards. Older hotel with 140 newly-decorated rooms; TV movies, room phones, desks. **By the Square Restaurant** serves 7 a.m. to 10 p.m., California-Italian, dinners $15 to $25.

Commodore Hotel ● △△ $$ **(downtown)**
825 Sutter St. (Jones), SF 94109; (800) 338-6848 or (415) 923-6800. Doubles $45 to $90, singles $40 to $85. Major credit cards. Older, refurbished 113-unit hotel with TV and phones in rooms. **Coffee shop** serves breakfast and lunch from 7 to 2; American, meals from $6; full bar service.

Day's Inn San Francisco ● △△△ $$ Ø **(near park and zoo)**
2600 Sloat Blvd. (Great Highway), SF 94116; (800) 325-2525 or (415) 665-9000. Doubles and singles $60 to $80, suites $105 to $130. Major credit cards. New 33-room motel across from San Francisco Zoo. TV, room phones, microwaves, refrigerators; free continental breakfast, free parking.

Great Highway Motor Inn ● △△ $$ **(near Golden Gate Park)**
1234 Great Highway (Lincoln), SF 94122; 731-6644. Doubles $60 to $78, singles $54 to $72. Major credit cards. Located near ocean beach and Cliff House; 54 rooms with TV and room phones; free parking.

King George Hotel ● △△△ $$$ (downtown)

334 Mason St. (Geary), SF 94102; (800) 288-6005 or (415) 781-5050. Doubles $99, singles $89, suites $194. Major credit cards. Charming English style hotel, with a tinkling lobby piano, marble staircase and cage elevator. TV movies and phones in rooms. **Bread and Honey Tearoom** serves buffet breakfast from 7 to 10 and English High Tea, Monday-Saturday afternoon 3 to 6:30.

Lombard Motor Inn ● △△△ $$ (Marina)

1475 Lombard St. (Franklin), SF 94123; (800) 835-3639 or (415) 441-6000. Doubles $70 to $82, singles $60 to $65. Major credit cards. On Lombard Street's "Motel row"; 48 rooms. TV, room phones, free coffee; free indoor parking.

Miyako Inn ● △△ $$$ Ø (Japantown)

1800 Sutter St. (Buchanan), SF 94115; (800) 528-1234 or (415) 921-4000. Doubles $83 to $89, singles $73 to $79. Major credit cards. Formerly the Kyoto Inn; near Japan Center; 125 rooms. TV, room phones. **Cafe Mums** serves from 7 a.m. to 10 p.m.; continental-Japanese; dinners $12.50 to $25.

Pacific Bay Inn ● △△ $$ (downtown)

520 Jones St. (Geary), SF 94102; 673-0234. Doubles $65 to $75, singles $55 to $65. Major credit cards. Attractive small hotel with 84 rooms; TV, room phones, free continental breakfast. **Dottie's True Blue Cafe** serves breakfast and lunch weekdays 7 to 2 and weekends 7 to 1; American menu; Fifties decor; meals from $7; wine and beer.

Phoenix Inn ● △△△ $$$ (Civic Center)

601 Eddy St. (Larkin), SF 94109; (800) 248-9466 outside California only, (415) 776-1380. Doubles $89 to $125, singles $79 to $125, suites $110 to $125. Major credit cards. Small full-service inn with 44 rooms, garden, free parking, heated pool, continental breakfast. TV movies, room phones. **Miss Pearl's Jam House** serves 11:30 to 2 and 6 to 11; Caribbean fare; dinners $5 to $16; full bar service.

Quality Hotel ● △△ $$$ Ø (Marina)

2775 Van Ness Ave. (Lombard), SF 94109; (800) 221-2222 or (415) 928-5000. Doubles $79 to $130, singles $67 to $118. Major credit cards. Free guest parking; 132 rooms. TV movies, room phones; continental breakfast. **Brandi's Restaurant** serves from 5 to 9 p.m.; American; dinners $14.70 to $21.70.

The Queen Anne ● △△△△ $$$ (Pacific Heights)

1590 Sutter St. (Octavia), SF 94109; (800) 227-3970 or (415) 441-2828. Doubles and singles $94 to $125. Major credit cards. European-style guest house in beautifully restored Victorian; 49 rooms. TV, room phones; continental breakfast and morning newspaper; afternoon tea and sherry; attractive living room lobby with fireplace.

The Raphael Hotel ● △△△ $$$ Ø (downtown)

386 Geary St. (Mason), SF 94102; (800) 821-5343 or (415) 986-2000. Doubles $94 to $115, singles $81 to $102, suites $135 to $195. Major credit cards. A 33-room European-style refurbished hotel with modern and period furnishings. TV, room phones; some refrigerators; free coffee in lobby. **Mama's Restaurant** serves from 7 a.m. to 11 p.m. daily; American; dinners $15 to $22.

Royal Pacific Motor Inn ● △△ $$ Ø (Chinatown)

661 Broadway (Grant), SF 94133; (800) 545-5574 or (415) 781-6661. Doubles $68. Major credit cards. Located on the outer edge of Chinatown; recently re-decorated rooms. TV, room phones, in-room coffee; sauna, coin laundry; restaurant next door.

San Remo Hotel ● △ $$ (Fisherman's Wharf)

2237 Mason St. (Chestnut), SF 94133; 776-8688. Doubles $55 to $75, singles $35 to $45, weekly rates from $100. MC/VISA, DIN. European-style hotel with 62 rooms, shared baths. **New San Remo Restaurant** serves from 8 a.m. to 10 p.m. daily; Italian-continental; dinners $7 to $16; Victorian decor; full bar service.

Seal Rock Inn ● △△△ $$ (Ocean beach)

545 Point Lobos Ave. (48th Avenue), SF 94121; 752-8000. Doubles $66 to $87, singles from $62, kitchenettes $4 more (two-day minimum). Major credit cards. Attractive inn near the Cliff House with 27 ocean-view rooms. TV, room phones, refrigerators, some fireplaces; pool, free parking. **Seal Rock Inn Restaurant** serves weekdays 7 a.m. to 4 p.m. and weekends 7 to 6; breakfast and lunch, specializing in omelets.

Sheehan Hotel ● △△△ $$ (downtown)

620 Sutter St. (Mason), SF 94102; 800-848-1529. Doubles $50 to $90, singles $40 to $60, suites $85 to $90. Major credit cards. Refurbished older hotel with 61 attractive rooms. TV movies and room phones; Olympic-sized indoor pool, workout room, free continental breakfast. **Tea room** serves light fare.

Star Motel ● △△ $$ (Marina)

1727 Lombard St. (Laguna), SF 94123; (800) 835-8143 or (415) 346-2950. Doubles $70 to $74, singles $62 to $66. Major credit cards. Fifty-one rooms; TV, room phones; refreshment room; free parking.

Town House Motel ● △△ $$ (Marina)

1650 Lombard St. (Gough); SF 94123; 885-5163. Doubles $55 to $80, singles $55 to $70. Major credit cards. Free continental breakfast is served in this 24-room motel; TV movies and room phones.

Valu Inn ● △△ $$ Ø (Civic Center)

900 Franklin St. (Eddy), SF 94109; (800) 223-9626 or (415) 885-6865. Doubles $66 TO $72, singles $55 to $61. Major credit cards. Motel with 59 rooms; TV movies, room phones and coffee, some refrigerators; spa, free parking.

York Hotel ● △△△ $$$ Ø (downtown)

940 Sutter St. (Leavenworth), SF 94109; (800) 227-3608 or (415) 885-6800. Doubles and singles $95 to $175, suites $175 to $195. Major credit cards. Free continental breakfast; 96 rooms. TV movies, room phones; free newspaper, evening wine hour, exercise gym, morning limo service.

ROOMS UNDER $50

Alpine Motel ● △ $ (south of city)

560 Carter St. (Geneva), SF 94134; 334-6969. Doubles $34. Thirty-five room motel seven miles south, off the Bayshore; TV movies; free parking.

Essex Hotel ● △△ $ (downtown/Civic Center)

684 Ellis St. (Larkin), SF 94109; (800) 44-ESSEX in California, (800) 45-ESSEX elsewhere; (415) 474-

4664. *Doubles $42 to $56, singles $38 to $46, suites $80. MC/VISA, AMEX.* Refurbished 100-room hotel; TV, room phones; free coffee in lobby.

Grant Plaza Hotel ● △△ $ (downtown/Chinatown)

465 Grant Ave. (Bush), SF 94108; (800) 472-6805 in California and (800) 472-6899 elsewhere, locally 434-3883. Doubles $42 to $65, singles $37 to $55, suites $82. Major credit cards. Budget-priced, attractive hotel; 72 rooms with TV movies and room phones; near entrance to Chinatown.

Lombard Plaza Motel ● △ $ (Marina)

2026 Lombard St. (Fillmore), SF 94123; 921-2444. Doubles and singles $39 to $69. Major credit cards. Thirty-two rooms; TV movies, room phones; guest parking.

Temple Hotel ● △ $ (Financial District/Chinatown)

469 Pine St. (Kearny), SF 94109; 781-2565. Doubles $35 to $45, singles $30 to $40. No credit cards. Clean, older hotel with 88 rooms, 19 with private baths.

BED & BREAKFAST INNS

Alamo Square Inn ● △△△ $$ Ø (Alamo Square)

719 Scott St. (Fulton), SF 94117; (415) 922-2055. Doubles $70 to $150. Some private, some shared baths; full breakfast. MC/VISA, AMEX. Restored Victorian mansion; fifteen rooms furnished in Victorian and early American antiques with Oriental rugs. Attractive parlor and dining room with wood burning fireplaces; landscaped gardens; patios; decks. Tea and wine service.

Albion House ● △△ $$ (Civic Center)

135 Gough St. (Oak), SF 94102; (415) 621-0896. Doubles $65 to $110. Private baths; full breakfast. MC/VISA, AMEX. Eight rooms in a refurbished German meeting hall; Edwardian decor; attractively-furnished parlor with fireplace; evening wine service.

Art Center Bed & Breakfast ● △△ $$ Ø (Marina)

1902 Filbert St. (Laguna), SF 94123; (415) 567-1526. Doubles $65 to $85, suites $115 to $155. Private *baths; full breakfast. Major credit cards.* Five rooms with a mix of antiques, modern furnishings and artworks in a restored Colonial-style home. Comfortable sitting room, library. Full kitchen in each unit.

Bayside Boat & Breakfast ● △△△ **$$$$ (Fisherman's Wharf)**

c/o 40 Jack London Square, Oakland, CA 94607; (800) 262-8233 or (415) 291-8411 AND 444-5858. Doubles $115 to $275. Private baths; continental breakfasts. MC/VISA, AMEX On-the-water lodgings aboard private yachts berthed at Pier 39 and Oakland's Jack London Square. Various amenities, including TV, stereo, continental breakfast, some microwaves. Validated parking; meal service available. Bay cruises may be arranged.

Bed & Breakfast Inn ● △△△ **$$ Ø (Marina)**

Four Charlton Court (Union), SF 94123; (415) 921-9784. Doubles $70 to $90 with shared baths; $115 to $140 with private baths; penthouse $215. Light breakfast. No credit cards. Cozy B&B in the heart of Union Street's shopping area, offering ten rooms with cheery English decor. Mix of modern and antique furnishings; patio garden. It brims with country inn charm.

Chateau Tivoli ● △△△△ **$$$$ Ø (near Alamo Square)**

1057 Steiner St. (Golden Gate), SF 94115; (800) 228-1647 or (415) 776-5462. Doubles $100 to $125, suites $200 to $300. Some private, some shared baths; expanded continental breakfast. MC/VISA, AMEX. Striking 1892 French Renaissance chateau-style mansion with five rooms and two suites. Furnished with Victorian and French antiques and rare artworks. Canopy beds, marble baths and fireplaces in some rooms.

Dolores Park Inn ● △△△ **$$ Ø (Mission)**

3641 Seventeenth St. (Dolores), SF 94114; (415) 621-0482. Doubles $59 to $89. Some private, some shared baths; full breakfast. Major credit cards. European and American antiques in five handsomely-furnished rooms in an Italianate Victorian. Sunny patio, afternoon wine service, spa.

Visitors can sleep in Victorian elegance at several bed and breakfast inns; this is Chateau Tivoli at Steiner and Golden Gate.

Edward II Bed & Breakfast ● △△△ $$ (Marina)

3155 Scott St. (Lombard), SF 94123; (800) GREAT-INN or (415) 922-3000. Doubles $67 to $169. Some private, some shared baths; continental breakfast. MC/VISA, AMEX. English-style inn with 30 rooms. Country wicker decor; some rooms with spas and kitchens. Old English style **Bloomers** pub and **Cafe Lily** bakery-cafe.

Inn San Francisco ● △△△ $$ (Mission)

943 S. Van Ness Ave. (20th), SF 94110; (800) 359-0913 or (415) 641-0188. Doubles $68 to $160. Some private, some shared baths; expanded continental breakfast. MC/VISA, AMEX. Italianate Victorian; 22 rooms handsomely furnished with Victorian and American antiques. Room phones, TV and refrigerators; fireplaces and spas in some rooms. Sherry and hot beverage service; English garden; hot tub in gazebo; roof-top sun deck with city view.

Mansions Hotel ● △△△△ $$$ (Pacific Heights)

2220 Sacramento St. (Laguna), SF 95115; (415) 929-9444. Doubles $89 to $225. Private baths; full breakfast. Side-by-side Victorian mansions with 29 guest rooms. Fully restored and delightfully overdone with antiques, a stuffed monkey, live macaw and Lawrence Welk bubble machine. It's the city's only bed and breakfast with a sense of humor. Sculpture garden; antique-filled sitting rooms. **Mansions Restaurant** features continental fare with pre-dinner concerts or comedy entertainment.

Millefiori Inn ● △△ $$$ (North Beach)

444 Columbus Ave. (Vallejo), SF 94133; (415) 433-9111. Doubles from $75. Private baths; continental breakfast. Major credit cards. Fifteen-room inn with Italian Provincial decor and intimate courtyard.

Obrero Hotel ● △ $ Ø (Chinatown-North Beach)

1208 Stockton St. (Pacific), SF 94133; (415) 989-3960. Doubles from $45. Share baths; full breakfast. No credit cards. Small European-style pension with homey decor, room sinks. **Obrero Basque Restaurant** serves family-style dinners for $13; nightly seating at 6:30.

Petite Auberge ● △△△△ $$$$ Ø (downtown)

863 Bush St. (Mason), SF 94108; (415) 928-6000. Doubles $105 to $155. Private baths; full breakfast buffet. MC/VISA, AMEX. Posh French country-style inn with 26 rooms; antique furnishings; some fireplaces. Morning newspaper, cookie jar, other amenities.

Red Victorian ● ⌂⌂ $$ Ø **(Haight-Ashbury)**

1665 Haight St. (Cole); SF 94117; 864-1978. Doubles $50 to $125. Some private, some shared baths; large continental breakfast. MC/VISA, AMEX. Some rooms are simply furnished and affordable, others rather elegant with Victorian decor. The whimsical Aquarium Bathroom and Gallery of Transformational Art are appropriate to the laid-back Haight-Ashbury scene. The inn is smoke-free.

Spencer House ● ⌂⌂⌂⌂ $$$ Ø **(Haight-Ashbury)**

1080 Haight St. (Baker), SF 94117; (415) 626-9205. Doubles $95 to $155. Private baths; full breakfast. MC/VISA (for reservations only.) Six rooms handsomely furnished with antiques in an 1890 restored Queen Anne. Opulent decor with padded wall coverings, thick coverlets on beds, oak paneling and stained glass.

Union Street Inn ● ⌂⌂⌂ $$$$ Ø **(Marina)**

2229 Union St. (Fillmore), SF 94123; (415) 346-0424. Doubles $135 to $225. Private baths; expanded continental breakfast. MC/VISA, AMEX. Six rooms with Victorian and contemporary decor in a restored Edwardian mansion. Set in an attractive garden in the Union Street shopping district. Spas in two rooms. Tea and cookie and wine service.

Victorian Inn on the Park ● ⌂⌂⌂⌂ $$$ **(Haight-Ashbury)**

301 Lyon St. (Fell), SF 94117; 931-1830. Doubles $81 to $138. Private baths; large continental breakfast. MC/VISA, AMEX. Impeccably restored 1897 Queen Anne with Victorian furnishings. Twelve rooms, some with fireplaces; wine served evenings before a parlor fire. Near Golden Gate Park panhandle.

Washington Square Inn ● ⌂⌂⌂ $$$ **(North Beach)**

1660 Stockton St. (Filbert), SF 94133; (800) 388-0220 or (415) 981-4220. Doubles $75 to $160. Some private, some shared baths; continental breakfast. MC/VISA. Fifteen rooms; contemporary decor with French and English country antiques; afternoon tea and evening wine service.

White Swan Inn ● ⌂⌂⌂⌂ **$$$$** Ø **(down-town)**

845 Bush St. (Mason), SF 94108; (415) 775-1755. Doubles $145 to $160. Private baths; full buffet breakfast. MC/VISA, AMEX. Sister inn to Petite Auberge; 26 handsome rooms done in English antiques, four-poster beds. Library, afternoon tea, morning newspaper.

WHERE TO—CAMP?

San Francisco RV Park ● ⌂⌂ **$** **(South of Market)**

250 King St. (Fourth), SF 94107; (800) 548-2425 or (415) 986-8730. RV sites $30 a night, $168 a week or $500 a month; MC/VISA. No, you can't pitch a tent here, but you can park your RV or camper in the only rec vehicle park near downtown San Francisco. Facilities include full hookups, picnic tables, barbecues, showers, rest rooms and a convenience store.

LODGINGS OUTSIDE THE CITY

Americana Inn Motel ● ⌂⌂ **$$** Ø **(South San Francisco)**

760 El Camino Real (W. Orange), South San Francisco, CA 94080; 589-0404. Doubles $55 to $65, singles $45 to $60. Major credit cards. Seventeen-room motel; TV movies, room phones, refrigerators; free coffee; spa; free parking.

Apple Inn ● ⌂⌂ **$$** Ø **(Oakland)**

1801 Embarcadero (Fifth Avenue exit from I-880), Oakland, CA 94606; (800) 323-8622 or (415) 436-0103. Doubles $63 to $70, singles $59 to $66. Major credit cards. Near waterfront; 95 rooms with TV, phones; spa, free continental breakfast.

Motel Orleans ● ⌂⌂ **$$** Ø **(Sunnyvale)**

1071 E. El Camino Real (Henderson Avenue; 35 miles south of city), Sunnyvale, CA 94087; (408) 244-9000. Doubles $52 to $60, singles $44 to $48, kitchenettes $50 to $59, suites $55 to $59. Major credit cards. Southern Colonial style motel; 64 rooms. TV movies, room phones, refrigerators; continental breakfast; pool; free parking.

San Carlos Inn ● △△△ $ (San Carlos)

1562 El Camino Real (Central; 15 miles south of city), San Carlos, CA 94070; (800) 554-8585 in California only, or (415) 591-6655. Doubles $46 to $48, singles $42 to $46, kitchenettes $55, suites $65. Major credit cards. Thirty-two well-equipped rooms with microwaves, refrigerators, TV movies, VCR. Spa, sauna; free parking.

Townhouse Motel ● △△ $ Ø (Palo Alto)

4164 El Camino Real (Oregon Expressway off U.S. 101), Palo Alto, CA 94306; (415) 493-4492. Doubles $45, singles $37 to $40. Major credit cards. Thirty miles south of city; 23 rooms; TV, room phones, refrigerators and microwaves.

The Trees Inn ● △△△ $$ Ø (Concord)

1370 Monument Blvd. (off Highway 24, 25 miles east of city), Concord, CA 94520; 827-8998. Double and single kitchenettes $49 to $78, suites $78 to $88. Major credit cards. All-kitchenette motel; 58 rooms. TV movies, room phones, free coffee and newspapers; pool, laundry.

SEVENTEEN

RESTAURANT GLOSSARY

*Cafes are listed by type.
Some are listed in more than one
category. All restaurants also are
listed alphabetically in the index.*

AMERICAN
(including California nouveau)
Asuka Brasserie (Japanese-
California) 170, 172
Bagel (Jewish deli), 147
Balboa Cafe (California-American
regional), 29, 212
Bepple's Pie Shop (American,
desserts), 213
Big Four (American-continental), 43,
63, 65
Bill's Place (American), 187
Bix (American), 100
Buena Vista (American), 120, 127
Cafe Majestic (California cuisine),
213
Cafe Picaro (American), 154, 155
Caffe Trieste (coffee house), 96, 100
California Culinary Academy
(American-continental), 144
Chestnut Street Grill (American), 29,
214
China Moon Cafe (California-
Chinese), 66
City Picnic (American), 144
Clement Street Bar & Grill (California
cuisine), 189
Cliff House (American, seafood,
pasta), 206
Dish (American regional), 186
Elite Cafe (Cajun-Creole), 171, 173
Faz (American), 67
Garden Court (California cuisine),
45, 60, 67

Greens (Vegetarian), 201, 206
Hamburger Mary's (American), 134
Hard Rock Cafe (American), 29, 147
Harrington's Bar & Grill (American),
114
Harris' (American), 147
Hell's Kitchen (American), 180, 186
Holding Company (American), 114
Ivy's (American regional), 144
Java House (American), 133
John's Grill (American-continental),
49, 55, 68
Julie's Supper Club (California
cuisine), 134
Kimball's (California cuisine), 146,
149
Kuleto's (northern Italian-California),
55, 68
Le Piano Zinc (French-California),
160, 162
Lefty O'Doul's (American Hofbrau),
57, 69
Lehr's Greenhouse (American), 58,
69
Little City Antipasti Bar (Italian-
Californian), 102
Mission Rock Resort (American),
134
New Dawn (American), 154, 157
Olive Oil's (American), 135
Pat O'Shea's Mad Hatter
(American), 29, 42, 190
Patio Cafe (American), 160, 162
Perry's (American), 29, 216
Polk Street Beans (American), 148
Pork Store (American), 187
Red's Java House (American), 133
Ryan's (American nouveau), 160,
162

House of Piroshki (Russian-
   Mideastern deli), 186
Kasra (Persian), 189

ITALIAN *(and pizza parlors)*
Bardelli's (Italian-continental), 48, 65
Basta Pasta (Italian), 47, 100
Bonta (Italian), 213
Cafe Riggio (Regional Italian), 189
Caffe Roma (Italian coffee house),
   96, 100
Calzone's Pizza Cucina (Italian), 101
Ciao (northern Italian), 66
Circolo (northern Italian), 66
Enoteca Lanzone (regional Italian),
   144
Fior d'Italia (northern Italian), 101
Gold Spike (Italian), 101
Iron Horse (Italian), 61, 68
Kuleto's (Italian-Californian), 55, 68
Little City Antipasti Bar (Italian-
   Californian), 102
Little Joe's (Italian), 44, 102
Little Rio Cafe & Pizzeria (Italian-
   Brazilian), 127

Mamma Tina (Italian), 103
Marina Cafe (Italian-seafood), 215
Mario's Bohemian Cigar Store
   (Italian), 97, 103
Mayes (Italian-seafood), 49, 148
New Joe's (Italian), 70
North Beach Restaurant (northern
   Italian), 103
Olive's Gourmet Pizza, 215
Pietro's Ristorante (Italian), 216
Pizzeria Uno (pizza), 128, 216
Prego (Italian), 216
Ristorante Donatello (Italian), 70
Ristorante Grifone (Italian), 103
Spada (American-Italian), 128
Tarantino's (seafood-Italian), 128
Umberto Ristorante (Italian), 116
Vicolo Pizzeria (pizza), 129
Washington Square Bar & Grill
   (American-Italian), 41, 97, 104

JAPANESE *(and Korean)*
Asuka Brasserie (Japanese-
   California), 170, 172
Benihana of Tokyo (Japanese), 170,
   173

Hahn's Hibachi (Korean barbecue),
   147
Iroha (Japanese), 173
May Sun (Teriyaki-Mandarin), 174
May's Coffee Shop (Japanese), 169
Mifune (Japanese), 170, 173
Ten-Ichi (Japanese), 174

MEXICAN *(and other Latin)*
Alejandro's (Latin mix), 187
Cadillac Bar & Grill (Mexican), 47,
   134
Carlos Golstein's (Mexican), 66
Corona Bar & Grill (Regional
   Mexican), 67
Don Quijote (Mexican), 155
El Toreador (Mexican), 162
Il Pollaio (Italian-Argentinian), 102
La Barca (Mexican), 215
La Bodega (Spanish), 102, 105
Little Rio Cafe & Pizzeria (Italian-
   Brazilian), 127
Los Guitarras (Mexican), 157
Tia Margarita (Mexican), 191

SEAFOOD
Adriatic, 147
Bentley's, 65
Cliff House (American, seafood,
   pasta), 206
Hayes Street Grill, 44, 145
Neptune's Palace, 127
Pacific Cafe, 190
Pacific Heights Bar & Grill, 171, 174
Pompei's Grotto (seafood, pasta),
   128
Scott's Seafood, 217
Tarantino's (seafood-Italian), 128
Waterfront, 111, 116
Yuet Lee (Chinese seafood), 91

SOUTHEAST ASIAN
Bali Restaurant (Indonesian), 187
Khan Toke Thai House (Thai), 47,
   189
Singapore-Malaysian (Malaysian),
   190
Thai Spice (Thai), 148
Thai Stick, (Thai), 71
Thep Phanom (Thai), 174

INDEX

REMARKABLY USEFUL GUIDEBOOKS
by Don and Betty Martin

Critics praise the "jaunty prose," "pithy writing" and "beautiful editing" of Don and Betty Martin's guidebooks. You can order their other popular books or additional copies of *Inside San Francisco* by sending a personal check or money order to Pine Cone Press. If you wish, the authors will autograph your book. Indicate the dedication you'd like them to write.

THE BEST OF SAN FRANCISCO — $9.95

This humorously irreverent guide to everybody's favorite city names its best attractions, cafes, nightspots and shopping, walking and biking areas. It even lists the ten naughtiest and dumbest things to do in the city. **196 pages**

BEST OF THE GOLD COUNTRY — $11.95

It's a "complete, whimsical and opinionated guide to California's Sierra gold rush area and old Sacramento." This informative book covers historic Highway 49, listing its attractions, cafes, campgrounds, gold rush hotels and other lodgings. **208 pages**

SAN FRANCISCO'S ULTIMATE DINING GUIDE — $9.95

The Martins surveyed the *real* dining experts to compile this upbeat guide: chefs and other restaurant personnel, hotel concierges, cafe critics and community leaders. It lists more than 300 restaurants in the city and nearby communities. **224 pages**

THE BEST OF ARIZONA — $12.95

It's the complete guide to the Grand Canyon State, written in the Martins' typically opinionated, humorous style. This illustrated guide covers attractions, scenic drives, dining, lodgings and campgrounds. A special "Snowbird Directory" helps retirees plan their winters under the Arizona sun. **336 pages**

Include $1 postage and handling for each book; California residents add 1/2 percent sales tax. Please give us a complete mailing address and phone number, in case there's a question about your order.

Send your order to: *Pine Cone Press*
P.O. Box 1494, Columbia, CA 95310